MW00422919

WASHINGTON'S ENGINEER

WASHINGTON'S ENGINEER

Louis Duportail and the Creation of an Army Corps

NORMAN DESMARAIS

Prometheus Books
Guilford, Connecticut

Prometheus Books

An imprint of The Rowman & Littlefield Publishing Group, Inc.
4501 Forbes Blvd., Ste. 200
Lanham, MD 20706
www.rowman.com

Distributed by NATIONAL BOOK NETWORK

British Library Cataloguing in Publication Information Available

Library of Congress Cataloging-in-Publication Data

Names: Desmarais, Norman, author.
Title: Washington's engineer : Louis Duportail and the creation of an Army
  Corps / Norman Desmarais.
Other titles: Louis Duportail and the creation of an Army Corps
Description: Lanham, MD : Prometheus Books, 2021. | Includes bibliographical
  references and index. | Summary: "This is a unique biography about an
  overlooked, even obscure, French officer that was instrumental in the
  American cause for independence. As a complete biography, it covers Louis
  Deuportail's time as the first Commandant of the Army Corps of Engineers, his
  return to France, and his service in the French army."—Provided by publisher.
Identifiers: LCCN 2020033020 (print) | LCCN 2020033021 (ebook) | ISBN
  9781633886568 (cloth) | ISBN 9781633886575 (epub)
Subjects: LCSH: Duportail, Antoine-Jean-Louis Le Bègue de Presle, 1743–1802.
  | United States—History—Revolution, 1775–1783—Campaigns. | United
  States—History—Revolution, 1775–1783—Engineering and construction.
  | United States. Continental Army. Corps of Engineers—History. |
  United States—History—Revolution, 1775–1783—Participation, French. |
  Generals—France—Biography.
Classification: LCC E207.D9 D47 2021 (print) | LCC E207.D9 (ebook) |
  DDC 973.3092 [B]—dc23
LC record available at https://lccn.loc.gov/2020033020
LC ebook record available at https://lccn.loc.gov/2020033021

I have a high opinion of his merit and abilities, and esteem him not only well acquainted with the particular branch he professes, but a man of sound judgment and real knowledge in military science in general.

—George Washington, in a letter to the president of Congress, November 16, 1778 (Washington, *Papers*, 18:168)

CONTENTS

Introduction   ix

1   Early Years   1

2   Valley Forge   17

3   West Point and the Hudson   53

4   The Campaign of 1779   71

5   The Campaign of 1780: Charleston   95

6   The Corps of Engineers   109

7   Prisoners of War   139

8   The Campaign of 1781: Yorktown   151

9   Peace   185

10 American Citizen and Farmer   201

Appendix A: Cargoes of Two of Beaumarchais's Ships Sent to America   211

Appendix B: Chiefs of the Corps of Engineers, 1774–1893   213

Notes   215

Glossary   245

Works Cited   251

Bibliographic Essay   257

Index   263

INTRODUCTION

Since the Battle of Hastings in 1066, the British and the French were arch-enemies; the French victory resulted in a French king ruling England for more than three centuries. In the eighteenth century, American colonists, being British subjects, shared the same prejudices and dislike of the French. Moreover, the French were also their enemy in the colonial wars, particularly the French and Indian War, which was begun by George Washington. As many of the colonists came to America to escape religious persecution, especially the Catholic Church's Inquisition, they were loath to ally themselves with the French, most of whom were Catholic. So why did the Americans turn to France for assistance in their struggle for independence?

Following the basic military principle "the enemy of my enemy is my friend," the colonists turned to France, hoping that she would desire to avenge her defeat in the French and Indian War and try to regain lost territory. Further, the French had the best military engineers, and the colonists desperately needed engineers. Sébastien Le Prestre de Vauban (1633–1707) was generally regarded as the best military engineer in the seventeenth and eighteenth centuries, his influence extending into the mid-nineteenth century.

Military engineering in the eighteenth century combined the skills of the artilleryman and the engineer and focused on three main areas: fortification, artillery, and cartography. Defensive activities normally involved erecting small, temporary structures, such as earthwork batteries, at vulnerable points along the Atlantic coast and palisaded outposts along the interior frontier. Engineers also created less permanent field fortifications to provide advantage on the battlefield. They also reinforced and strengthened existing houses and constructed blockhouses. Examples of their work include those by British, Hessian, French, American, and Spanish engineers:

- Fort Chambly, Île aux Noix, Les Cèdres, Louisbourg, and Québec (Canada)
- Fort Phoenix (Massachusetts)
- Fort Butts (Rhode Island)
- Fort Griswold (Connecticut)
- Forts Clinton/West Point, Montgomery, Niagara, Ontario, Salonga/Slongo, Stanwix/Schuyler, Stony Point, and Ticonderoga (New York)
- Fort Lee, Monmouth, Morristown, and Red Bank/Fort Mercer (New Jersey)
- Brandywine/Chadds Ford, Fort Mifflin, and Valley Forge (Pennsylvania)
- Yorktown (Virginia)
- Guilford Courthouse (North Carolina)
- Camden, Fort Dorchester, Fort Sullivan/Fort Moultrie, Kings Mountain, and Ninety Six (South Carolina)
- Fort George/Fort Morris and Spring Hill Redoubt (Georgia)
- Castillo de San Marcos (Florida)
- Fort Michilimackinac (Michigan)
- Fort Laurens (Ohio)
- Point Pleasant (West Virginia)

As it was common to destroy fortifications when they were no longer needed, most of these examples are now reconstructions. A number of Revolutionary War–era fortifications were replaced by fortifications during the War of 1812 and the Civil War.

An engineer's main duty during battle was to command the artillery. He selected the type of shot (round, grape, canister, bar, sliding bar, chain, star, mortar/bomb) to be used and determined the size of the charge (amount of powder to use). He also calculated the distance and trajectory to the target.

Cartographers in the military were known as topographical engineers, and their job essentially involved making maps. General Washington appointed Robert Erskine as "Geographer and Surveyor-General to the Continental Army" on July 19, 1777. He was commissioned as "Geographer and Surveyor to the Army of the United States" the following week, on July 27.

The military engineer was the most difficult staff officer to obtain because of the highly technical skills required. American engineers knew a great deal about civil construction and could erect simple fieldworks, but

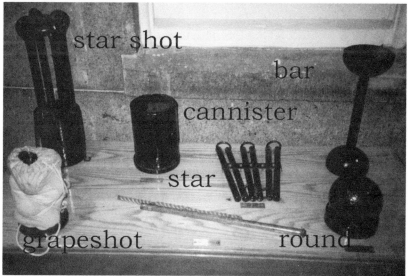

Types of artillery shots. *Photo courtesy of the author.*

their skills were not on par with those of formally trained European military engineers. American engineers created earthworks that the Crown forces sometimes chose not to attack, but they could not conduct a formal siege of a town. Their lack of skill turned operations into a mere blockade.

Pierre-Augustin Caron de Beaumarchais (1732–1799), the son of King Louis XVI's watchmaker and better known as playwright of *The Barber of Seville* and *The Marriage of Figaro*, wrote a lengthy memo to King Louis XVI on February 29, 1776, outlining why France should help America. He concluded, "[T]he saving of a few millions [livres or francs] to-day would surely result in the loss of more than 300 within two years."[1] He also emphasized the Americans' need of arms, powder, and especially engineers, stressing that without engineers, the Americans could not even defend themselves, let alone win.[2]

The Congressional Committee of Secret Correspondence appointed Silas Deane to the Secret Committee of Congress (which also included Benjamin Franklin, Benjamin Harrison, John Dickinson, John Hay, and Robert Morris). Deane was commissioned on March 2, 1776, "to go to France, there to transact such business, commercial and political as we have committed to his care, in behalf and by authority of the Congress of the thirteen united Colonies."[3]

PHILIPPE CHARLES JEAN BAPTISTE TRONSON DU COUDRAY

Silas Deane and Benjamin Franklin were instructed to hire skilled professional soldiers in addition to soliciting material assistance as part of their diplomatic mission to France in the summer of 1776. Beaumarchais and Jean-Baptiste Vaquette de Gribeauval (1715–1789), the leading artillery expert of the century, advised Deane to contract Philippe Charles Jean Baptiste Tronson du Coudray (1738–1777), one of Gribeauval's protégés, to organize and lead a group of volunteers to America. Despite his extravagant claims, du Coudray was actually a military theorist whose rank was equivalent to that of an artillery major. Deane granted him a generous contract promising him essentially a free hand in artillery and engineer operations and the title of general of artillery and ordnance.

Meanwhile, Beaumarchais, operating under the corporate name of Roderigue Hortalez et Cie., wrote to the Committee of Secret Correspondence on August 18, 1776, to tell them that the company was founded for the sole purpose of serving them in Europe to meet all their needs there and to see that all the goods, cloth, canvas, powder, munitions, guns, cannons, and even some gold to pay the troops could be obtained rapidly and under concession. Whenever possible, Beaumarchais would remove any obstacle that European politics might present. He also told Deane and Franklin that he had procured about 200 bronze four-pounders, which he would send at the earliest opportunity, along with 200,000 pounds of cannon powder; 20,000 excellent guns; some bronze mortars, bombs, cannonballs, and bayonets; plates, cloth, linen, and so on to clothe the troops; and some lead to make musket balls. He also found an artillery and engineer officer who would leave for Philadelphia before the arrival of the first shipment, accompanied by lieutenants and officers, artillerymen, gunners, and so on.[4]

Franklin conveyed du Coudray's request to the Comte de Saint-Germain, the French minister of war, in December 1776. Saint-Germain allowed four French engineers to volunteer for service in America: Louis le Bègue de Presle Duportail; Louis-Guillaume-Servais des Hayes de La Radière; Jean-Baptiste de Gouvion; and Jean Baptiste Joseph, Comte de Laumoy.

Du Coudray embarked for America with twenty-nine officers and twelve sergeants of artillery, with assurances from the commissioners that he would be commissioned a major general and given command of the artillery. The group arrived in Philadelphia in May 1777, but some American generals resisted du Coudray's appointment. They were reluctant to appoint a Frenchman as commander of artillery above American general officers. Generals John Sullivan, Nathanael Greene, and Henry Knox wrote to Congress on July 1, expressing their reservations. Sullivan threatened to resign his commission if du Coudray were promoted over Knox. Congress reacted on July 3 by resolving that the

> president inform General Sullivan that Congress have not been accustomed to be controlled by their officers in the measures which they are about to take in discharge of the important trust committed to them by the United States; that they mean not to be controlled by his letter in their proceedings respecting Monsr. du Coudray; for that whatever those proceedings may be, General Sullivan's resignation will be accepted by Congress whenever he shall think it proper to transmit it to them.[5]

Congress also directed General Washington

> to let those officers know that Congress consider the said letters as an attempt to influence their decisions, and an invasion of the liberties of the people, and indicating a want of confidence in the justice of Congress; that it is expected by Congress the said officers will make proper acknowledgments for an interference of so dangerous a tendency; but if any of those officers are unwilling to serve their country under the

authority of Congress they shall be at liberty to resign their commissions and retire.[6]

Congress appointed a committee on July 15 to meet with du Coudray to inform him that the agreement offered by Silas Deane could not be carried out, but Congress would "cheerfully give him such rank and appointments as shall not be inconsistent with the honour and safety of these States, or interfere with the great duties they owe to their constituents."[7] The committee delivered its report to Congress on July 21, requesting that du Coudray

> be appointed a Major General with the Powers, Emoluments and Privileges, annexed to that Rank, and that a Train of Artillery be allotted for his Command separate from that under the Command of Brigadier General Knox. That the officers accompanying Mons Du Coudray should have the Ranks proposed for them in France together with the Pay and Emoluments annexed to those Ranks in the service of the United States.[8]

Congress postponed consideration of the report for a few weeks. Du Coudray was appointed inspector general with the rank of major general on August 11. Congress later commissioned Thomas Conway and Philippe Huber, Chevalier de Preudhomme de Borre, as brigadier generals and appointed du Coudray as inspector general of ordnance and military manufactories. Du Coudray's accidental death on September 15, 1777, ended the controversy over rank.

SECOND AND THIRD GROUPS

The Comte de Saint-Germain, the French minister of war, sent a second group of technical experts to America under the command of Louis le Bègue de Presle Duportail.[9] He formally "loaned" four military engineers to the Continental Army. This was more than a year before France officially declared war against England. Unlike the previous volunteers, these men received contracts that called for promotions to a grade only one step higher than their French commissions, and Saint-Germain had carefully picked them for their skills. Duportail was commissioned a colonel on July 8, 1777, and given command over all engineers in the army shortly thereafter. Duportail's obvious expertise and cooperative attitude led to his promotion to brigadier general on November 17, a status equivalent to that of General Knox.

Major General Marie Jean Paul Joseph du Motier, Marquis de Lafayette (1757–1834) led a third contingent from France in 1777. He and the Bavarian-born Major General Johann, Baron de Kalb (1721–1780), were talented protégés of Charles-Jacques-Victor-Albert, Comte de Broglie, one of France's top military officers. Although nineteen-year-old Lafayette had limited military experience, he had powerful political connections in the French court. Consequently, Deane offered him and de Kalb, an experienced officer in the French Army, major general's commissions.

By the time this third group reached Philadelphia, the failure of some of the first volunteers and the controversy surrounding du Coudray led to a cold reception by Congress and the army. But Lafayette's enthusiasm, his and his companions' offer to serve as unpaid volunteers, and their demonstrated competence eventually earned commissions for most of these Frenchmen. Because the Americans had little practical experience and no training that could match the British engineers' at Woolwich or those in France, where the science of military engineering was being perfected, these foreign volunteers made their most immediate impact in military engineering.

FIRST CHIEF ENGINEERS

The first chief engineers of the Continental Army were self-taught Americans. Colonel Richard Gridley had had a principal role in the siege of Louisbourg in 1745 and was responsible for laying out the siege works around Boston in 1775, but his advanced age limited his active service thereafter. Colonel Rufus Putnam (1738–1824) eventually received the post on August 5, 1776, partly in recognition of his efforts to help lay out the defenses on Manhattan Island and Long Island that summer. Congress commissioned Andrew Thaddeus Kosciusko (or Kosciuszko; 1746–1817) a colonel of engineers on October 18, 1776. He was a young Polish captain who had been trained in France and was qualified by European standards. Colonel Putnam chose to return to infantry duty in 1777. Congress, now more cautious, halted the commissioning of untested volunteers. Washington had only Colonel Jeduthan Baldwin (1732–1788), Kosciusko, and a number of detailed infantry and artillery officers to choose from until Duportail's group arrived at Philadelphia.

Duportail became chief of engineers on July 22, 1777, and continued in that post until October 10, 1783. He was Washington's chief engineer at the siege of Yorktown, where he worked closely and effectively with his artillery counterpart, Henry Knox, and his former colleagues in the French expeditionary force. Washington was so impressed with him that he wrote, "I shall ever retain a grateful sense of the aids I have derived from your knowledge and advice to me."

1

EARLY YEARS

Antoine-Jean-Louis Le Bègue (sometimes misspelled Lebèque) de Presle Duportail, better known as Louis, was born at Pithiviers en Gâtinais (now in the department of Loiret), a small town near Orléans, France, on May 14, 1743. He was the son of Sédillot, a merchant's daughter, and Jacques Guillaume Le Bègue de Presle Chevalier du Portail.[1] His father was an attorney specially charged with the Orléans forest. The Duportail family was recognized as nobility from the seventeenth century, when one of Louis's ancestors was appointed advisor secretary to the king (*Conseiller-secrétaire du roi*).

Louis was the ninth of ten children, several of whom died very young. A notarized document drawn up on May 17, 1782, after the death of his father on December 20, 1781, indicates that he had three surviving brothers and one sister. His next older brother, Jacques Louis, Le Bègue d'Oyseville, was chosen as godfather for his baptism. The eldest, Achille-Guillaume Le Bègue de Presle, became a physician and chair of the faculty of medicine in Paris and maintained regular correspondence with Benjamin Franklin and his family. (Several of his letters are at Yale University.) His younger brother, Pierre, Le Bègue de Villiers, was a learned priest in the Society of the Sorbonne and vicar general of Comminges. Louis's only known sister was Marie-Elisabeth Le Bègue de Presle. She married Julien, François Boys, a Paris attorney. The document also reveals that Louis inherited revenues, titles, and property totaling 61,000 livres (a private soldier in the French army earned about 1 livre per week in 1780), which permitted him later to buy a very large parcel of land on the banks of the Scioto River in Ohio. However, the Montgomery County archives (where the property was located) has no record of what happened to the land.

Louis must have undertaken rigorous classical studies at a religious school, as he was able to read and write Latin. In letters to Benjamin Franklin on January 16 and 19, 1777, he proposed to communicate in Latin to maintain a certain secrecy in their correspondence and because he didn't understand English at the time.

Louis began studies as an engineer at the Military School of Mézières in 1761 at the age of eighteen. The school was founded in 1690 by the king's engineers, who succeeded Vauban. It was established at Mézières to benefit from a battlefield in total reconstruction for military exercises. Many children of the lower nobility had little hope of attaining high military rank, so the school of the Royal Corps of Engineers, open only to nobility, was often a path for career advancement. Because the number of candidates far exceeded the limited number of places in 1751, the academic program required an entrance exam and two years of study. (Duportail drew up an order on December 31, 1776, making the king's engineers officers of the Royal Corps of Engineers.)

Duportail was appointed second lieutenant (*lieutenant en second*) on January 1, 1762. Two naval engineers who were admitted on their titles denounced him and some friends in February 1763. They opposed the admission of students of doubtful nobility to the school. One of the accusers was the son of a postmaster who barely escaped bankruptcy. The other was the son of a merchant who still bore the social stigma of a bankruptcy. As a result of the anonymous accusation, Duportail and two other "ringleaders" were separated and sent to prison for one year in March 1763: one to Ham, another to Sedan, and Duportail to Bouillon Castle in the Luxembourg province of Belgium. All the students at the military school decided

Ducal palace at Charleville-Mézières. The city, located on the banks of the Meuse River, is a commune in northern France and capital of the Ardennes department in the Grand Est region. *Wikimedia.*

to join their fellow students in prison. After completing their sentences, the three students were exonerated by the king and readmitted to the school at Mézières. An inquiry later revealed the allegations were totally unfounded, but Duportail benefited from his time in prison by reading and studying military science at a high level, which advanced his career.

GRADUATION AND ASSIGNMENTS

Louis Duportail graduated as a regular engineer in 1765 at the age of twenty-two. He served two years with the infantry at Bayonne and Marseille, working pretty much as a modern engineer does and learning much through the communications with the authorities who employed him. He continued studying, edited memoirs, evaluated costs, and made maps. He had assignments at Strasbourg (1769); Gex (1770), where he was dismayed by the useless works at Versoix (a village on the Swiss border that the Duc de Choiseul wanted to fortify); Montpellier (1771); and Metz (1774). He was promoted to captain on August 25, 1773, at the age of thirty. He was assigned to Aire in 1775, then to Bethune in 1776.

The Comte de Saint-Germain, the minister of war, summoned him on July 15, 1776, to prepare a new edition of a training manual for the Royal Corps of Engineers. It was to contain every bit of knowledge that an engineer needed to know and to reflect the changes being instituted in the military. Duportail proposed reducing the number of officers from 400 to 329 and the number of fortifications from 20 to 12. He also recommended basing promotions solely on merit and organizing internships to complete the course of training. The manual was published on December 31, 1776, just as Duportail was beginning his negotiations with Benjamin Franklin.

NEGOTIATIONS WITH FRANKLIN AND DEANE

Duportail was recognized and appreciated for the quality of his work, just as he was for the memorandum that he wrote for the minister of war in December 1773, in which he proposed a complete organization of the engineers. The manual was poorly received by the engineering officers, but his minister greatly appreciated it for its intellectual discipline and strength of reflection and his ability to analyze and synthesize. The Americans later translated it and used it to organize their own Corps of Engineers.

When Benjamin Franklin arrived in Paris in December 1776, he informed the Comte de Saint-Germain that Congress wanted him to "secure skilled engineers, not exceeding four," who might serve in the Continental Army. The minister of war agreed to this request if it could be done in secrecy, without arousing the suspicions of the British ambassador, whose ubiquitous spies kept him informed. Saint-Germain suggested that Duportail go to America and authorized him to deal directly with the American agents. Duportail quickly agreed and was admitted into the Royal Corps of Engineers with the rank of lieutenant colonel.

Silas Deane, however, did not take the necessary precautions to adhere to the strict and precise demands of Congress. He was immediately besieged by many candidates whose qualifications he would not take the time to verify. One of them particularly impressed him: Philippe Charles Jean Baptiste Tronson du Coudray, the pretentious duc d'Artois and former tutor of the king's brother. This theorist of artillery authored several books on the topic, such as *L'artillerie nouvelle et L'ordre profond et l'ordre mince considérés par rapport aux effets de l'artillerie*. He was an expert on making gunpowder and on metallurgy for canons. He also had access to the arsenals and promised to supply 200 pieces of artillery; material to clothe 25,000 men; and 12 engineers, 4 captains, and 4 lieutenants to satisfy Deane's needs.

Du Coudray's application was quickly accepted with great enthusiasm, and Deane wrote a letter to the Secret Committee of Correspondence of Congress, in which he specified the reasons for his choice: Du Coudray would secretly recruit engineers and, on Vergennes's recommendation, contact Beaumarchais about his operations for recruitment and reinforcement. Beaumarchais would then ship the promised armaments and equipment through Roderigue Hortalez et Cie., a new trading house, which would essentially act as a front for the French government. Deane concluded an official agreement with du Coudray on September 11, 1776, in which he promised him the command of the artillery and the future Corps of Engineers. Every plan or project related to the fortification and artillery would then be submitted to du Coudray for his approval before execution.

However, du Coudray's plans soon became known to his superiors and risked compromising the secrecy that the king wanted concerning aid to the colonies. Du Coudray was recalled to his garrison at Metz, but instead of complying, he evaded the order and departed incognito on a vessel going to the West Indies, where he found the means to join his staff at Philadelphia, where they had arrived in April. The British ambassador's frequent complaints forced the French government to prohibit the young

Marquis de Lafayette from leaving France and to order the unloading of Beaumarchais's supply ships bringing secret aid to America.

Franklin joined Deane in Paris in December 1776 to negotiate a treaty of alliance with France and to recruit four engineers, as requested by Congress. The French court was informed a month earlier about the American colonies' Declaration of Independence, so Louis XVI was less reluctant and consented to Franklin's request. Franklin wrote to General Washington, hoping that four experienced, motivated, and volunteer officers of the Royal Corps of Engineers would bring sufficient support to the Continental Army.

In his first letter to Benjamin Franklin, in the third person and dated Sunday, December 29, 1776, at Versailles, Duportail introduced himself, outlined his qualifications, and offered to serve the American colonies. He only requested employment at a higher rank than the one he had in France. He also offered to bring with him two other engineering officers of lower rank who would be chosen for their knowledge and ability. He requested further instructions on how to proceed.

In his second letter, which was undated but written shortly after the first, he invited Franklin to verify that none of the volunteers recruited by Silas Deane had the engineering qualifications demanded by Congress and General Washington. Fearing that other volunteers might enter their candidacy and seek to replace him, Duportail immediately wrote another letter dated January 2, 1777, requesting a response to his proposal of four days earlier. He also reminded Franklin that if his response was positive, he was ready to go to Paris to begin preparations. He concluded by begging Franklin not to show anyone his letter or the one of December 29.

FRANKLIN'S RESPONSE

Franklin's response cannot be found among his or Duportail's papers, but there are undated notes taken by Franklin's secretary at working meetings following the correspondence of the two men. The meetings were probably held in Paris at the Hôtel d'Entraigues at Rue de l'Université, where Franklin resided, or at the Ministry of War at Versailles. The room was in the building formerly occupied by the chief of engineers at number 3 of the street that would become Rue de l'Independance Americaine (American Independence Street). Franklin had an office there on the left of the ground floor overlooking the courtyard. The distance between the ministry and the

Red Horse Inn (Hôtel du Cheval Rouge), where Duportail was lodged, was less than two hundred yards, which facilitated their meetings.

Franklin's notes, taken about January 11, 1777, comprise five paragraphs:

1. M. de Portal demands to be at the Head of the Corps d'Ingenieurs in America: and under the Orders only of the General, or the Commander-in-Chief in the Place where he may be.
2. He demands a Rank superior to that he enjoys at present, which is Major in the marine Infantry.
3. He proposes to take two Captains of the same Professions with him: to whom should be given in America the Rank superior.
4. That himself and his Friends shall be at Liberty to quit the Service and return to France when they please except in the middle of a Campaign.
5. The Gentlemen are willing to give the Chevalier de Portal the rank of Lieutenant Colonel and the Gentlemen he mentions that of Major, when their names are made known to them so that they may inform themselves of their qualifications which they shall do with every necessary precaution. They cannot do so much in justice to Gentlemen who have been from the beginning in the service of the States as to advance Strangers suddenly above them.

Another undated letter written by Duportail around January 12 specified further conditions, probably stemming from changes made by the Ministry of War when Duportail became aware of the status of his negotiations. It confirms that matters should be kept in utmost secrecy, as Duportail was known rather well, having served in the Ministry of War for six months, writing a new manual for the Corps of Engineers, which was soon to appear. Any rumor arising about his departure for America would cause the ministry to prevent him or any other officer of the corps to depart.

The complementary conditions, undoubtedly demanded by the ministry were

1. The American government will grant the men a rank one step higher than the one which they hold at the time they leave France.

2. It is understood that the officers are free to return to France when they so desire except during a campaign or during the construction of works. Of course this is left to the appreciation of the feelings of honor well-known and always practiced by the French officers. On its part, the American government will also be free to cashier them if desired.
3. In case of capture or imprisonment by the British, Congress will do its utmost to obtain a prisoner exchange.
4. The American agents will ensure that the officers are well-lodged and well-treated during their voyage.

The officers requested to be kept informed of what they needed to bring, necessary clothing, and so on. Foreseeing that their future army might not have the necessary instruments, such as graphometers, compasses, and the like and the difficulties of procuring them on location, Duportail proposed that he be authorized to purchase them before his departure.

The final document stipulated that the remuneration of these gentlemen would be the same as that of the officers holding the same rank in the American army. They would select the most convenient ships for their crossing at their own expense, and their compensation would begin on the day of their departure. These conditions were all dated January 12, 1777, but Franklin's agreement was not immediate. Duportail became impatient and begged Franklin, four days later, to give him a response as soon as possible so as not to waste valuable time to prepare for the voyage.

Duportail entered into frequent correspondence with Franklin between December 29, 1776, and May 15, 1777, to maintain secrecy and not to arouse the British ambassador's suspicions through frequent visits. He provided Franklin with a list of officers of the French Corps of Engineers and emphasized that no artillery or infantry officer could replace an engineer in matters of attacking or defending places or in the design and construction of fortifications and entrenchments. He stressed that the skill of an engineer was particularly important in a defensive war, such as the one America was fighting, because a poorly fortified city or post could be decisive. He requested to be at the head of the Corps of Engineers and to report only to the commander in chief. He also sought a rank one level higher than his French rank and proposed to take two captains of engineers with him. Duportail would receive the rank of lieutenant colonel, and the others, that of major. This was not out of line, as other foreign volunteers were getting appointments to superior ranks. However, it would make it more difficult for Duportail and his companions to get noticed for promotion.

Duportail had a friend who knew English and could translate for him but suggested that Franklin could respond to him in Latin, indicating that he had better facility with that language than with English. Franklin's response, though, came in English at a time when Duportail's friend was absent. His attempt at "decrypting" Franklin's response was atrocious and could have changed the course of his career, as he totally misunderstood the message, thinking that Franklin had rejected his conditions.

He wrote to Franklin again on January 19 to request further clarification. Duportail was now in Paris for a month at the Hôtel de Hollande, where he was probably preparing for his departure.[2] He reminded Franklin that he would find no other officer in the Corps of Engineers who was better qualified. Franklin might find somebody calling himself an engineer but really wasn't or one who studied at the school of engineering a short while but not long enough to absorb the principles of fortification.

Franklin must have responded quickly, or the friend returned, for there is no record of the response. Duportail wrote to Franklin again on January 21, expressing his regrets for having misunderstood his letter of the nineteenth and causing him to lose valuable time. He departed that night for Versailles to consult with the minister of war, as well as with his companions to get their agreement, after which he would send their names to Franklin. In the meantime, he vouched for their character and skills.

THE KING'S APPROVAL

Four days later, on January 25, King Louis XVI signed his orders, granting him two years' leave to take care of his personal business (*pour aller vaquer à ses affaires particulières*) and to thank him for completing the work for the Corps of Engineers.[3] This is the first time that the king signed a document that committed France to supporting the young nation's fight for independence. The king also granted him the title of lieutenant colonel of the Royal Corps of Engineers. Duportail identified his companions (Jean-Baptiste de Gouvion; Louis-Guillaume-Servais des Hayes de La Radière; and Jean Baptiste Joseph, Chevalier de Laumoy), the youngest of whom was thirty, and their ranks, along with a request that they receive the next-higher rank in the Continental Army. Their recruitment was confided to the minister of war, the Comte de Saint-Germain, and approved by the

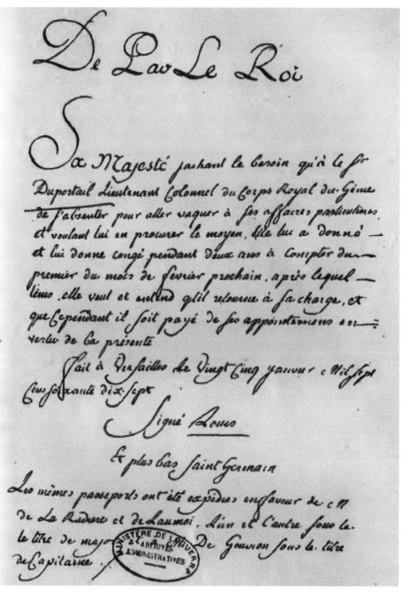

King Louis XVI's order granting General Duportail, Major de La Radière, Major de
Gouvion, and Captain de Laumoy leave to take care of their "personal business."
Ministère de la Guerre, Archives Administratives, *General Du Portail's dossier*;
Archives des Affaires Étrangères, États-Unis, correspondence politique, *vol. 2,
no. 66, in André Lasseray*, Les Français Sous Les Treize Étoiles, 1775–1783
(Macon: Imprimerie Protat frères, se trouve à Paris chez D. Janvier, 1935), 276.

king. The three received the same orders as Duportail, signed by the king. They were the only French officers obtained under the direct instructions of Congress and approved by the king.

Duportail also recommended that if Franklin made any inquiries about them, that he do so with the utmost secrecy because the slightest rumor could result in the failure of the enterprise. He concluded by requesting an immediate response. If it arrived before 6:00 p.m., then he would go visit Franklin that very night to make further arrangements. He also requested the exact time he should arrive and that Franklin ensure that no stranger be present, as it was important that Duportail not be seen.[4]

He announced to Franklin in a new letter dated January 26 that he was going twenty leagues outside Paris to prepare for his departure, that he received the king's permission that very morning, and that he would be ready to depart in less than fifteen days.

The correspondence became more frequent as the departure approached. Duportail wrote from his parents' house in Pithiviers on February 1 that Mr. Laumoy, one of his companions, wanted to meet Franklin at 7:00 p.m. on Monday, February 3, to tell him that they expected to be at Nantes or Bordeaux, ready to embark about February 15.

Having completed his recruitment mission, Franklin was now in Paris. Duportail returned to Paris on February 7 and requested to meet with him at 7:00 that evening to discuss the matters of their departure. He may not have been able to meet with Franklin that evening, as he wrote another letter to him the following morning to finalize some details. He notified Franklin that he and his companions would sail out of Nantes, which offered greater security and more amenities. He also specified that he located three protractors, three compasses, and three azimuth reading devices for about fifteen louis (a louis d'or equals six livres). He asked whether Franklin wanted to arrange for their purchase or whether he should purchase them and be reimbursed, in which case, the instruments would belong to the state. He then offered to meet with Franklin the following Monday evening to sign their agreement. He suggested that if Franklin drew up the agreement in advance, he should use their French titles and leave a space after their real name to indicate another name that they would assume.

Duportail met with Franklin on February 12, but there is no record of the proceedings. The contract between Duportail and his friends was signed with the American ministers on February 17, 1777. In fact, all of the members, except La Radière, had already signed the agreement on the thirteenth. La Radière feared being delayed by the formalities and signed on the seventeenth, not having secured his leave of absence before that date:

Agreement between the American Commissioners
and Duportail, Laumoy, and Gouvion

[February 13, 1777]

Agreement Convention

1st. It is agreed that the Congress of the United States of America shall grant to the Chevalier du Portail now Lieutenant Colonel in the Royal Corps of Engineers of France, the Rank of Colonel in their Service.

2. The Congress of the United States of America will grant to Monsr. de Laumoy now Major in the Royal Corps of Engineers of France, the Rank of Lieutenant Colonel in their Service.

3. The Congress of the United States of America will grant to Monsr. de Gouvion now Captain in the Royal Corps of Engineers of France, the Rank of Major in their Service.

4. Messrs. Le Chevalier duportail, de Laumoy, and de Gouvion, shall be at liberty to quit the Service of the united States provided it is not during a Campaign or during any particular service, unless ordered so to do by the King of France: and the Congress may dismiss them or any of them whenever they may judge it proper.

5. If all or either of these Gentlemen should be made prisoners by the King of Great Britain the Congress shall use all due means to obtain their Liberty.

6. These Gentlemen shall use all possible dilligence in preparing for their embarkation in order to reach Philadelphia or wherever else the Congres of the united States may be to obey their orders.

7. The pay of these Gentlemen shall be such as is given to officers of their Rank in the Service of the States of America, and shall commence from the date of this agreement.

8. These Gentlemen shall procure and provide for their own passages in such Ships, and in such manner as they shall think proper.

The above agreement was entered into and concluded by us at Paris this 13 February 1776.

signed
B Franklin
S Deane
le che du Portails
Gouvion l'ainé
signé pour Mr. de Laumoy

Copy Note Mr la Radière was afterwards agreed with on the same terms with the within officers and is to be a Lieutenant Colonel.[5]

VOYAGE TO AMERICA

The voyage to America encountered many difficulties, either because Beaumarchais had no ships available until April or because of increased British surveillance of all French ports as a result of learning of the recent capture of Beaumarchais's ship *La Seine*.[6] Duportail wrote to Franklin from Nantes on March 6 that he could not find a ship that was going directly to the colonies and that he must board a ship bound to Saint-Domingue (Haiti), whence he could easily get to Philadelphia. He also noted that in the event that they had to throw their papers overboard and assume a different identity, Duportail would assume the identity of Le Chevalier Derford; Mr. Radière, that of Baillard; Mr. Launoy [Laumoy], that of Le Thur; and Mr. Gouvion, that of d'Otry, and that they would maintain those identities until they were safely in America and even longer if it proved advantageous. The crossing must have been uneventful, as the secret identities seem not to have been used.

Once in the West Indies, Duportail wrote to Franklin from Saint-Domingue on May 15 to report that he was having difficulty finding a vessel to take them to Philadelphia and that Mr. Carabas, Beaumarchais's agent at Cap François (Cap Haïtien), equipped a small vessel loaded with foodstuffs and nothing that would make them suspect if they were stopped. Mr. Carabas acted quickly, as the party was to depart on the seventeenth, minus Laumoy, who became ill with malaria. Mr. Carabas promised to take care of him and give him the means to rejoin his companions as soon as his health improved, which turned out to be the end of the summer.

Duportail recruited Lieutenant Castaing and two sergeants at Saint-Domingue. Lieutenant Castaing became Duportail's aide-de-camp. The party then sailed to New Bern, North Carolina, where they received help from Governor Richard Caswell, the local representative to Congress, to go to Philadelphia. When they arrived at Philadelphia in July, Congress was in turmoil, and the army was seething with unrest because the country had just declared its independence the previous year and was going through birthing pains.

Two of Beaumarchais's ships, the *Amphitrite* and the *Mercure*, carrying secret aid to America, managed to sail from France unnoticed and landed at Portsmouth, New Hampshire, in April with huge cargoes of military supplies (see appendix A) and about thirty volunteer officers, including Louis Antoine Jean Baptiste, Chevalier de Cambray-Digny; Étienne Nicolas Marie Béchet de Rochefontaine (later known as Stephen Rochefontaine); Jean-Bernard Gauthier de Murnan; François-Louis Teissèdre de Fleury;

Jean-Louis-Ambroise de Genton de Villefranche; Pierre Charles L'Enfant; Gilles-Jean Barazer, Chevalier de Kermorvan; Antoine-Joseph Mauduit du Plessis; Antoine Félix Wuibert de Mézières; and Henri Dominique Marius de Palys de Montrepos. They were all capable men who expected to receive important positions in the Continental Army, as the American agent Silas Deane had promised them.

Du Coudray had come out alone on a French ship bound for one of the French West Indian ports. As soon as he arrived in Philadelphia, he presented himself before Congress and was received June 2, 1777. The officers of his staff soon joined him, as well as other volunteers who had come over independently. However, only a few of these men spoke English, and they waited three months for Congress to make their appointments. Many had depleted their funds, and all were more or less dissatisfied. Ten days after the arrival of the Royal Engineers, another band of eleven volunteers, led by the Marquis de Lafayette, arrived at Philadelphia. Silas Deane had commissioned several of these volunteers as major generals before they left France.

General Charles Lee said that these engineering officers did not know the difference between chevaux-de-frise and a field of cabbage. Colonel Richard Gridley, a fine draftsman, was appointed commandant of sappers and miners in 1775 and became a topographer. He was trained in the British artillery and then joined the Corps of Engineers, but he admitted to General Thomas during the French and Indian War that he had never read a single page of a treatise on fortification. Colonel Rufus Putnam, twenty-eight years younger, replaced him in 1776, and was among the first to realize the need for a Corps of Engineers for the Army to accomplish its missions.

The army had too many senior officers, and some of the younger men preferred to resign their posts rather than serve under a foreigner, regardless of their training or capability. Duportail arrived on July 5 to present his credentials to Congress, which was torn by factions and not inclined to grant the commissions sought by the volunteers. It faced insubordination on the part of the American officers and the danger of offending America's newfound ally if the Frenchmen did not receive commissions. Moreover, the army badly needed trained engineers. Most of them spoke only French, and everyone had suffered great hardships before du Coudray's arrival.

Duportail and his companions fulfilled Congress's and the army's needs for a few engineers. They had come with the express consent of the French government, and their demands were modest. Three days after they had presented themselves, Congress resolved to confirm their appointments and appointed Duportail to command all the engineers, while du Coudray directed the field fortifications.[7]

From this date on, Duportail's dispatches were written in English, either translated by an American officer knowing French (John Laurens, Washington's aide-de-camp) or written by himself, as he was learning English, but he always took the precaution of having his messages reviewed. One of the peculiarities of his writing is that he usually wrote in lowercase letters, even for the personal pronoun *I* and for proper names. He had a tendency to employ what might be considered a capital letter when an *R* or a *C* or sometimes a *D* begins a word. He always dotted the personal pronoun, though it sometimes appears to be a little larger than at others. There was never any recognition of the necessity of beginning a new sentence with a capital. The grammar often reflects French construction, and the spelling of cognate words usually use French spelling: for example, *americain* for *American*. French drafts of the documents are rarely located, if they ever existed, and many documents mentioned in his letters have disappeared.

DEFENSE OF PHILADELPHIA

Duportail and his companions arrived at Washington's headquarters at Coryell's Ferry on the Jersey side of the Delaware to present themselves on July 29. Du Coudray was already there, constructing defenses. Washington sent the French engineers to General Gates at Philadelphia to assist him and General Mifflin in reviewing the grounds on the west side of the Delaware River and selecting proper places for encampments and defenses so as not to interfere with du Coudray's work on the Jersey side. He thought a "Jealousy between them, and setting them to work together would only create confusion and widen the Breach."[8] Duportail and his men worked at any odd jobs that were given them during the remainder of the summer. On the morning of September 14, 1777, Washington ordered Duportail to Major General Armstrong to construct "some small Works along the Schuylkill which must be such as can be most speedily executed."[9]

DU COUDRAY'S DEATH

Du Coudray, returning from an inspection of Fort Ticonderoga, arrived on the bank of the Schuylkill River on September 18. He embarked on a barge to cross the river but, too proud to dismount, remained on horseback.

His mount became frightened during the crossing and darted forward. Du Coudray was unable to control it, and both went into the water. Despite the efforts of his escorts to save them, both the horse and rider drowned. His companions now found themselves in dire straits, as they were deprived of their representative to the American authorities. Congress offered to pay their expenses back to France if they so desired, but most decided to remain under Duportail's command and served faithfully.

The engineers' situation might appear more comfortable after du Coudray's death, but their problems continued to multiply: They were not yet paid, and they incurred the cost of horses for travel and transport.[10] Duportail despaired, seeing that Congress was not giving any serious thought to his employment and his reasonable requests. He and his companions seriously considered returning to France at the end of the campaign in January.

In the meantime, Duportail made another attempt to induce Congress to improve their situation. He sent a memorial that was read in Congress on November 13, in which he expressed his frustration at the inaction of Congress in their regard and their intention of returning to France. He also requested the rank of brigadier general for himself, the rank of colonel for Mr. Radière, and the rank of lieutenant colonel for Mr. Gouvion, as previously promised to them. He noted that the chief engineer should have a respectable rank in the army, that army and militia colonels refused to follow his directions, and that soldiers and some officers insult them and their servants using foul language.[11]

The previous day, he had written to the minister of war, the Comte de Saint-Germain, giving his analysis of the Continental Army. He reported that the American victories were not so much due to the good conduct of the army but to the bad decisions of the British generals. He emphasized the need for men and supplies of all kinds to prosecute the war. This would cost France many millions but would be greatly repaid by the destruction of Britain's naval domination. Without any colonies, she would soon have no navy, and American commerce would be conducted with France, which would then have no rival.

He mused that France might sign a treaty with the United States and send 12,000 or 15,000 men to her aid, but he concluded that this would be the best way to ruin everything. He noted that even though America was at war with Britain, the Americans hated the French more than the British and that despite everything that France did and would do for them, they would prefer to reconcile with their former brothers than to find themselves among crowds of people they fear more.[12]

Congress responded immediately on November 17, by appointing Duportail to the rank of brigadier general; Laumoy and Radière, to that of colonel; and Gouvion, to that of lieutenant colonel. This was the turning point in their fortunes. They now had a rank that commanded respect and were soon indispensable to the commander in chief. They then took a leading part in every phase of the war and continued to be indispensable to the Continental Army for the duration of the war.[13]

2

VALLEY FORGE

General Duportail joined the Continental Army at Whitemarsh after its defeat at Germantown and attended his first council of war on November 24, 1777. The terrible winter of 1777–1778 was approaching, and the future of the United States seemed precarious. The army already lacked clothing, food, hospital accommodations, and transportation facilities. Military victories seemed more like defeats, contributing to poor morale. The commander in chief reported the state of affairs to the assembled generals (Armstrong, de Kalb, Duportail, Gates, Greene, Knox, Lafayette, Lee, Mifflin, Scott, Stirling, von Steuben, Wayne, and Woodford) and asked them to consider the question "What measures had best be pursued in the present emergency?" He asked them to put their responses in writing and to give their opinion regarding the "expediency of an attack upon Philadelphia." Eleven of the generals were against making the attack, and only four (Scott, Stirling, Wayne, and Woodford) were in favor.[1]

Duportail's memorial shows his skill of analysis and synthesis on this matter, a quality that stands out more clearly when his memorial is compared with those of the other council members. Washington was impressed. It was not simply that Duportail was a trained officer, as there were several other important European officers at the council, including de Kalb; Lafayette; and, later, von Steuben. But Washington wrote only of Duportail when he recorded, "I have a high opinion of his merit and abilities, and esteem him not only well acquainted with the particular branch he professes, but a man of sound judgment and real knowledge in military science in general."[2] This statement was not to disparage his other officers' qualities, which he also valued, but Duportail stood out among them.

Duportail's first memorial analyzes all aspects of the problem: the terrain, the report and preparation of the troops, the enemy, the motivation

Louis le Bègue de Presle, Duportail (1743–1802), by Charles Willson Peale, probably from life, c. 1781–1784. Duportail is wearing the uniform of a major general in the Continental Army. The ribbon attached at the second button on the coat facing bears the Croix de St. Louis (a reward for exceptional officers with at least ten years of service, notable as the first decoration that could be granted to non-nobles). *Courtesy of Independence National Historical Park.*

and level of training of the combatants, the weather conditions, and possible operations, among other things. He deemed that an attack would result in certain defeat and risk the reversal of any preceding gains. This first memorial (to be followed by many others of similar quality) is as follows:

To attack the Enemy in their Lines appears to me a difficult and dangerous Project. It has especially this very considerable Inconvenience, the
exposing our Army in case it does not succeed, to a total Defeat. This is
easily demonstrated—one of the principal means proposed, is to throw
two thousand men in the rear of the Enemy—if we do not succeed,
these are so many men absolutely lost—as to the main body of the Army
which is to attack in front, it must pass through the intervals left in the
Abattis and Redoubts, which they say, form very narrow Passages—if
after penetrating we should be repulsed, can Troops in disorder return
easily by the Passages through which they were introduced?—Will it
not be very easy for the English to cut off their Retreat—Our whole
Army then may be destroyed or made prisoners—Now does it become
this Army which is the principal one, to run such Risques—*does it
become it to stake the fate of America upon a single Action*? I think not—for
my part I never would place this Army in a Situation where its Rear was
not perfectly free—much less where it will be inclosed on all sides without means of Retreat—to justify such an Enterprise the Success must
be almost certain—to judge of this we have only to take a view of the
dispositions which must be made for this attack—This view will render
the Difficulties evident—first two thousand men are to be introduced by
a River of which the Enemy are wholly Masters—if we embark them
near the Enemy the noise may alarm them—if at a distance, the cold
which they will undergo, will render the use of their arms exceedingly
difficult in the morning—besides can we flatter ourselves that the River
Side is unguarded—let us reflect that a single man is sufficient to make
this Project miscarry and cause us the loss of two thousand men.

As to the Attack in front—these are nearly the Dispositions which
would be followed—We should march upon so many Columns as
there are Roads leading to the Enemy—Upon our arrival in their presence, each Commanding officer of a Column, according to the size of
the works before him, and the number of men which he judges are
contained in them, divides his troops into two parts, one of which sur-
rounds his works and attacks them vigorously while the other marches
boldly through the Intervals and falls upon the Troops in the Rear—But
every one sees how much harmony is required in all these dispositions—how much presence of mind in the Superior officers, how much
firmness in the Troops who have to execute all their manoeuvers under
the fire of an Enemy who are in a great measure covered.

If the Enemy Works are not inclosed, the Enterprise would be much
less dangerous—if they are, the Enterprise is too hardy.

His Excellency, I think, desired us to say a word respecting the
operations in Jersey. In general it seems to me that we can do nothing
better than to endeavor to attack the Enemy's Force there with superior

numbers—but there is a very important observation to be made, which is that we should not weaken ourselves too much here, for we are to consider that the Enemy may recross their Troops in one night and attack us by daybreak with their whole force.

The Chevalier du Portail

P.S. If however an attack be determined upon, the Enemys Works should be more particularly reconnoitred.[3]

Duportail's suggestion must have been acted upon, as Colonel John Laurens, Washington's aide-de-camp, wrote in a letter to his father, then president of Congress, on November 26:

> Our Commander-in-Chief wishing ardently to gratify the public expectation by making an attack upon the enemy yet preferring at the same time a loss of popularity to engaging in an enterprise which he could not justify . . . went yesterday [November 25], to view the works. . . . we saw redouts of a very respectable profile, faced with planks, formidably fraised, and the intervals between them closed with an abattis unusually strong. General Duportail declared that in such works with five thousand men he would bid defiance to any force that should be brought against him.[4]

WINTER QUARTERS

General Washington abandoned any immediate thought of attacking the enemy and turned his attention to selecting a site for winter quarters. He convened another council of general officers on November 30, in which many places were suggested and their various claims to acceptance discussed. They included Wilmington on the Delaware, positions back of Chester and Darby, Lancaster and Reading. These latter places were much farther removed from the enemy lines. Again, the commander in chief requested that his officers give their opinions in writing.

No minutes of the meeting have been found, but Robert Hanson Harrison, Washington's aide-de-camp, summarized the officers' preferences. Generals Armstrong, Duportail, Greene, Lafayette, Scott, Smallwood, and Wayne favored Wilmington. Generals de Kalb, Knox, Maxwell, Muhlenberg, Poor, Sullivan, Varnum, Weedon, and Woodford favored the Lancaster-Reading line. Varnum preferred "Reading to Easton." Lord Stirling was the only one to favor the "Great Valley or Trydruffin." Generals

Duportail and Irvine were "for hutting in a strong position," and Pulaski favored a winter campaign.[5]

Duportail responded,

> By taking Winter Quarters from Lancaster to Reading, we abandon to the Enemy Jersey and all the Country adjacent to Darby, Chester and Wilmington, one of the richest Tracts in this part of the Continent—By establishing them at Wilmington we cover the Country, and do not so completely abandon that part of it which is before Philadelphia, nor even Jersey because our proximity to the Enemy and the ease with which we could throw ourselves upon the rear of their lines in case the Schuylkill should be frozen, will keep them in respect, and put it out of their power to send considerable detachments on the other side of the Delaware from the fear of weakening themselves too much. . . . The position then of Wilmington answers the end of making very difficult the subsistence of Genl. Howe. . . . This position further deprives him of the means of recruiting in the Country,—extending himself in it, adding to the number of his Partisans, in a word, gaining the Country—It has besides the advantage of rendering his communication with his fleet difficult. . . . I should not omit mentioning . . . should War be declared between France and England, and Genl. Howe, from a dread of finding himself blocked up in the Spring by a French Fleet, should wish to quit Philadelphia, we shall be within distance at Wilmington for hindering his embarcation. . . .
>
> This Position [of Wilmington] then unites great Military Advantages—but . . . to ask whether it is eligible is to ask whether we should expose ourselves to an Action, and perhaps more than one— . . . at present . . . if we should gain an advantage we should be unable to pursue it—if we experience a check we run the risque of seeing our army dissipated in the rude marches consequent on a defeat. Consistently with the plan which we ought to form of putting our army in good condition this winter and preparing it for a good Campaign we ought not to have its Repose preceeded by a Defeat.
>
> As to the other points to be considered in this Question, whether Wilmington or Lancaster will be the most proper situation for furnishing the Army with every necessary, I cannot decide, being ignorant of the Country, but it appears to me in general that this point deserves our most serious attention—it is much better to lose Soldiers in Combats with the Enemy to whom we cause a loss at the same time than to lose them by Disorders or Desertion arising from their Misery. Misery, destroys part of an Army and leaves the other without Vigour, without Courage and without good will—we should find ourselves then in the Spring with a Body of an Army incapable of anything, and consequently have no right to expect a successful campaign.[6]

COUNCIL OF WAR

As a brigadier general, Duportail was present at every council of war convened by the commander in chief and gave his opinion in writing, along with the other generals, regarding every matter discussed. Lafayette was impressed with his abilities and called him one of the most honest officers upon this continent.[7]

Washington sent the following circular letter to his general officers on December 3, 1777:

WHITEMARSH

Sir;

> I wish to recall your attention to the important matter recommended to
> your consideration sometime ago—namely the advisability of a Winter's
> Campaign, and practicability of an attack upon Philadelphia with the aid
> of a considerable body of Militia, to be assembled at an appointed time
> and place—Particular reasons urge me to request your Sentiments on
> this matter by the morning, and I shall expect to receive them in writing
> accordingly by that time.[8]

Surviving responses to the circular include letters from Generals Cadwalader, Duportail, Greene, Kalb, Knox, Lafayette, Stirling, and Varnum on December 3 and from generals Armstrong, Irvine, Maxwell, Muhlenberg, Patterson, Poor, Potter, Scott, Smallwood, Sullivan, Wayne, Weedon, and Woodford on December 4. Joseph Reed also presented an opinion on December 4.

Duportail analyzed the situation and provided a concise response in less than an hour in his memorial:

> I have examined anew with all the attention of which I am capable,
> the Project of attacking the English and it still appears to me too dan-
> gerous,—the great body of Militia with which we might be reinforced
> for this purpose does not give me any additional hope of succeed-
> ing—it is not the number of troops which is of importance in this
> case, but it is the quality, or rather, their nature and manner of fight-
> ing. The Troops wanted are such as are capable of attacking with the
> greatest vivacity, the greatest firmness—Troops that are not astonished
> at suffering a considerable loss at the first onset, without causing any
> to the Enemy—for this must be the case in an attack of Intrench-
> ments—although when the Works are carried the Chance turns and
> the loss is on the side of the intrenched.—now, are the Militia or even

our Continentals capable of undergoing this trial, in which the best Troops in the world cannot always support themselves—I am very sorry, in giving the motives for my opinion to be obliged to speak so unfavorably of our Army But the Battle of German Town ought to be a Lesson to us—if our Army had proceeded with vigour on that occasion, would not the English have been completely defeated? The Disposition was excellent—Your Excellency in that instance really conquered General Howe, but his troops conquered yours—if then notwithstanding the advantage of a complete Surprise, notwithstanding the advantages of ground we were repulsed—what would happen before a Line of Redoubts well disposed in all appearance, and the Intervals of which are closed with Abbatis.

There is, however, a case in which I think we might attack the Enemy with Success—I mean if the Schuylkill should be sufficiently frozen below their left to admit of our throwing our greatest Force on their Rear at the same time that we should make an attack in front. Gentlemen acquainted with the Country must decide this point—if indeed the Schuylkill is sufficiently frozen every year to afford a passage for Columns of Troops with Artillery—my opinion is fixed—I think the Army ought to be marched to the other side of the Schuylkill, to be reinforced with all the militia that can be collected, while we wait for the favorable moment.

I would go more minutely into the Subject, if Your Excellency did not order me to send my Answer this morning I did not receive Your Excellency's letter until half after twelve and it is now half after one.[9]

The lesson was "Patience, and train your army before you attempt deliberately to attack seasoned troops." Duportail and the ministry in France both realized that the Americans possessed, in General Washington, not only a military genius but also a man of such character that he could endure apparent defeat with equanimity and that his foundation principles were such that he could be relied on to lead the army through all difficulties to final success.

While the army was waiting at Whitemarsh, uncertain regarding the movements of the British, Duportail went to reconnoiter the positions at Chester and Darby for possible fortification. Two undated pencil sketches from his hand, with explanations, are in the Washington papers in the Library of Congress. The report was not sufficiently favorable for these locations to receive further attention.

On Monday afternoon, December 8, 1777, after having hovered about for several days as though intending to attack Washington, General Howe "changed front and by two or three routes marched his army back to

The artillery park at Valley Forge was placed at the center of
the inner line of defense so the guns could be moved quickly to
wherever they were needed. *Photo courtesy of the author.*

Philadelphia."[10] Washington left Whitemarsh on the twelfth. The engineers
first constructed a bridging train during the night of December 11–12,
1777. It consisted of two bridges over the Schuylkill River at Swede's
Ford. One comprised a roadbed laid across floating rafts; the other involved
thirty-six wagons in the shallow water of the ford with rails across them.
The engineers later constructed more sophisticated flat-bottomed pontons
with special wheeled carriages at Albany. (These pontons accompanied the
troops to Yorktown in 1781.)

GULPH MILLS

By sunrise, the army had crossed the river and stopped at a place known as
the Gulph Mills. Here, General Washington decided on Valley Forge for
winter quarters. His camp overlooked a bleak and desolate winter land-
scape with a beating rain driving in on the men, who had pitched tents
to make themselves a little more comfortable. Heartbroken at abandoning

his plan of action for 1777 and fully realizing the hardships they both already endured and were yet to face, he wrote an address to the army with heart and mind buoyed by confidence. Nowhere does the simplicity and moral grandeur of the character of this great man shine forth more strikingly:

Head Quarters at the Gulph,
Dec. 17. 1777—

The Commander-in-Chief with the highest satisfaction expresses his thanks to the officers and soldiers for the fortitude and patience with which they have sustained the fatigues of the campaign—Although in some instances we unfortunately failed, yet upon the whole Heaven hath smiled on our Arms and crowned them with signal success; and we may upon the best grounds conclude, that by a spirited continuance of the measures necessary for our defence we shall finally obtain the end of our warfare—Independence—Liberty and Peace—These are blessings worth contending for at every hazard—but we hazard nothing. The power of America alone, duly exerted, would have nothing to dread from the power of Britain—Yet we stand not wholly upon our ground—France yields us every aid we ask, and there are reasons to believe the period is not very distant, when she will take a more active part, by declaring war upon the British Crown. Every motive therefore, irresistibly urges us—nay commands us to a firm and manly perseverance in our opposition to our cruel oppressors—to slight difficulties, endure hardships, and contemn every danger—The General ardently wishes it were now in his power to conduct the troops to the best winter quarters—But where are these to be found? Should we retire to the interior parts of the State we should find them crowded with virtuous citizens, who, sacrificing their all, have left Philadelphia, and fled thither for protection. To their distresses humanity forbids us to add—This is not all; we should leave a vast extent of fertile country to be despoiled and ravaged by the enemy, from which they would draw vast supplies, and where many of our firm friends would be exposed to all the miseries of the most insulting and wanton depredations—A train of evils might be enumerated, but these will suffice—These considerations make it indispensably necessary for the army to take such position, as will enable it most effectually to prevent distress and to give the most extensive security, and in that position we must make ourselves the best shelter in our power—with activity and diligence Huts may be erected that will be warm and dry—In these the troops will be compact, more secure against surprises than if in a divided state, and at hand to protect the country. These cogent reasons have determined the General to take post in the neighborhood of this camp; and influenced by them he persuades himself, that the officers and soldiers, with one heart, and one mind, will resolve to surmount every difficulty, with a fortitude and patience, becoming their profession, and the sacred cause in which they are engaged. He himself will share in the hardship, and partake of every inconvenience.—

Tomorrow being the day set apart by the Honorable Congress for public Thanksgiving and Praise; and duty calling us to devoutly express our grateful acknowledgements to God for the manifold blessings he has granted us—the General directs that the army remain in its present quarters, and that the Chaplains perform divine service with their several corps and brigades—and earnestly exhorts all officers and soldiers, whose absence is not indispensably necessary, to attend with reverence the solemnities of the day.[11]

VALLEY FORGE

Valley Forge was selected, and the army set up headquarters there on December 20, 1777. Before leaving the Gulph, orders were issued regarding the building of huts, which the soldiers were immediately to construct for themselves. Thomas Paine, who was at Lancaster and York during the winter of 1777–1778, wrote a letter to Benjamin Franklin regarding the encampment at Valley Forge: "I was there when the army first began to build huts; they appeared to me like a family of beavers; every one busy; some carrying logs, others mud and the rest fastening them together. The whole was raised in a few days."[12]

Immediately after erecting shelters for the men, the work of providing defenses began. Duportail was assigned the task of bolstering those defenses to prepare against an enemy attack because the army was encamped in a place easily accessible from the enemy's headquarters in Philadelphia. Washington expected an attack the following spring, but it never happened. This was among the most significant of all of Duportail's services and established his reputation.

General Washington's order book for January 15, 1778, specified,

The works marked out by the Engineers for the defense of the camp are to be erected with all possible dispatch and the Commander-in-Chief requests the favor of General Greene, Lord Stirling and the Marquis de la Fayette (General Sullivan being upon other duty) to consult with

The soldiers built two thousand huts similar to these to house 20,000 men and officers. Each hut sheltered nine to twelve men. Construction was completed in a month, and the encampment became the fourth-largest city in America after Philadelphia, New York, and Boston. *Photo courtesy of the author.*

Genl. Portail on the proper means and number of men necessary to execute the works in the different Wings & second line and gives orders accordingly—and that each of them appoint proper officers to superintend and push forward the defences.[13]

Later, when General William Howe returned to England, he came under severe criticism for not having driven Washington from his entrenchments before his departure from Philadelphia. His excuse was that the place was naturally strong and had been so strengthened by "artificial works" that he did not judge it prudent to attempt an attack "during the severe season"; later, it would have been impossible. He said, "[H]aving good information in the spring that the enemy had strengthened his camp by additional works and being certain of moving him from thence when the campaign opened, I dropped all thought of attack."[14] This gives "indirect but decisive testimony to the wisdom of the selection of this site" and to the "deterrent effects" of the entrenchments so laboriously constructed and constantly strengthened by additional works of a defensive character carried on during the winter.[15]

The Duportail House (297 Adams Drive, Chesterbrook, Pennsylvania), is now a venue for weddings. The plaque on the left of the door reads, "Headquarters of Brigadier General Louis Lebègue Duportail, chief of engineers of the American Army who planned the defenses at Valley Forge 1777–1778." *Photo courtesy of the author.*

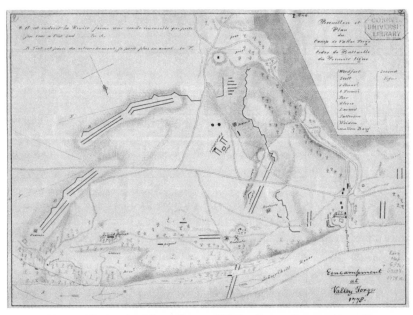

Duportail's sketch of the defenses of Valley Forge. *Courtesy Cornell University Library, https://digital.library.cornell.edu/catalog/ss:545278.*

Duportail was staying on the farm of a Welsh Quaker named John Havard Jr. at Chesterbrook at the time. The house came to be known as the Duportail House. General Duportail's original map of the Valley Forge defenses was found in the attic rafters during renovations in 1903 and has been in the collections of the Pennsylvania Historical Society since 1908.

SAPPERS AND MINERS

Duportail also proposed to supplement the engineer officers with companies of combat engineers and called them companies of sappers and miners, according to European custom. The sappers dug the entrenchments (saps) for a formal siege; the miners constructed underground tunnels. These companies, which would become a permanent part of the Continental Army, could execute small projects or supervise infantry details in more extensive undertakings. Duportail submitted the paper to the commander in chief about January 18, 1778:

> If fortification is necessary in any Armies, it is peculiarly so in those, which like ours, from a deficiency in the practice of manoeuvres cannot oppose any to those of the enemy being necessitated therefore to receive him on their own ground, they ought always to be protected either by a natural or artificial Fortification, if it were only to have (under favor of the resistance of this fortification) sufficient time to ascertain the Result of the Enemy's movements—where his principal force is directed—and where his greatest effort is to be made. With respect to natural fortification, all Situations do not afford it—and to rely entirely upon it, would involve prodigious restraint in the choice of Positions and exclude many excellent ones considered relatively to the operations of War—it is therefore much more advantageous to have recourse to artificial Fortification which is applicable in all Situations.
>
> The very great difficulties which I experienced in the last Campaign, both in setting on foot the most simple work and having it executed with the necessary Conditions, induce me to propose to His Excellency an establishment which is absolutely indispensable, if he chooses to derive hereafter those succours from Fortification which it holds out to him.
>
> I would desire to have three Companies of Sappers formed—they should be instructed in every thing that relates to the construction of Field works—how to dispose of the Earth to cut the Slopes—face with Turf or Sods—make fascines—arrange them properly—cut and fix Palisades &ct.

The Sappers should be distributed in the different works, and a sufficient number of fatigue men drawn from the line should be joined to them to work under their direction, by which means the work would be executed with a perfection and celerity which otherwise will ever be unknown in this army—it is, I believe, altogether useless to enlarge upon a matter so obvious—I proceed therefore immediately to the principal Conditions on which the Corps should be formed.

1st. The pay ought to be greater than that of ordinary foot soldiers because the Service is exceedingly hard—this is the practice in Europe, and they receive besides extraordinary pay when they work.—Choice ought to be made of vigorous Soldiers and the preference should be given to Carpenters and Masons.

2. The Non-commissioned officers ought all to read and write, and be intelligent persons of good Characters.

3. The Companies of Sappers ought to be altogether under the Command of the Head Engineer—for if the Major Generals had a right to employ them as they pleased, each, from a desire of fortifying his Camp in his own way, would ask for Sappers and they would all be taken from the Engineers.

Besides as such partial works do not enter into the general plan of the position they are for the most part useless, ill concerted, and sometimes even dangerous.

4. The Captains of Sappers will be charged with the detail of their Companies, and each of them will be accountable to the Commanding officer of the Engineers in order that he may always know the State of the Companies, their Strength etc.

5. Each Company should always have its Tools with it, carried on a Waggon provided for the purpose—The Company should be answerable for all Tools lost—and in case any should be broke, the pieces are to be produced to the Officer to whom the detail of the Company is to be committed.

The Camp of the Sappers to be assigned by the Commanding officer of Engineers adjacent to the place where they are to be employed.

Of the Officers.

If it be important to choose the Privates in these Companies—it is much more so to choose the Officers—The Congress ought, in my opinion, to think of forming Engineers in this Country to replace us when we shall be called home—The Companies of Sappers now proposed might serve as a School to them—they might there acquire at once the practical part of the Construction of Works, and if choice be made of young men, well bred, intelligent and fond of Instruction, we shall take pleasure in giving them principles upon the choice of Situations, and the methods of adapting works to the ground.

If His Excellency approves my Plan—I would advise the speedy execution of it—in order that the Companies may have served their Apprenticeship before the opening of the Campaign.

These Companies ought not to be composed of Recruits—but Soldiers answering the description above should be taken from the Line for the purpose.

While I am employed in representing the defects of my branch of the Army—I entreat His Excellency to observe that four Engineers are not sufficient—of the four, one is always detached and sometimes two, which is the case at present—and I am left with only one Officer—it is impossible for us to do the Service of the Army. There is at York Town a French officer who was brought by Mr. Du Coudray and introduced by him as an Engineer—for my part I do not give him out as such, because he was not in that character in France and has no such pretensions himself—but he studies with a view to become a Member of the Corps—he has studied Geometry, understands surveying and Drawing and therefore might be very useful to us.

I entreat His Excellency to ask the Congress for this Gentleman—he has on his part made applications which have hitherto proved fruitless. His name is Ville franche and he brought a particular recommendation from General R. How to the President of Congress.

Signed Chevr. du Portail[16]

Duportail did not await a response to this memorial, as he was aware of the responsibilities that would be required of the engineers in future combat. He created a school of engineering to start the next campaign off on good footing. Gouvion undertook the administration and could instruct the corps in a rigorous and homogeneous manner, faithful to the principles of conformity of action instructed at Mézières.

CORPS OF ENGINEERS

Washington, keenly aware of the need for an effective Corps of Engineers in the army, particularly liked Duportail's plan to train officers as apprentice engineers, thus ensuring a steady supply of native-born engineers. He readily accepted Duportail's plan and urged Congress to consider its importance, but that body was too busy with the many demands made upon it to give the matter immediate attention. In the meantime, Mr. Villefranche, in response to a demand made to Congress some time previously, received his appointment as major of engineers. But more officers were needed.

Congress approved the formation of three companies on May 27, 1778, but the army moved slowly, and Washington appointed officers only on August 2, 1779, after Duportail had personally interviewed the candidates. Washington transferred the carefully selected enlisted men from infantry regiments a year later.

Each company was authorized a captain, three lieutenants, four sergeants, four corporals, and sixty privates. Congress took the final step to regularize the "corps of engineers" on March 11, 1779. In response to Washington's continuing pressure, it resolved "that the engineers in the service of the United States shall be formed into a corps, styled the 'corps of engineers,' and shall take rank and enjoy the same rights, honours, and privileges, with the other troops on continental establishment."[17] This legislation gave the engineers the status of a branch of the Continental Army, with the same pay and prerogatives as artillerymen to prevent any jealousy between the technical branches. As commandant of the Corps of Engineers, Duportail supervised the engineer officers and the companies of sappers and miners, functioned as a special adviser to the commander in chief, and assigned individual officers to specific posts before the start of each campaign.[18]

France began rigorously training a small corps of topographical engineers, the Ingénieurs Géographes (distinct from the Corps Royal du Génie), after the Seven Years' War, setting a precedent for a separate topographical section. These topographical engineers prepared a systematic map reference library for planning operations. Washington, a former surveyor,

Reenactors, portraying the Department of Geographers, survey a redoubt. *Photo courtesy of the author.*

particularly understood the value of accurate maps. He asked for a topographical staff on July 19, 1777, and Congress authorized him to appoint a "geographer and surveyor of the roads, to take sketches of the country, the seat of war," as well as necessary subordinates six days later. Robert Erskine, a civil engineer and inventor, accepted the job but did not report to headquarters until June 1778. His maps were as accurate as those of the French and vastly superior to anything available to British commanders.

JEAN-BERNARD GAUTHIER DE MURNAN

Duportail discovered another young Frenchman who had come over independently as a volunteer and who possessed all the necessary qualifications for an officer of engineers. Duportail wrote a letter on February 23, 1778, strongly recommending him to the commander in chief:

> M. de murnan, in whose favor I take the liberty of soliciting your kindness, has gone through the necessary studies for entering into the Corps of Engineers in France—he even obtained his license for examination, which is never granted until satisfactory papers are delivered at the War office setting forth that the person is of noble family. France does not receive into the Corps which is charged with the precious Trust of her fortified places and every thing that relates to the defense of her frontiers, any other subjects than those whose birth and education are pledges of their Sentiments and Conduct. This license is at the same time a proof of his studies, because it can only be had in consequence of certificates given by professors who are liable to be called upon—The reason why this gentleman was not admitted was because the arrangement of the Minister underwent a considerable change at that time—and that after having intended to make a considerable promotion in the Corps of Engineers, he confined himself to making a very small one.—This officer then entered into the King's household Troops, but this Service not suiting his tastes which inclined him to engineering, he went to Russia which was then at war with the Turks. He there served in the capacity which he liked—he was Captain Engineer, but peace being made he returned to France where he was preparing to reenter the Service when called by some business to one of the Sea port Towns. The Enthusiasm which prevailed there in favor of this country took possession of him and he was persuaded to come here; a Vessel was ready, he embarked, contenting himself with barely writing to his friends to recommend him to Messrs. Franklin and Deane, as well as to the principal officers of his own Country here, among others, to the Mquis. de la Fayette, but none of these letters are arrived.

This officer may be very useful here, he possesses sufficient theoretical knowledge to make him an exceedingly good Engineer, and he
acquired some practice in Russia. He asks for the rank of Major, which
appears reasonable. In all the States of Europe, a grade is readily given
to an officer and especially to an Engineer whose service is wanted, and
it is easily conceived that this is necessary, as no one would expatriate
himself and go into a new service without reaping a benefit from it.

I am with great Respect
Your Excellency's etc.
DUPORTAIL.[19]

Washington passed the application on to Congress. As he received no
answer, Washington added the following postscript to his March 1 letter
to Congress: "As Genl. Portail is pressing to know the Comee. Decision
relative to Engineer recom. by him and a real want of these people appear
I should also be glad to know what to expect & say to him."[20]

Congress still paid no heed, but Mr. Murnan, the Frenchman in question, was willing to enter into the service immediately, expecting Congress
would give him his commission later. Congress did not consider his case
until January 13, 1778, and passed the following resolution: "That M. John
Bernard de Murnan be appointed major in the corps of engineers, to take
rank as such from the first day of March last, and to receive pay and subsistence from the 1st day of February last, the latter being the time he was
directed by the Commander-in-Chief to act as major."[21]

OATH OF ALLEGIANCE

Congress adopted a resolution on February 3, 1778, requiring that every
officer in the military take an oath of allegiance before the commander in
chief or any major general or brigadier general:

> Resolved, That every officer who holds or shall hereafter hold a com-
> mission or office from Congress, shall take and subscribe the following
> oath or affirmation:
>
> I, do acknowledge the United States of America to be free, indepen-
> dent and sovereign states, and declare that the people thereof owe no
> allegiance or obedience, to George the third, king of Great Britain; and
> I renounce, refuse and abjure any allegiance or obedience to him: and
> I do swear (or affirm) that I will, to the utmost of my power, support,
> maintain and defend the said United States, against the said king George

the third and his heirs and successors, and his and their abettors, assistants and adherents, and will serve the said United States in the office of which I now hold, with fidelity, according to the best of my skill and understanding. So help me God.[22]

As France had not yet declared war against Great Britain, French officers were not required to sign the oath until after the Treaty of Alliance with France was promulgated. Duportail signed it on May 12. His signature on this document would later play an important role, as it conferred American citizenship on him ipso facto.

DEFENSES OF VALLEY FORGE

The defenses of Valley Forge were practically completed by the end of March. Henry Laurens, president of Congress, wrote to a friend on April 7, "The present newly adopted encampment Genl. Duportail assures me, is tenable against the enemy's utmost efforts by their present powers."[23]

The work was accelerated because General Washington expected the enemy would attack the Continental Army in their entrenchments as soon

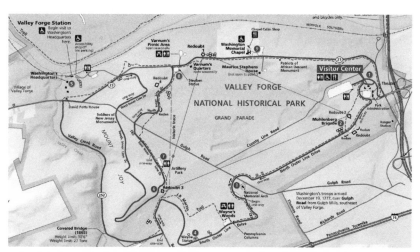

The defenses of Valley Forge consisted of five redoubts (highlighted) connected by miles of trenches and earthworks designed to strengthen the natural advantages of the terrain. The redoubts were arranged in a triangle and were all visible to each other because the ground had been cleared of trees for miles around to build the huts and earthworks and for firewood. Enemies approaching the encampment could be spotted miles away. *Valley Forge National Historical Park Visitors' Brochure.*

as the good weather returned. Washington also thought that an enclosed work on a particular height ("Joy Hill" or "Mount Joy") might add to the army's security. General Duportail wrote a note on April 13, expressing his concern that such a work would be a hindrance rather than a help, as it only allowed viewing an enemy advance on one or two sides. They could mount an attack on the other sides under cover, which were incapable of defense.[24]

The situation at Valley Forge was very tense during April 1778. The so-called Conway Cabal attempted to replace Washington with General Gates as commander in chief. The debate roiled in Congress during February and March and was still on everyone's mind when news of a new menace reached camp. After news of the surrender at Saratoga reached London, Parliament considered Lord North's Conciliatory Bills, and General Howe was sending out notices from Philadelphia about them. There were also reports of commissioners from Parliament coming to restore peace. They were due to arrive shortly, with full powers to grant any demand short of independence and to pardon all who would immediately lay down their arms.

Washington wrote a private letter to John Banister, a personal friend and a delegate from Virginia, a few days later, emphasizing his distress:

> The enemy are beginning to play a game more dangerous, than their efforts by arms . . . which threatens a fatal blow to the independence of America, and of course to her liberties. They are endeavoring to snare the people by specious allurements of peace. . . . Nothing short of independence, it appears to me, can possibly do. A peace on other terms would . . . be a peace of war. The injuries we have received from the British . . . are so great and so many, that they can never be forgotten.

He then thinks of France, and his outlook brightens immediately:

> I think France must have ratified our independence and will declare war immediately, on finding that serious proposals of accommodation are made. . . . It cannot be fairly supposed that she will hesitate to declare war if she is given to understand, in a proper manner, that a reunion of the two countries may be the consequence of procrastination. An European war or European Alliance would effectually answer our purpose.[25]

General Washington proposed on April 20, 1778, three plans and related questions for his general officers to consider for the upcoming campaign:

1. [A]ttempt to recover Philadelphia and destroy the enemy army there. What mode of execution to pursue and what force will be

required against an estimated 10,000 men, exclusive of marines and seamen, whose aid may be called in? Attempt an attack by storm, by regular approaches or by blockade, and in what manner?

2. [T]ransfer the war to the north by attacking New York. Should this be done by a coup de main, with a small force, or make an attack with a large force? How large a force would be necessary in either case, estimating the number of the enemy in and around New York at 4000 men, and how to dispose of the troops to achieve the desired result, and to protect the country and secure the stores at the same time?

3. [R]emain quiet in a secure, fortified camp, drilling and disciplining the army. What post shall be taken so as to keep the army secure, to cover the country and magazines and to be in a position to counteract any future movements of the enemy?[26]

Duportail's memorial on this occasion was a very significant document, as it had a profound influence in shaping Washington's policy. It also indicated that Duportail was imbued with the American cause during the five months he had been in the Continental Army because he saw the cause of France in it. He understood English very well by this time and had listened to all the arguments of the officers in camp regarding the situation of America. He thought the victory at Saratoga blinded the people in the north to the true character of the American troops. His memorial emphasized, "Let us take care that the successes in the North do not occasion defeats here, where the circumstances are by no means the same."[27]

He wrote the "Supplement" in English and in his own hand. This version of the memorial is Colonel John Laurens's translation, which includes Duportail's interlined corrections. It also shows how carefully he watched Laurens's work to ensure that his ideas were conveyed accurately in the English version that the commander in chief would read. The memorial intended to state that England could never reduce America by arms if proper care were taken of the men and if France continued to keep England on guard by warlike preparations so that she retained a large part of her troops in Europe.

DUPORTAIL'S MEMORIAL

The memorial is as follows:

In all great Enterprises, the first thing to be done, is to form a general Plan of Conduct, to which all the particular operations are to have reference. This general plan is as it were the touch Stone by which all the subordinate projects are proved—according as they agree or disagree with it they are good or ill, deserve to be approved or rejected: now in this great Enterprise of supporting American Liberty by arms, I do not see that we have established the principles which ought to guide us in war, or, to speak more frankly, it appears to me that we have adopted defective principles. Almost every one considers the American Army in the same light as the British, thinks it capable of the same things, and would have it act in the same way; thus we see from time to time bold projects formed, rash resolutions proposed, which are the better received as they flatter those to whom they are proposed, by shewing them that the Nation is judged capable of vigorous actions—but this flattery may have fatal consequences, it may ruin America. Let it be our endeavor in this important business, to consider things in their true light.

It is an Axiom among Military men, that Troops which are not what are called *Regular Troops* cannot make head against regular troops in level ground or in any Situation that does not offer them very considerable advantages. The American Army therefore cannot stand against the British who are composed with British or German troops all Regular. perhaps some person too much prejudiced in favor of their Country, or not sufficiently instructed, will ask me, why I refuse to call the American Troops regular; I have no answer for the Persons who make this question; it proves that they do not know what Troops are—I address myself only to those who have an idea of what is understood by Discipline, Theory and Practice of Manoeuvres, System, Pride of Corps etc. . . . Such Persons will grant that the American Army new in every respect, and not having had a foundation of formed officers and Soldiers, cannot as yet claim the Title of regular Troops, and that it is therefore incapable, as I remarked above, of resisting the Enemy on equal ground. besides has not experience manifestly proved it? we were beaten at Brandywine—we were beaten at German Town altho' we had the immense advantage of a complete Surprise. if any action is to enlighten us in respect to our troops, it is this—The dispositions on our side were excellent. General Washington was truly victorious over General Howe, since the latter was absolutely in fault and completely surprised, but his troops conquered ours and thereby they have saved the glory of their general and [they] gave a great proof of their superiority in plain [in even contest]. Let us therefore avoid committing ourselves in this way again—for it is farther a principle of war cautiously to avoid doing what your Enemy would have you do—Now let General Howe be asked whether he would like to meet the American Army on nearly equal ground for the issue of the present dispute, he will answer that it is the wish of his heart—that he desires only two or three such opportunities to decide the cause of America—because he is sure of beating us, and that the loss of general actions will soon have ruined our party without recourse. I know very well that many persons are not of this opinion, and that they say, that having more men than the English and greater facility of procuring them we cannot fight the Enemy too often because even if we should be beaten, the loss of the Enemy, though less in itself would be greater relatively to their whole number, and consequently they must soon be ruined—but this opinion is built upon a foundation altogether false. our numbers are not superior to those of the English. doubtless measures were taken last year to get as great a number as possible, yet at Brandywine we scarcely had 12,000 men, the English had as many—besides let us remark one thing; we received in the month of October 1500 men from General Putnam's army; in November 3000 from the Northern army; these added to the 12,000 men we had in the month of September would amount to 16,000 men. however when we quitted Whitemarsh we were scarcely between 8000 and 9000 men—that is to say, that in three months, the diminution from Battle and principally sickness and Desertion, has been half the Army; thus if the Campaign instead of opening in the month of September had commenced in the months of April or May we should not have had a man left at the end of the campaign. This proves that if we get men easily, we lose them in the same manner. besides with respect even to the facility of getting them, I do not see that many recruits arrive. On the contrary I hear that they experience great difficulties in procuring them. nevertheless the last Campaign, all things considered, was not unlucky, and the northern successes keep up the spirits of the people. if then notwithstanding these things, there is so little eagerness in enlisting, or so much facility in quitting the army; what would be the case if we were to be unfortunate in general actions the loss of which will not always be made up by great success in another part. What we ought to propose to ourselves, is to defend the country inch by inch, to endeavor to hinder the enemy from rendering himself master of it, consequently never to receive him but when we are protected by a natural or artificial fortification, in other words to carry on what is styled a defensive War. this is our true part and it is so obvious that in Europe, all Military men and even those who are not so, suppose this to be our Conduct—if the Americans could consult the modern daily publications, they should there find that the model offered to General Washington is principally Fabius, that wise Roman who ruined Hannibal by refusing to fight him in plain. Fabius however commanded Romans, but these Romans had been thrice defeated, they were disheartened, dreaded the Enemy, and were nearly reduced to the condition of new and unformed Troops. The Consul conducted himself accordingly, avoided general Battles, kept himself on the defensive, always occupying strong positions and where the Enemy could not attack him but with considerable disadvantage—it is true that this kind of war was not approved of at Rome; Men of leisure who loved to be amused by great events, men of impetuous dispositions, men whose discernment was not sufficient to judge of what circumstances required, in a word the particular enemies of the Consul, turned him into ridicule, affixed to him insulting surnames, but the sage General was unmoved by them. he knew that after all, the event would determine his reputation in the world—he therefore invariably pursued his plan, and by his firmness which was crowned with success, he merited the appellation of Savior of Rome.

Application of the foregoing Principles to our present Situation and what we ought to propose to ourselves.

Ought we to open the Campaign by an attack on the Enemy's lines as I hear sometimes proposed?

If the English army were out of its lines at the distance of one or two miles in front, from the reasons just mentioned we ought not to attack them for we should expose ourselves to almost certain Defeat (I suppose our army so large as in its last Campaign): and because this army is covered by lines, because it has added to its natural Strength that of Fortification we would attack it? This is manifestly unreasonable. Fortification is the means used by the weak to enable them to resist the strong. We Engineers count that a good fortified place enable those who defend it to resist ten times their own number.—Field Engineering does not afford such considerable advantages, but according as the ground is more or less judiciously chosen, as the Engineer has traced his work with more or less skill, and afterwards as the Profiles are more or less respectable, executed with more or less care, this kind of fortification renders one equal to two, three, four, and sometimes more—I am not acquainted with the English lines in their whole extent, but I may judge by what I have seen, because it is a principle in fortification to establish as perfect an equality as possible in the different parts, so that no one be more attackable than another; now by what I have seen of the English Lines, I judge that the defenders may at least hold them against double their numbers. Their army may at present be 10,000 strong, consequently they may defend themselves against 20,000 composed of troops equal in every respect (I mean Regular Troops). Let us make the comparison and judge.

I cannot forbear making an observation here which is, that to judge by the rash or rather the [paper torn] Projects of certain Persons they would think, that they had originally imagined that the establishing of

American Liberty was to be the business of one or two years. that being deceived in this respect they begin to grow tired of the war, and wish to bring the matter to a speedy decision one way or the other. in effect, if their projects were followed, the matter would soon be decided. instead of free Citizens the Americans would in a little time be a conquered people, and consequently obliged to submit to the conditions imposed on them by their Subduers.

I know very well that those who propose to attack the English in their lines, deduce their arguments from the American Troops having attacked and carried lines in the North, but let us take care that successes in the North do not occasion defeats here, where the circumstances are by no means the same. the Northern Troops may perhaps have attacked and carried some portion of Intrenchments, either illy made or injudiciously disposed, or not sufficiently lined with troops;—or perhaps they attacked with vastly superior numbers—but that they ever attacked with a number nearly equal to that of the enemy (which would be our case), Intrenchments such as those of the English at Philadelphia, supported on each flank by a River, secure from being turned and attackable only in front, is what I will never believe. I will add to this by way of explaining my idea, that if I were General Howe, and the Americans should advance to attack me in my lines, I would not give myself the trouble of defending them. I would retire some four or five hundred yards in the rear to some covered place, I would only leave a few poppers to deceive them and make them think they had forced the lines, and when they had once got within and were preparing to push their imaginary advantage, I would fall upon them like a thunderbolt. The aim of this conduct which at first appears whimsical, is as follows: General Howe by defending his lines seriously would soon disgust the Americans and oblige them to desist from the attack, which would produce nothing decisive for the English—whereas if they were once within the Lines and were repulsed to effect a retreat every one must regain the breaches made in the Entrenchments and abbatis, which is not very easy and exposes the greatest part of the army to be slaughtered or made prisoners.

Second Question—

Ought we at the opening of the campaign to approach Philadelphia? No. We ought not. we are even too near already, and for this reason— would we approach the enemy in order to be more certain of fighting him? this is altogether useless—he will certainly come to seek us. The English Minister does not send Genl. Howe with his army into America, to remain inactive in Philadelphia. he must fight us—must endeavor to destroy us. he must conquer the Country; not to do it, is to be conquered himself. it is to give gain of cause to the Americans. therefore General Howe will make it his business to find us. but at present I say, to wait for him ten or twelve miles nearer to or farther from Philadelphia makes for us the difference of having about two thousand men more or less to engage. this is clear. . . . supposing us more than thirty miles from Philadelphia, it will no longer be practicable for him to come upon us in one march, he must leave the City at a great distance; then if we had a sufficient body of militia conveniently posted for the purpose, at about fifteen miles from the Town, this body as soon as Genl. Howe should be at proper distance, might march to the Lines, destroy them, enter Philadelphia and burn the Magazines. To prevent this Genl. Howe would be obliged to leave a sufficiency of troops to guard the Lines and the Town, that is to say, about 2500 or 3000 men—this would be 2000 men less . . . which is certainly worth attention—on the other hand, as long as Genl. Howe has only to move twenty miles from Philadelphia to attack us—his rear, his Communications with the town are secure; we venture to interpose any Troops, as in case of a sudden retrograde motion of the Enemy such parties would be entrapped between his army and the Town or the Rivers. whereas if he were at the distance proposed, we might convert our numerous Militia which cannot be opposed in front of the enemy, to harrassing his Flanks, attacking his baggage, Convoys etc.

These are real advantages; what are those expected from approaching Philadelphia which can counterbalance them? To cover ten or twelve miles of Country? what a pitiful consideration is that in competition with the powerful interests above mentioned—To close in upon the Enemy, and render their subsistence difficult? we ought not to be seduced by this reason—this made us take and occupy the position of White marsh until the month of december, and it was very much better founded at that time, nevertheless what end did it answer—the Enemy still procured nearly all that they wanted—and for our part, by remaining in that camp, in a season already cold, in which the Soldiery suffered greatly, when the proximity of the Enemy and the dread of being attacked, obliged us to keep Tents, baggage, and provision waggons at a distance—by having amused ourselves that Camp, with the absurd plan of attacking the Enemy his Lines with an inferior Army—by having too long delayed to come and build our barracks and form Magazines of every kind—the Camp of White Marsh may be charged with the loss of three or four thousand men perhaps, of which we have been robbed by sickness, misery and Desertion—it may be charged with half the horses of the Army, which emacerated by the hunger they have suffered this winter, will perish on our first movements in the Spring, and leave, may be, our waggons and Artillery in the roads.

We ought therefore in my opinion to keep ourselves between 30 and 40 miles distance from Philadelphia, and since we have the advantage at present of obliging the enemy to march to our own ground to fight us, it is our part always to post ourselves in such a manner as that he cannot attack us but under considerable disadvantages; and for this purpose to always choose Situations strong in themselves, and besides avail ourselves of the Succors of Art. We should farther prefer positions in which we might avoid a general Battle if we thought proper—we should esteem it an essential quality in our positions to have the Rear free and an easy Retreat in order that an unlucky action might not be attended with too extensive consequences. if we should discover in our position any capital Defect which did not at first appear, or which only became such in consequence of the movements of the Enemy, we would immediately decamp and go elsewhere.—we should be cautious not to give into the Snare, which our Enemies will not fail to lay for us, endeavoring by their Raillery on our Retreats, to make us establish it as a point of honor, rather to keep a bad position than to make a retrograde movement. we should not forget that in war, to advance or retire are neither honorable or dishonorable; that it is at the end of a Campaign that the Prize is given, and that Glory is his reward who has gained his end—besides if the Enemy in the movements which he should make to try us, to turn us, should give us an opening, should expose any of his Troops, Posts, Baggage, to be attacked with advantage; we should never fail to do it—for one must not imagine that defensive war consists in never forming any Enterprise against the Enemy, but in such war the whole army (I Confess) should not form enterprises against the whole ennemy's army—enterprises are formed with Detachments, whenever you can assure yourself of attacking with greater numbers—these expeditions even ought to be sought for, and frequently repeated, for it is thus that new Troops are by degrees enured to War.—Care must be taken, only, not to expose them to too severe marches, excessive bad weather or the want of Provisions. it appears to me that this kind of War would greatly embarrass the Enemy: for at length, as it is absolutely necessary that he attack us, he would do it; but as we are supposed to be always well fortified, and choose positions in which the whole Army cannot be attacked at once as we support the points only as long as it can be done with advantage, and retire whenever the Enemy begins to get too great an ascendancy over us, he is always liable to suffer considerable Loss without procuring decisive Success—in fact if we retire, even if the greatest part of the Army should have been successfully employed in supporting the point attacked, it is after all no battle—it is a post forced—a particular Corps repulsed—and this has no consequence—the Retreat is peaceably conducted—another post is taken hard by, and the business is to begin again—but General Howe has not a sufficiency of Troops, to purchase ground so dearly—it is easy to see that by these means 20 miles of Country would cost him half his Army—it is when weakened to this degree, and advanced into the interior of the Country he would tremble to see himself surrounded by those clouds of Militia useless at other times, but serviceable then, that he would be forced to yield the Country to us, and retire to shut himself up in his lines—and this is all that we have to desire, because it would prove to the English their inability to reduce this State, and consequently America—for what would happen in this State would in like manner happen in any other by pursuing the same Conduct. Nothing therefore would be better calculated [to] disgust them from continuing useless Efforts; whereas if we pique ourselves upon making war as equal European Armies do, if we will engage in general Actions, attack the Enemy or receive him in any kind of ground and unprepared, we shall experience some considerable Check—the Enemy will not always commit the fault of which he was guilty at Brandywine (where he might have cut off our Retreat, made himself master of our baggages and have reduced us to a ne plus ultra between the Delaware and the Chesapeak Bays), he will pursue us vigorously, hinder our reassembling, dissipate us, drive us from the Pennsylvania State, then availing himself of the disaffection of the majority of the inhabitants, make it declare for the King, and perhaps take arms in his favor—an event of the greatest consequence relatively to the other States of America, which would not be unshaken by such an example—relatively to the English who would be encouraged by it to make the greatest Efforts. and lastly considered with reference to foreign powers who not being near enough to estimate such Events according to their real value—and distinguishing in them only a proof of the great Superiority of the English, or inconstancy of the Americans, would not perhaps involve themselves further by giving them unavailing Succors—

This translation is interlined here and there by Duportail, who adds with his own hand and in his faulty English the following:

Supplement

the more i reflect upon the matter above treated, the more it seems to me impossible that the English can reduce America by arms, at least so long as the Americans behave himself properly. provided also that the Court of france will not Change her political system and by the awe of War which she gives to England, will hinder its sending to America more troops than it has sent hytherto. if there is any cause of reducing it, we should look for that Cause in the American army itself. i have observed just now that in three or four months our army diminished one half without doubt principally by desertion. that is very frightful for everybody sees that if it continues so all America will soon be exhausted of men. there can be certainly many Causes of that prodigious desertion, but the most Considerable and which can be Remedied is the bad situation of the Soldiers, the want of cloathing that (besides he must bear all the intemperatures of the weather) abases his profession in his own eyes and makes him disdain it—the want of provisions During many Days the more hard to be borne as when he has any he has too much—the want of Cleanliness in his tents which causes us shameful sicknesses that are the appendices of the extreme misery. the proofs of what I mention are before our eyes. we see that there are a great deal less depression in some battalions of artillery who are generally better provided with every thing and whose officers take more care of their Soldiers.

i will say no more on this subject because it is within reach of every body i thinck that great many persons have taken notice of it and proposed the means necessary to remedy the inconveniency above mentioned. as for me I have mentioned them only because I had an opportunity to share them in a prospect very striking since every body can perceive that upon this depends most the fate of America.

LE Ch^vr. DUPORTAIL[28]

In a separate paper, Duportail addresses the several questions proposed and disposes of them by referring to this quoted memorial. He adds the following general observations:

it appears to me that there is a previous important point to be decided because all our operations ought to be subordinate to it—this point is to know, in case of our army suffering a check and not being able to maintain its ground here, in what direction our Retreat is to be made in preference—towards the blue mountains?—on the other side of the Susquehannah?—on the side of the Delaware? by determining this, we shall determine where the grand magazines of the army are to be formed—and then we shall be governed by these two considerations in the choice of our positions as well as in all our movements.

As for the determination of this capital point, viz. *whether in case of a check we are to go to the North, to the South, or to the West mature deliberation is required*—we are to consider, supposing the communication between the Northern and Southern States cut off, which of the two will be able to furnish the most numerous army, and provide it best with subsistence and stores—

as this is not proposed for our examination I shall say nothing more on it.

CH^vr. du PORTAIL[29]

FRANCE RECOGNIZES THE INDEPENDENCE
OF THE UNITED STATES

This memorial was ready on April 23, several days before Washington received all the responses. While Washington was still considering the responses, Simeon Deane, brother of Commissioner Silas Deane, brought news from Bethlehem, Pennsylvania, on May 1 that France had recognized the independence of the United States and had signed a Treaty of Alliance with her. Deane had been entrusted with the precious treaties and secretly sent from France with them. He crossed on the frigate *Sensible*, landing safely on the shores of Casco Bay at the mouth of the St. Lawrence. He then proceeded on horseback as quickly as possible toward York, Pennsylvania, where Congress was sitting, spreading the good news as he went. Washington waited for authorization from Congress before announcing the event to the army.

That authorization arrived on May 5, and he proclaimed the following day as a day of rejoicing by the whole army. The day began with religious exercises to thank God for having "raised up among the Princes of the Earth a great and mighty friend." There would be a feu de joie, cheers, and feasting, and every soldier was to receive a gill of rum.

Duportail gave his written report three days later, as did most of the other officers:

> As to the first question—whether we ought to attack General How in his lines—I adhere to what is contained in my last memorial—Unless we have 25 thousand resolute men armed with good muskets and bayonets (for the latter will be necessary here) we ought not to think of it.
>
> It is not in my power to discuss the second relative to the Attack on New York, as I am not acquainted with the topography, nor have ever seen any particular plan of the Town, or the fortifications in its vicinity and at Kingsbridge—I shall remark only that the expedition against N. York ought not to be attempted at the expence of the Army opposed to General How, for if this army should cease to be in condition to make head against the british—the latter would attack it, dissipate it, and march uncontrouled through Pennsilvania and Jersey—it is I presume needless to point out the consequences.
>
> but if without prejudicing this army, we may have besides, a number of Troops which intelligent and experienced Officers acquainted with N. York and its vicinity, judge sufficient to attack it—in that case doubtless the attempt may be made—but measures must be prudently taken.

Lastly, as to the third object of discussion—*what are the positions to be taken by this Army acting on the defensive*—it appears to me that there is a previous important point to be decided—because all our operations ought to be subordinate to it—this point is, to know, in case of our armys suffering a check and not being able to maintain its ground here, in what direction our Retreat is to be made in preference—towards the blue mountains? on the other side of the Susquehannah? On the other side of the Delaware? by determining this, we shall determine where the grand magazines of the army are to be formed—& then we shall be governed by these two considerations in the choice of our positions as well as in all our movements.

As for the determination of this capital point, vizt *Whether, in case of a check we are to go to the North, to the South, or to the West*—mature deliberation is required—we are to consider, supposing the communication between the Northern and Southern States cut off, which of the two will be able to furnish the most numerous army, and provide it best with subsistence and Stores—as this is not proposed for our examination, I shall say nothing more on it.[30]

The officers (John Armstrong, Johann Baron de Kalb, the Chevalier Duportail, Horatio Gates, Nathanael Greene, Henry Knox, the Marquis de Lafayette, Thomas Mifflin, Friedrich von Steuben, and William Alexander Lord Stirling), in a rare display of unanimity, signed a joint communication on May 9, recommending "to remain on the defensive and wait events; without attempting any offensive operation of consequence."[31]

Neither Congress nor the army had any positive knowledge of what was going on in Europe. They had not received any dispatches from their commissioners at Paris in almost a year, since May 26, 1777. While a packet boat arrived at the beginning of 1778, it had no letters of political significance. The Committee of Foreign Affairs had written, announcing their stupefaction on January 12, 1778,

> GENTLEMEN: Not having received any letters from you since the 26th of May, we were severely chagrined yesterday, upon the arrival of Captain John Folger, who, under the name of dispatches from the commissioners at Paris, delivered only an enclosure of clean white paper, with some familiar letters none of which contained any political intelligence. . . . We cannot yet prove whether he [Folger] was willfully connected with the robbers of the packet.
>
> We shall endeavor to find whether the roguery was committed after Folger left France; but we must depend upon you to trace the circumstances from the time of your sealing till that of his embarking.[32]

This incident remained a mystery for many years, until the British spy correspondence relating to this phase of England's struggle to maintain control of her American colonies became accessible. Franklin and Deane trusted Joseph Hynson, a young American privateer sea captain, but he was a secret agent for the British. He had orders to use any means to get control of any message sent by the commissioners to Congress.

When Hynson received a package of dispatches to be given to Captain Folger onboard his ship, he had a paid expert substitute blank papers for the dispatches without arousing suspicion. Folger took the package, unaware of what had happened. Hynson returned to London, where the British secret service gave him a handsome reward. In the meantime, he wrote a lying letter to the commissioners, relating an imaginary accident that prevented his immediate return to Paris.

Duplicate dispatches were sent soon afterward aboard another vessel, but they were cast into the sea when the vessel was chased by a British cruiser. A third set reached America after news of the Treaty of Alliance had been received. Had the stolen dispatches been delivered as sent, they might have wrecked the cause of independence. They contained news regarding the attitude of France toward America that was so discouraging that Congress, if it had received the dispatches, might have accepted Lord North's Conciliatory Bills when they arrived in April. America had the added advantage that England was thrown off her guard because the American commissioners had almost given up hope of France forming an alliance with America.

Neither Washington nor Duportail knew any of these facts in April 1778. Congress had spurned the Conciliatory Bills, and the army was eager to attack General Howe in Philadelphia. Washington knew that public opinion and his generals supported him if he attempted any such action.

It began to seem certain that the enemy would soon evacuate Philadelphia without striking a single blow. The question then became, Will they march across New Jersey or go to New York by sea? The scouting parties watched every move intently and faithfully reported every detail to headquarters.

BRITISH COMMISSIONERS

The British commissioners sent to restore friendly relations between England and the Americans reached Philadelphia in early June. They immediately sought to enter into relations with the leaders of Congress. General

Washington convened a Council of War on June 17 to discuss the situation.[33] As usual, the officers were asked to send their opinions in writing. Duportail wrote,

> I think we ought not to quit our position of Valley Forge—before the enemy has evacuated Philadelphia—he must have lost his reason to remain in that city without the means to defend it. Thus, either the intelligence which says there are no more than 2 or 3000 men there, is false—or the English have it in their power by the measures which they have taken, signals agreed upon, number of boats to recross in sufficient force—in case of our advancing to attack them—
>
> The matter is besides reducible to this—Either the English are not going away—or they are—if the former be the case all that has hitherto been done is a feint on their part and conceals some snare into which they would draw us—
>
> if they are really determined to go away—what can we desire more— here is a certain immense advantage—let us not risk the loss of it, by procuring another, which even should we obtain it, would not change our affairs—
>
> However, as we have here 12,000 men and that our position may be defended by a smaller number, I think it would be well to send 1500 men into the Jerseys, to reinforce what is there already—the whole should be commanded by a person well acquainted with the Country—they ought not in general to oppose the enemy in front, on his march—but to follow him on his left flank—
>
> When the English shall have passed the Delaware, we ought in my opinion to move to the banks of that River and prepare to pass it likewise—but certain precautions are necessary—if we learn that the English are advancing hastily towards N. York—we may likewise pass with celerity but if they should halt, or appear to march slowly—in that case I think our troops ought not to pursue the enemy as fast as they could cross the River but post themselves advantageously near the River, and wait till the whole Army has passed in order to advance in force—
>
> In Jerseys as well as every where else, I think we ought always to avoid General actions—to seek advantageous posts—to have the Roads of Retreat well reconnoitered, and to have secure communications with our magazines. After all, I find it difficult to believe that the Enemy mean to cross the Jersies and go to New York—unless there is deficiency of transports—but we have the same conduct to observe in case the Enemy should march down the left shore of the Delaware to embark below—
>
> DUPORTAIL[34]

That same day, the entire camp at Valley Forge was put into condition to leave on the shortest possible notice. A returning scout brought intelligence at 11:30 the following morning that the enemy had evacuated Philadelphia earlier that morning. General Washington immediately put six brigades in motion while the "rest of the army prepared to follow with all possible dispatch."[35] All the troops converged at Coryell's Ferry, about forty miles from Valley Forge and thirty miles north of Philadelphia. The whole army had crossed the Delaware by the twenty-first. After they "had cleaned their arms and gotten matters in Train," the main body moved on toward Princeton, while General Poor, aided by Lafayette, led a detachment forward to come up with the enemy's rear and left flank, giving them "as much annoyance as possible."[36]

Colonel John Laurens, Washington's aide-de-camp, and General Duportail went to reconnoiter the slopes of the Sourland Hills, while Washington passed through Princeton with the main body and took up headquarters at Hopewell. They each sent their reports to Washington, both dated June 23, 1778. Colonel John Laurens summarized Brigadier General Duportail's observations on the other side of Duportail's letter:

> By General Duportail's leave I inclose a rude sketch of the Road and the principal points, which have relation to the ground your Excellency desired to have reconnoitred. The chain of Sourland hills as nearly as I can judge runs north by east—its nearest distance from Prince Town is five miles—General Duportail has reconnoitred as well as time will permit a position in that part of the chain—the front is generally good—the flanks can only be made so by art—Roads of Retreat could not be examined—water is not very abundant, but might be sufficient for a short stay—there is an inferior range of hills in front of those above mentioned, upon which stands a Militia Alarm Post. A good position might perhaps be found there but the Rocky Hill from all accounts promises the strongest ground—Genl. Duportail proposes to await further orders 'till 8 o'clock tomorrow morning.[37]

The army did not use the position on the Sourland Hills.

At about the same time, the officers held discussions to determine the feasibility of launching an attack against Philadelphia. Some, including Duportail, Nathanael Greene, Henry Knox, and John Sullivan, opposed the offensive. General Washington, after listening to their reasons, concurred and abandoned the plan. The two sides clashed in a major battle at Monmouth, New Jersey, on June 28. Two days after the battle, Duportail was sent to ascertain what defenses would be necessary for its security and to plan fortifications for the Delaware, as Washington feared the British might send a fleet to attack Philadelphia after the return of Congress. The army later took up its position at White Plains near the Hudson River north of New York.

While Duportail was engaged fortifying the Delaware, Congress received news that a French fleet, under the Admiral Comte d'Estaing, was approaching American shores. A short while later, on July 12, Conrad-Alexandre Gérard landed at Chester, Pennsylvania, the first foreign representative to be received by the United States. A delegation from Congress received and escorted him in a carriage to the nearly ruined city that the British had demolished before leaving.

A completely new phase of the American struggle with Great Britain was set to begin. After only a year in America, Duportail, having been chosen as a captain, had become the commander in chief's most valued advisor, a confidence that would never be betrayed.

3

WEST POINT AND THE HUDSON

General Washington funneled available resources to the field army after the defeats of 1777. He refortified the Hudson Highlands to make the area the strategic pivot for the main army. A large portion of the engineer corps worked on the fortress at West Point from the winter of 1777–1778 until the end of the war. Instead of a single large fort, which could be lost in one stroke, Duportail's engineers erected a complex of smaller, mutually supporting works for in-depth defense.

These defenses were the most important during the whole extent of the war because the line of fortifications extending along Lake Champlain had originally served the British in their struggle with France for supremacy on the continent. The Hudson River also provided an inland waterway from New York to Canada. British control of the river could also control communications between the northern and southern colonies, thereby dividing the country.

Philadelphia received news on May 18, 1775, of the capture of Fort Ticonderoga a few days after the Second Continental Congress convened. Congress resolved on May 25, "that a post be immediately taken at or near King's Bridge."[1] General Clinton began constructing defensive works in the summer of 1777 but abandoned and destroyed them when he realized he could no longer hold them after Burgoyne's surrender at Saratoga on October 16, 1777.

Congress requested on October 6, 1777, that Washington send an officer of engineers to take charge of the works of the north following the retreat of the Continental Army from Germantown. The commander in chief immediately sent Lieutenant Colonel Louis-Guillaume-Servais des Hayes de La Radière to serve at Fort Montgomery and take charge of the defensive works on the Hudson. He was promoted to the rank of colonel the following November.

General Washington then wrote to General Israel Putnam on October 8 to inform the commander of the Highlands.[2] He was nearly sixty years of age when he was appointed to command the important Hudson defenses. He had led the defense of Bunker Hill, and his men adored him, but this was his last great exploit. He was not well fitted for conducting long-drawn-out campaigns that required definite knowledge and accuracy of details. He was impatient and peevish at times. Washington himself even had difficulties with him.

Lieutenant Colonel Radière was very different. His training and gifts were diametrically opposed to Putnam's, and the two could not understand one another. Radière was very punctilious and guided by knowledge of principles. He worked by exact rules and was used to weighing the pros and cons before beginning operations. He was incapable of comprehending Putnam's attitude and refused to allow himself to be disturbed. He persistently continued acting in his own meticulous way.

DEFENSES OF THE HUDSON

Radière's date of arrival in the Highlands is unknown because one or two early memorials have not been preserved. His first letter in the *Papers of the Continental Congress* is dated "New Windsor, December 13, 1777." He drew up an elaborate plan for the defenses of the Hudson River dated January 2, 1778, which begins,

> To the Honorable Major General Putnam and to the
> Council of War called for fixing a plan of
> Defence for Hudsons River.

The Memorial of Luis de la Radiere, Col. of Engineers, showing the reasons for fortifying the HILL upon which FORT CLINTON was, in preference to any other place.

GENTLEMEN

I have requested General Putnam to call a Council of War in order to lay before you my thoughts concerning the Settlement of a Fort for the defence of Hudsons River. It is the more necessary that I make you acquainted with the reasons on which my opinion is founded, as many of you may not concur with me in it. But am in hopes that the perusal of this memorial will accord our sentiment.[3]

Since Radière's plan was not followed, it has been omitted here.

• • • • • • • • •

Conclusion:

You have certainly observed, Gentlemen, in this Memorial that there are many arguments for fortifying the Hill upon Fort Clinton, & very few for fortifying West Point; as also the arguments for fortifying Fort Clinton are stronger than those for fortifying West Point. Therefore I think that you will conclude with me that a fort must be built on Fort Clinton.

I will read to you Gentlemen a Memorial about all the preparations necessary for the building of this Fort & for the Obstructions of Hudsons River. I have two others ready concerning different parts of the same subject. After the reading of which I will request General Putnam to settle a general plan of what is to be undertaken & of the necessary preparations. Yet if any among you Gentlemen does not think that the place which I propose to you to be fortified is the best, I request you will again examine the reasons above mentioned and shew me Cause why they think my opinion is not well grounded, then I will adopt another. This business is of too great consequence not to be unanimous in our opinions.

I beg General you will direct to me your orders about the place to be fortified. I will execute them. It was my duty to make this representation, at present it is my duty to draw and take under my direction the works that shall be deemed advantageous by the Commander in Chief.[4]

WEST POINT FORTIFICATIONS

General Putnam and the other officers, together with the governor of New York, decided to fortify West Point, and the French engineer could not change their decision. When Radière asked them, as he practically did near the end of his memoir, "Show me your reasons for preferring West Point to Fort Clinton; if your arguments are stronger than mine, I will adopt your decision," they had nothing to say because their minds worked in a totally different manner than his. They had made up their minds, and that was the end of it so far as they were concerned. Matters practically came to a standstill. General Putnam wrote to General Washington at Valley Forge,

Dear Sir
★★★★★★★★★★★★★★★★★★★★★★

I wrote Your Excellency that the place agreed upon to obstruct the navigation of the Hudson's River was at West Point—Previous to that I had been with Governor Clinton, his Brother, the French Engineer and several others, to view that place. It was the opinion of all except the Frenchman, that it was the best and only effectual on the River. He could not prefer any other place but thought it was necessary to take more time to examine the ground etc. and it was near a month before we could have his opinion—which he at last gave in favor of Fort Clinton. This being contrary to the sentiment and expectation of every general officer, I was advised to wait on the Council and Assembly of this State for a final Determination. They at my Request, appointed a Committee for that purpose who have been these three days Reconnoitering the River and have now unanimously determined on West Point.

I have directed the Engineer to lay out the fort immediately—but he seems disgusted that every thing does not go as he thinks proper, even if contrary to the judgment of every other person. In short he is an excellent paper Engineer and I think it would be as well for us if he was employed wholly that way—I am confident if Congress would have found Business for him with them, our works would have been as well constructed & much more forward than they now are.[5]

Work on the fortifications progressed all through February 1778 but under great difficulties. During a temporary absence of General Putnam, the command devolved on another Connecticut man, General Samuel Holden Parsons. He wrote to General Washington on March 7,

Col. Laradiere finding it impossible to compleat the Fort and other Defences intended at this Post in such manner as to effectually withstand the attempts of the Enemy to pass up the River, early in the Spring and not choosing to hazard his reputation on Works erected on a different scale, calculated for a short Duration only, has desired leave to wait on Your Excellency and Congress which I have granted him. In justice to Col. Laradiere I ought to say he appears to be a gentleman of Science and Knowledge in his Profession and disposed to render us every Service he is able to do.[6]

General Washington responded to General Parsons's letter on March 18, announcing the appointment of General Alexander McDougall to take the command at the Highlands "to reconcile all matters and to obviate the jealousies and prejudices that whether well or ill founded, have taken place."[7]

THE SITUATION IN THE NORTHERN DEPARTMENT

The situation in the Northern Department had been rendered difficult not only because of the differences between the commanding officer and the engineer in charge of the works but also because of the confusing and, at times, conflicting orders issued by the Continental Congress. General Gates was president of the Board of War, and some of his friends in Congress wanted him to replace Washington. Gates admired and preferred another foreign engineer, Thaddeus Kosciusko, who had come to America a year before Duportail and his companions. Congress gave him the rank of colonel on October 18, 1776.

Kosciusko had gone north with General Gates in 1777 and had been responsible for the fortifications at Saratoga. He was greatly liked by the men who served under him as well as by his superiors, and there was a distinct effort put forward by his friends in Congress to have him made brigadier general in reward for his services at Saratoga. When news of the difference between Colonel Radière and the officers on the Hudson became known in Congress, without consulting Washington, it was decided that the Polish colonel should be sent north to replace the Frenchman. The visit of the latter to camp, indicated in the permit given him by General Parsons, offered the opportunity. Congress ordered Kosciusko north as Radière arrived at Valley Forge.

General Washington hoped that General McDougall's command of the Highlands would smooth away all difficulties. He easily persuaded Colonel Radière to return to his post and the fortification of West Point, giving him at the same time the following letter of introduction to the new commanding officer:

Head Quarters, 21st March, 1778

Sir

This will be delivered to you by Colonel de la Radiere of the Corps of Engineers who was employed to superintend the fortifications on the North River—but from some misunderstanding between him and the late commanding officer, in which he thought his own honor and the public interest were committed, he determined to renounce the work, and return to Camp. I can safely recommend him to you as a man who understands his profession, and make no doubt of his giving you satisfaction, both in projecting and executing the works required for the defence of the River.[8]

Kosciuszko, acting under orders from Congress, immediately set to work on the fortifications already begun, expecting to be made brigadier general. Then, Colonel Radière returned with express orders from General Washington, who later learned, in some unexplained way, of the double command and ordered General McDougall, "The presence of Colonel de la Radiere rendering the Services of M. Kosciousko as Engineer at Fishkill unnecessary,—you are to give him orders to join this army without loss of time." He added the following postscript: "P.S. However desirous I am that Mr Kosciousko shd. repair to this army if he is specially employed by order of Congress or the Board of War, I wd. not wish to contravene their commands."[9]

Congress placed General Gates in charge of the Highlands soon afterward, so that the two friends were together again. Kosciusko followed Gates to the south in 1780, and after the latter's defeat at Camden, North Carolina, he served under General Nathanael Greene. He never came close to Washington.

General McDougall replied to Washington's communication,

Fishkill 13th April 1778

Sir

I have lately been three days at West Point, the Fort is by this time so enclosed as to resist a sudden assault of the Enemy. But the Heights near it are such that the Fort is not tenable, if the Enemy possess them. For this reason we are obliged to make some work on them. It will require 5,000 men effectually to secure the ground near the Fort which command it. And these Objections are to almost all the Points on the River, proper to erect works to annoy the Shipping. Mr. Kosciousko is esteemed by those who have attended the work at West Point, to have had more practice than Col. Delaradiere, and his manner of treating the people more acceptable, than that of the latter; which induced Genl. Parsons and Governor Clinton to desire the former may be continued at West Point. The first has a Commission as Engineer with the rank of Colonel in October 1776—Colonel Delaradiere's Commission I think is dated in November last,[10] and disputes rank with the former, which obliges me to keep them apart; and avail the services of their assistance in the best manner I can devise. This seems to be the Idea recommended by the Board of War in consequence to a reference of Congress to them, on the Subject of Disputes relative to the construction of the works. If Your Excellency should think proper in this State of those Gentlemen, to order Mr. Kosciousko to join your army, whenever I am honored with your Commands on this Head, I shall despatch him.[11]

GENERAL GATES COMMANDS THE
ARMY OF THE NORTH

General Washington wrote to McDougall on April 22, informing him that Congress had appointed General Gates to command the Army of the North, with orders "to repair forthwith to Peekskill." McDougall was therefore ordered to return immediately after Gates's arrival to join the army at Valley Forge. In regard to the two colonel engineers, he wrote, "As Col° La Radiere and Col° Kosuisko will never agree, I think it will be best to order La Radiere to return especially as Kosuisko is better adapted to the Genius and the people."[12]

The Continental Army repossessed Philadelphia after the British evacuated, and General Washington sent General Duportail to Congress on June 30, 1778, with a letter recommending securing the Delaware River against enemy assaults.[13] He also gave the general and principal engineer ample instructions, but seven weeks later, Congress still had not read the instructions. General Duportail was soon called away, and Colonel Jean Baptiste Joseph, Comte de Laumoy, was left in charge of the works. Congress paid very little attention to the matter. President Laurens wrote to the governor of South Carolina on August 11,

> Immediately after we had repossessed this city, General Washington, in the spirit of a wise and watchful Commander-in-Chief, sent General Duportail with a letter to Congress recommending the immediate securing the river against Assaults from the Enemy, and for that purpose gave the General, who is principal engineer, ample instructions. We have been here upwards of 7 weeks & I have repeatedly urged Congress to hear the instructions read, yet to this moment no step is taken.[14]

The French fleet of ten ships of the line and three frigates under Admiral Comte Jean Baptiste Charles Henri Hector d'Estaing (1729–1794) was badly damaged in a hurricane on August 11, 1778, while they were attempting to engage the British fleet off the coast of Rhode Island. The British fleet went to New York to refit, while the French fleet departed Newport on August 21 for Boston for repairs. Duportail thought the British might attempt to block the port of Boston with a fleet and to embark troops at New York to go to Rhode Island, where they would debark and march directly toward Boston. He recommended ordering General John Sullivan to take all the necessary measures to hinder their debarkation; to reconnoiter positions to be occupied on the route to Boston; to have cut up, or hold himself ready to cut up, all parallel and detour roads leading there; and to fortify any place that could be favorable to fighting the British Army. He also recommended sending three thousand to five thousand men toward the Connecticut River to be ready to cross to reinforce General Sullivan. He also suggested that he (Duportail) go immediately "to General Sullivan's army to assist in choosing and fortifying a good position on the route to Boston. When that should be done—That I should go myself to Boston to see what may be done for the defence of the town itself."[15]

Soon afterward, General Duportail was sent to oversee the works on the Hudson with the following orders:

> Head Quarters, White Plains,
> 27 Augst. 1778
>
> Sir,
>
> You will proceed as speedily as possible to the Highlands and examine the several fortifications carrying on there for the defence of the North River. When you have done this, you will make me a full report of their state and progress, with your opinion of any alterations or additions which may appear to you necessary in improvement of the present plan. In doing this you will of course, consider the labor and expense which have been already incurred, the advanced season of the year & the resources of the country for carrying any plan which may be formed into execution.
>
> It is my wish you should also take measures without delay for executing the instructions given you the [thirtieth] of June last relative to a plan for the defense of the River Delaware and the City of Philadelphia.—In performing which you will also view the Subject in a maritime point of light; in order as far as natural circumstances will permit, to provide a secure Port capable of excluding the enemy's vessels and receiving or protecting our own or those of our allies.—To this end you will make such arrangements as the good of the service and the state of your department will best warrant.[16]

General Washington wrote to Colonel William Malcom on September 7, advising him that he was ordering Duportail to visit the posts in the Highlands to examine the state of the fortifications there. Duportail arrived two days later and examined all the works, then went to Windsor with Colonel Malcom on the eleventh to view the chevaux-de-frise.

Chevaux-de-frise were used to block passageways and to serve as obstructions of troop movement on the battlefield. *Photo courtesy of the author.*

DUPORTAIL'S SURVEY OF THE WEST POINT DEFENSES

Duportail submitted the following report dated August 13, 1778 (it should be September 13, as his orders to undertake a survey of West Point defenses were issued on August 27, and he arrived on September 9):

> The Works which are in hand at West Point and some inconsiderable ones, which it is necessary to add to them, will, with the help of the chain, perfectly fulfill the object which is proposed,—that of hindering the enemy's remounting the North River.
>
> Fort Putnam, which is as it were, the key of all the others may be rendered almost impregnable. There is indeed a height, which commands it, but besides that this height may be taken possession of with a redoubt, it would be very difficult for an enemy, even when master of it to bring heavy cannon there. Besides it would be too far to make a breach. This fort has nothing to fear but a bombardment or escalade with respect to a bombardment, the mean(s) to make it ineffectual is to have bomb-proofs sufficient for three fourths of the Garrison, magazines, hospital, etc.—I am told Col. Koshucsko proposes, at this time to begin one; but

which will not suit more than 70 or 80 men. This is far from sufficient. There must be another, the place and size of which, I have pointed out to the Captain who conducts the works.—It will contain about two hundred men—with respect to the escalade, to prevent its success, the side of the fort which looks towards the river and is the most accessible, as well as that which looks towards Fort Arnold, must be raised a great deal more than it is, and besides the palisades and chevaux de frise, abaties must be made in front. The roof of the great bomb-proof, which I propose, may be made use of to collect the rain and conduct it into the Cistern. This will always be a small resource.

Fort Willis [Fort Webb] does not appear to me well traced. It ought to be put entirely upon the declivity which looks towards the River, the force next Fort Putnam following the ridge of the eminence. In this manner it would have overlooked equally all the valley between Fort Putnam and itself and all its interior would have been under cover of Fort Putnam; the face next the river would have extended to the very border of the declivity; and the work in every respect would have been a great deal stronger. In its present position it is too large, its parapet makes too large a circuit. It will be best perhaps to rebuild this fort altogether; if this is not done, to remedy its inconveniencies, the face opposite Fort Putnam must be raised not so as to cover the interior, which I am told Col. Kosciousko proposes, because it must be prodigiously elevated to answer that purpose—but instead of this, I would prolong the eminence which is in the middle of the work, and improve it into a Traverse to extend the whole length of the work—I would then reject a third of the work on the South as altogether useless—the bomb-proof will be backed by the traverse above-mentioned.

I should have preferred to the Redans which are in front of the Redout Willis, on the South side, and which require for their defense four or five hundred man—a small inclosed work to secure the possession of the eminence and protect the batteries in front—but for the present matters may be left as they are.

Fort Arnold appears to me to be pretty well situated and traced—but if the intention of Col. Kosciusko is to leave the sides next the River at the present height—(as appears to be the case) I cannot approve it—they are exceedingly liable to an escalade—it is proper to elevate them and even to make a small covert way without having good palisades in front, to secure the body of the place against all surprise.

The Scantlin for the Bomb-proof appears to me too feeble—the top will be almost flat—What is made of earth ought to have been of Masonry or bricks—however I forbear enlarging upon this subject, because time will hardly admit of a Remedy—the Stuff being squared and ready to be put together—observing only that the work should be sunk more in order to furnish a greater thickness of earth for the roof.

Reenactors assembled for inspection at Fort Putnam. Fort Putnam was part of a complex of forts and redoubts protecting West Point. *Photo courtesy of the author.*

There is below Fort Putnam a battery nearly round, which is extremely well placed for battering the Vessels which should approach the Chain—but its situation likewise exposes it to the fire of the Ships—at least as it is much advanced, the fire of the tops would injure the Gunners, and the more, as by the form of the battery they are collected within a very small space—it appears to me advisable, to raise the parapet of this battery several feet—and to cover the embrasures from the top of one Merlon to another—so as not to interfere with the working of the Guns—although it is equally necessary to secure the Chain on the left-hand Shore of the River—it seems to have been little attended to—there is no inclosed work on this side to hinder the enemy from debarking a sufficient number of men to get possession of the ground and cut the Chain—there is only a battery which may answer some good ends, but cannot prevent the enemy from doing as above mentioned—With three small works we shall render the point perfectly secure—the first to be placed where the block house of fort independence [Constitution] stood—it is sufficient for it to contain about sixty men—its end is to afford an immediate defense to the Chain and its extremity—against a hardy enterprise, which a few men are engaged sometimes to undertake by dint of money or other recompense—The parapets ought to be of wood in order to take less room—and sufficiently elevated to cover the area.

Links of the great chain that stretched across the Hudson to block British ships. The chain weighed 180 tons and was supported by log rafts. Trophy Point, US Military Academy at West Point. *Photo courtesy of the author.*

The *second* Redout should be placed on a steep eminence which commands all the other rising ground in the island.

the *third* on an eminence in the rear of the newly constructed battery—These two Redouts ought to be made for 150 men or 200 at most.

There was a battery, the remains of which are still in existence, (below Fort Independence) it was perfectly well placed for battering the enemy's Ships—it ought to be rebuilt, with a strong parapet of earth— and as this battery is low and exceedingly exposed to a plunging fire from the Tops of Ships—the Parapets must be high, and terminated by a Roof of thick plank for the protection of the Canoniers—this battery as well as that which is just finished, will be interlocked by the three Redouts—and be in perfection safety.—With these works we shall be completely masters of the Island.

As to the Chain itself, I would not have it floating on the surface of the Water—which exposes it to be laid hold of by machines prepared for the purpose, on board the Vessels which may approach—but the greatest danger arising from this would be the breaking it by Cannon Shot—when a vast number comes to be fired on both sides in a contest between the enemy Ships and the batteries—I should think it more eligible therefore to suspend the Chain three feet below the surface of the Water—because as the greatest number of the Shot, bound when they strike the water—there would be so many ineffectual in respect to it—besides, the matter would be very easily executed—by placing the floats above instead of below the Chain—and having another Chain made fast at each end to the great one, and carried above the floats—by these means the great Chain may be supported at the depth which is just suitable—if a Shot should carry away the Chain, by which the great one is made fast to the floats—the whole mischief that would result, would be that place would douse a few feet more.

There are so many accidents by which an iron Chain may be broken, that it would be prudent to have a stout cable in reserve, to supply its place, in part for a time.

Every thing which I have explained being finished—1800 men will render us completely masters of the River; and put us out of reach of the enemy's enterprises—at least, the resistence that may be made will allow ample time for the arrival of succours, however remote the Army may be.

The following is the distribution of these Troops as nearly as can be judged—

In Fort [Arnold]	700
Willis Redout	200
Fort Putnam	400
Small work above Fort Putnam	100
For the works on the Island or Peninsula on the left-hand shore	400
	1800

At the present moment, if we except the batteries against Ships—the works are not in a state of defence—but a little time would be sufficient for completing fort Putnam; which is the most important—the Redouts on the Island on the left hand shore—are likewise objects of the first attention.

His Excellency had ordered me to give him an account of the expenses arising from all these works to the present time—it is not in my power to present anything on this subject, not having seen Col. Kosciusko, who alone is possessed of these facts—I am going to write to him for this purpose.

I was likewise at New Windsor—The River appears to me very wide in this part for a defense of Chevaux de Frise besides the Chevaux de frise themselves appear to me to be very weak—I can with difficulty persuade myself that a Ship would be much embarrassed by them—and indeed until West Point is completed—I do not think we should occupy ourselves about New Windsor—I shall therefore forbear adding any thing farther relative to it.[17]

Chevaux-de-frise supplemented the great chain. They consisted of large coffers made of pine logs lined with planking. Long, heavy poles with iron-tipped spikes projected out of the coffers at a 45° angle. The coffers were floated to strategic positions in the river, filled with rocks, and sunk. The spiked logs, hidden two or three feet below the water's surface at low tide, punctured or damaged the hulls of ships striking them. This type of chevaux-de-frise was also used in the Delaware River to protect Philadelphia. *Photo courtesy of the author.*

Washington replied on September 19, 1778,

Fort Clinton West Point 19th September 1778

Sir I have perused the memorial which you delivered relative to the defence of the North River at this place—and upon a view of them highly approve what you have offered upon the subject—Col. Kosciusko who was charged by Congress with the direction of the forts and batteries—has already made such a progress in the constructions of them as wd. render any alteration in the general plan a work of too much time—the favorable testimony which you have given of Col. Kosciousko's abilities prevents uneasiness on this head—but whatever amendments subordinate to the general disposition that occur as proper to be made, you will be pleased to point out to Col. Kosciusko that they may be carried into execution.

The works proposed on the peninsula not being subject to the above mentioned inconvenience, you will desire Col. Kosciousko to show you his plan for approbation before he proceeds to the construction—or have them traced in the first instance conformably to your own ideas.[18]

After returning from the Highlands in September, General Duportail explained to the commander in chief that unless very strongly urged by Congress, he and his companions would return at the expiration of the present campaign, as their leave of absence would expire the first of February, and that if Duportail did not receive a "certain prospect of his being employed in a manner useful to the States and honorable to himself,"[19] then he would return to France. Duportail was also anxious that Congress take action with respect to his and his companions' pay and appointments. Washington wrote Congress,

Headquarters, Fredericksburgh Novemr. 16, 1778

Sir,

By the time this reaches you General Du Portail will probably be at Philadelphia. One part of his business is to prosecute the directions given him, sometime since, for forming a defence of the River Delaware, to be submitted to Congress, what may be their views and wishes with respect to his further continuance in America and that of the three other gentlemen attached to him. He informs me that the furlough, he obtained from the Court of France expires in February next, and that unless there is a certain prospect of his being employed hereafter, in a manner useful to the States and honorable to himself, he intends immediately to return.—He therefore wishes some explicit ideas to be realized on the subject. He is also anxious that something definite should be done, with respect to the pay and other appointments both of himself and of the other gentlemen with him; which have been hitherto undecided and have left them in an uncertain and disagreeable situation; added to this he is desirous to have some arrangement fixed for the rules and manner of service in his department.

He delivered me some days since a memorial intended for Congress and which I have now the honor to inclose, containing his ideas on a general system of fortification for these States and which he requests me to accompany with my sentiments.

But it includes questions of finance and considerations of policy the most extensive and important; of which Congress alone can form a competent judgment. I shall therefore only say, that considered merely in a military point of view, the plan appears to me worthy of very serious attention. It is but justice to General Du Portail to observe, that I have a high opinion of his merit and abilities; and esteem him not only well acquainted with the particular branch he professes, but a man of sound judgment and real knowledge in military science in general. I have also a very favorable opinion of the other Gentlemen.—I will take the liberty to add, that it appears to me, they will be extremely necessary and useful to our future operations, whether directed to offence or defence—whether to dispossess the enemy of posts in our frontier—to assist in carrying on the proposed expedition into Canada—or any other on a less extensive plan, which may be substituted in its stead, for the mere security of our frontier.

M. de Murnan has served in quality of Engineer under General Du Portail since the first of March last with the Promise of a majority from the Committee of arrangement at Valley Forge. He has never yet received his commission.

This, I promise has been forgotten in a crowd of more important matters. With the greatest respect and esteem—I have the honor to be

Sir, Your most Obed. Serv.
G. WASHINGTON.[20]

DUPORTAIL SENT TO BOSTON

General Washington ordered General Duportail on September 29 to go to Boston to examine the state of the fortifications and to form a plan to protect the town and the French fleet against a possible attack, especially on Dorchester Heights and at Roxbury. He was to concentrate on defense by land, while the Comte d'Estaing would focus on defense by water, thereby ensuring mutual support. He also wrote to Admiral d'Estaing and Major General William Heath, who commanded Boston, to inform them of his orders.[21]

Duportail reported his findings to Washington and Major General William Heath on October 20. He considered the possibilities of both sea and land attacks on Boston, made both with and without the French fleet present in the harbor, and he described fortifications that might be constructed on Boston Neck; the Dorchester, Charlestown, and Nantasket Peninsulas; and various harbor islands. He recommended the immediate construction of a redoubt for 50 men and an entrenchment on Boston Neck, two redans with batteries on Dorchester Heights, one work for 250 men on Noddles Island, and a fort on Peddocks Island. He noted that he learned the previous day the British had embarked five thousand or six thousand troops at New

York. He feared they were on their way to Boston but didn't think they would attack with that number of troops. He then thought that either they would embark more troops or would come to seize Newport. He decided to stay in Boston until he could ascertain British intentions.[22]

DEFENSE OF THE DELAWARE

General Washington's first care in June 1778, after the British had evacuated Philadelphia and Congress had returned to that city, was to provide for the defense of the Delaware River. To this end, he ordered General Duportail there immediately after the Battle of Monmouth. Washington wrote to Benedict Arnold, then in command at Philadelphia,

> I have sent General Duportail to examine what defences may be essential for its security and to make me a report as soon as the nature of the business will admit. In order to facilitate this, I am to request that you will give every aid in your power which he may consider material for informing his judgment and making a well digested plan. For particulars I refer you to General Duportail's instructions.[23]

He then sent the following letter to the president of Congress on October 22:

> Immediately after the action at Monmouth, I sent General Duportail to form a plan of fortification for the Delaware. While he was in the execution of this task, he was called away at General Lee's insistence as witness in his trial. After this was over, I thought it was necessary he should turn his attention to the Highland posts; and lately the possibility of an enterprise against the French fleet and the town of Boston determined me to send him to that place, to take measures for their common security. Previous to this, however, he had sent Colonel Laumoy to prepare the way, by taking plans of the river and the country adjacent to Philadelphia; these points I deemed it material to mention; and I submit to Congress the propriety, as Colonel Laumoy is not yet returned, of their directing a number of men to prosecute the defences.[24]

Washington didn't get Duportail's report until the end of October and concurred with General Heath that it was too late in the season to undertake a large construction project. He referred consideration of his proposal to General Gates, who was appointed by Congress to take command in Boston, which he did on November 6. Washington approved of

Duportail's decision to remain in Boston but expressed his ardent desire for him to come to Philadelphia as soon as possible to make that city secure.[25] Congress took no action on the plan of fortification, probably because it was too expensive.[26]

Two factions divided Congress in the fall and winter of 1778–1779. One supported Silas Deane and his transactions in France, and the other was bitterly opposed to him and his work there. Consequently, the important business of the country was delayed, and the French engineers found themselves practically ignored by Congress. Duportail and his companions decided they would return home. Washington's pleading induced them to defer their decision. The French minister, Conrad Alexandre Gérard, understood the situation in Congress and urged them to be patient, assuring General Duportail that everything would come right in the end.

4

THE CAMPAIGN OF 1779

General Duportail delivered his plan for fortifying Boston in October 1778 and requested clarification of his and his companions' status for the campaign of 1779. He stated that his furlough was to expire in February and that he and his companions would have to return to France if they were no longer needed in America. Congress did nothing about the plan for their continued service to the army.

Faced with the possibility of losing the French engineers, General Washington pleaded their cause to Congress. Duportail, Radière, and Laumoy expressed their gratitude in a letter dated January 15, 1779. Gouvion said that he would agree to whatever his companions did. They were pleased with Washington's efforts to allow them to remain in the service of the United States through the next campaign, and they consented with "no conditions to the continuance of our residence in America." They also considered it their duty to state "that being determined to remain here by our desire of serving and of being useful to the United States, if the means of usefulness should disappear on any account whatsoever we shall be desirous of preserving the liberty of returning into our country. Sensible of the interest which your excellency is so kind as to take in this affair, we beg you to accept our most humble thanks."[1] Minister of War Conrad Alexandre Gérard was also pleased with Washington's support and asked the king's consent, which the officers of engineers needed.[2]

Duportail wrote to Washington on January 27, 1779,

> The Inhabitants of Boston have a prejudice which may one day be fatal to them—they imagine their Town impregnable—Struck with seeing it at high Tide surrounded with water, and joined to the main only by a narrow neck—they appear not to have remarked that twice in twenty

four hours the water ebbs and leaves on each side of the Passage two or
three hundred yards uncovered—they repeat one after the other that the
ground is miry and impracticable—I have caused people to walk there
in several directions—and they did not sink at all—the bottom is very
good and as there is no fortification on the sides of the Town—I see no
difficulty in the enemys making himself master of it—if we suppose him
in possession of the adjacent Country.

Many people believed that the enemy would act as they had in the past
and expected that the British would only attack Boston by land. However,
they might send enough ships into port to capture whatever vessels may
be there and bombard and burn the town, or they could send a squadron
against French fleets coming to Boston.[3]

Congress passed an act on February 2, directing Washington to send
an engineer to South Carolina to serve in the Southern Department. He
directed General Duportail to send one of his engineers to Charlestown to
take orders from Major General Benjamin Lincoln or the officer commanding in that department. Duportail sent Laumoy.[4]

Busy completing a similar project for Boston, Duportail apparently
did not turn his attention to Philadelphia until early 1779. When he
approached the Board of War for men and equipment, the Board of War
wrote a letter to Joseph Reed, governor of Pennsylvania, on February 22,
requesting support from the Pennsylvania Supreme Executive Council for
the French military engineer.[5]

DEFENSES OF PHILADELPHIA

The commander in chief again sent General Duportail to Philadelphia
at the beginning of March 1779 with a message for Congress regarding
the defenses of the Delaware. The Board of War directed him to take his
request to Governor Reed, probably because of lack of funds. Governor
Reed at first promised to supply the chief of engineers with a boat and
men to conduct an examination, but he later recanted his offer, apparently
offended that the request did not come directly to him. Duportail explained
that he simply followed instructions and that, being a stranger, he knew
nothing of "what was due the different powers."[6]

Very much annoyed, Duportail wrote of his difficulties to Colonel
Alexander Hamilton, asking him to explain the situation to the commander in chief. He added that the governor was about to visit camp, and

he very much hoped that General Washington would speak to him about the importance of the work. Duportail's insistence on keeping virtually all information from Reed and his council members caused irritation and led them to withhold cooperation. His instructions requested and expected "that he will not Communicate the Knowledge he shall acquire of the depth of the River or other important Circumstances of our defence to more persons than are absolutely necessary for his assistance."[7]

Washington responded on March 30,

> I am sorry to find by yours of the 20th that you have met with so many delays and disappointments in the prosecution of your plan for taking a survey of the Delaware. Although I am anxious to see you in Camp I shall be very unwilling to recall you while there is the least prospect of your rendering any service. I must therefore desire you to point out to that public Body before which you may have your affair [paper torn] disadvantage of your remaining so long in Philadelphia and to request them to enable you to execute your Business immediately or if that cannot be done in a short time to permit you to return to the Army, where the preparations for the ensuing Campaign call for your attendance.[8]

In the meantime, Governor Reed visited headquarters and conferred with the commander in chief. The Pennsylvania Council soon made a favorable decision, and Washington wrote to General Duportail on April 17, "I am glad that the Council have come to a resolution which will enable you to proceed; and I hope you may receive every aid necessary to execute the Business with satisfaction and despatch. It is agreeable to me that you retain such of the Gentlemen as you think proper to assist you in your operations."[9]

Duportail completed his portion of the survey and presented a draft of the fortifications proposed for Philadelphia and the Delaware River to the Pennsylvania Council by May 14. The council adopted a resolution of gratitude on that date and authorized a $2,000 payment for Duportail and $1,000 and $600 for his assistants, Colonel Radière and Major Jean-Louis-Ambroise de Genton, Chevalier de Villefranche.[10]

Duportail's title was changed to commandant of the Corps of Engineers and Sappers and Miners on May 11, 1779. Later, he and Colonel Alexander Hamilton were sent to meet with Admiral d'Estaing and deliver confidential dispatches to him regarding a joint operation with the French fleet and the Continental Army and to confer with him about combined operations when the French fleet reached northern waters. However, the French and American forces were repulsed at Savannah on October 9, and only one ship made it to the Chesapeake. After a time, with no sign of the French fleet on the Delaware, the operation was aborted. There is no further mention of Duportail's connection with the defenses of the Delaware.

DUPORTAIL AT WEST POINT

As the British were beginning the systematic reduction of the South, Jean-Louis-Ambroise de Genton, Chevalier de Villefranche, was left in charge of the defense of the Delaware, while Laumoy proceeded south to assist in the construction of the defensive works there. Duportail went north to take command at West Point. He was ordered on June 9 to furnish a draft of West Point and its environs, including the communication with the camp. Washington was greatly relieved to have his commandant of engineers at that important post and had readily consented to allow Colonel Engineer Thaddeus Kosciusko to join General Gates at New York before accompanying him to the defense of the South.[11]

Brigadier General Anthony Wayne stormed Stony Point on July 16, capturing the British position with a vast amount of stores of all kinds. British retaliation prevented the Continental Army from garrisoning the height. They destroyed the fort after removing the stores and withdrew.

The British Army took possession again of both Stony and Verplanck Points, constructed new defenses, and replenished their magazines. As British troop movements to the south seemed to indicate the arrival of reinforcements, the American generals, uncertain of the enemy's intentions, wanted to attempt the recapture of Stony and Verplanck Points, hoping to repulse the British. Duportail was ordered on July 20 "to appoint engineers to superintend and direct the new works on the heights east and west of the river."[12]

The commander in chief convened a Council of War on July 26 to discuss the situation.[13] As was his custom, he requested opinions be sent in writing. Duportail's memorial, dated July 27, 1779, clarified the matter, as he saw it:

> West Point being to us a point which it is of the greatest importance to preserve and to put once for all in a state of defence. I think that we ought not to touch the fund of troops necessary to the defence of this post, in its present state, and to the construction of the works already undertaken. According to what his Excellency has been pleased to submit to our view, it appears that we have there about 5000 men—This

is perhaps more than sufficient to receive the enemy till the rest of the army can arrive to their succour, but it is not too much for the work we are carrying on—I therefore think it best to leave them there—The question then is what we can do with the rest—can we attack Stony Point or Verplank's point?

The English having augmented considerably the number of their troops at Stony Point, laboring to inclose their works and probably keeping themselves more upon their guard than heretofore, I think that we ought not to attack them, because we should be likely to lose a good many men and perhaps without success—Besides according to my conception of the matter we should not have any great advantage by gaining possession of Stony Point; because we must be also masters of Verplank's—Here then is another fort to be attacked and taken, which can hardly be hoped for, the enemy being advertised to go to the succour of the one by the capture of the other; and after all we should be masters of both places, I do not see what would result from it to us, so very advantageous. Our army (after leaving the necessary army at West Point) not being in a state to make head during the campaign below King's ferry, I do not see what good we should derive from the possession of these places—the army could not go farther down on this account and as to the communication by water, a single English frigate always has been able and always would be able to hinder it. If we should attack Stony point, it could only be to possess ourselves of the garrison and of the magazines, but though we have succeeded once without loss, we must not believe that we should succeed in the same manner a second time; and it would not be prudent to risk the loss of a great number of men upon hopes not well founded, who may become very useful to us.—The arrival of Lord Cornwallis and the strong appearances of an embarcation seem to indicate that the English have received, or are sure of receiving, a reinforcement which enables them to send troops to Carolina or elsewhere—Perhaps therefore until we know with what number of troops we shall have to do, it will be proper not to adventure our troops in expeditions more than uncertain.

We cannot propose to ourselves to attack Stony point by regular approaches.—The ground which is on a level with it, or which commands it, is too distant for the batteries erected there, to be able to batter the works with advantage and render them more easy to be carried with assault, in which it must ultimately end. Besides, by the disposition of the roads, we should run great risk of losing our cannon mortars etc.

What I say respecting the attack of Stony Point *sword in hand*, applies itself to Verplank's point—But as to attacks by means of batteries Verplank's point is very susceptible of them, and I think if the enemy should be imprudent enough to abandon Verplank's point to its own force, and there is no body of troops near enough to support it, we ought not to hesitate to make the attack because we risk nothing.—If the enemy arrives in time to bring them succour we get rid of the business by retiring; I think therefore we ought always to be ready for this enterprise.

Though I do not think that we ought to attack Stony point or Verplank's point by assault or otherwise unless in some extraordinary circumstances which may present themselves, nevertheless it appears to me essential to menace them continually.—I should then have been glad if 10 or 1500 men had been left at the outlet of the mountain about Stony Point and a like corps at the Continental village. These corps will absolutely risk nothing unless they should suffer themselves to be surprised—and even this would be very difficult—they could be turned on neither side and they have always their communication secure with West Point. By showing themselves, always ready to attack the forts, they oblige the enemy to have within reach to support them, corps of at least three thousand men to have nothing to fear.—Then, which will appear singular, the possession which the enemy have of Verplank's and Stony points will turn against them and become an advantage to us.— For here are 5000 men employed to maintain a point which is of no great consequence to us.—Let us add to these the number of men they must have at New York for the security of that place and on this side of King's bridge to support readily the three thousand men advanced, unless they keep their men upon the water; and we shall see that the enemy by having posted themselves at King's ferry have imposed on themselves the necessity of establishing a chain of posts from King's ferry to New York, which will prevent them from having so many for different operations; and thus we shall perhaps save the country from pillage.[14]

MEMORIALS

Duportail's memorial and those of the other officers must have completely answered Washington's questions because there was no further mention of an attack. The British abandoned both posts on October 21, justifying Duportail's judgment.

Major General Alexander McDougall was ordered on August 14, "with generals Knox and Du Portail [to] make a visit to all the works on both sides of the River, and ascertain the number of cannon and the sizes which will be necessary for their defence." They were "to distinguish between a full complement of cannon, which it would be *expedient* to have and the number which is *absolutely necessary*."[15] General Washington received the report on August 20 and decided that the forts receive a "speedy and ample supply of powder" because the scarcity of it prevented them from undertaking any offensive or defensive operations.[16]

Duportail sent his review of British options at West Point on the same day:

> To bar the river from the North in a suitable location is one thing the extreme importance of which everyone is presently aware. It is known that the depth of this river is considerable enough so that warships or frigates at least can go up it almost to Albany and that the breadth or the nature of its banks is such that enemy ships would find innumerable spots where in no manner would it be possible to damage them from the river bank. The enemy, by constant sailing of its frigates or small armed boats would prevent communication from the North to the south below Albany. Since the country above is still quite new sparsely populated and since there are few roads and besides the enemy, most of the river up to Albany, has the greatest facilities to reinforce and maintain the army of English, Tories and savages that he has within reach in these cantons, it follows that the passages above Albany would soon be in their possession, consequently, all communication between the lands situated on one side of the river and those of the other would be completely broken; which would have very fatal consequences: the main ones are that all parts of the United States thus separated would be left to their own forces, without being able to call on any aid one from the other, which would weaken them considerably, against an enemy Which can maneuver anywhere he desires. . . . When one reflects on that, one is surprised that the English have not turned their sights to that point, that they have not undertaken an operation so easy for a long time and so decisive. They could have done it up to the time of last May, for at that moment the works at West Point, even though I prepared them, and until then, there had never been enough troops to make up for the insufficiency of the works. Thus were we in a constant dilemma in regard to this valuable post. Happily, the time for fear is passed, and now far from being apprehensive about seeing the enemy march on this place, we infinitely desire it, assured that he would find there his ruin and his dishonor, and we an opportunity to weaken him so as to be unable to maintain himself any longer in New York, without receiving considerable reinforcements; this is what we are going to try to show by the following study:
>
> In order to judge correctly the effect of the fortifications built at West Point, . . . it is appropriate to examine the different undertakings that the enemy can plan against this post; the different means by which he can proceed in his operations, as much by the land as by water, and what we can contrast with if from our side, we supposing West Point left to

its own forces, that is defending itself with its garrison. [Here Duportail considered four alternatives open to the British and reached the following conclusion.]

. . . It must . . . be admitted that the different undertakings that [I] have just . . . described lead only to breaking the chain in a hurry, without having time to carry it away nor to detach it from the woods in order to sink it. It is not probable that the enemy would expose himself to so much danger in order to cause a damage that can be easily repaired, if we prepare the means. I am inclined to believe that if he undertakes something against West Point it will be in a more solid and decisive way. This will be to make himself master following operations against all the forts of West Point either to hold them or to destroy them completely and thus procure for himself a free passageway on the river. . . .

Fifth Undertaking. The 5th undertaking is the probable plan. If one examines the terrain above Fort Clinton, one will see that the heights which overlook it or which look down on each other, are occupied rather extensively in two directions. On one side Putnam, Rockhill and [a redoubt]; from the other side Webbs, Willys, but also one sees a mountain which begins at Rockhill and which extends behind Putnam, Webbs and Willys and which perfectly dominates these works, so that this array of fortifications which prescribes a great deal at first look, is reduced to little for effect, because the enemy, supposedly in possession of this mountain can establish at the same time cannon and mortar batteries against Rockhill, . . . Putnam, . . . Webbs and Willys. . . . [T]hese last two works are not even tenable for very long under these conditions, being too prolonged. It will be necessary then to abandon them early and consequently the enemy would advance along the slope . . . and can set up his batteries against Clinton without even having taken Fort Putnam. It is evident then that the real point of attack against West Point is from the mountain M, O in question, since one comes all of a sudden from it to the attack on Putnam instead of making successive attacks on all the Forts above or below this Fort, as would be necessary coming from the other side. Now with respect to the difficulty to the enemy to get to this place, if there were no works, there would be none. This mountain is most accessible from any side and its slope from the west is such that cannon can easily be brought there, so that supposing the enemy, disembarked opposite Robinson's, establishes himself on the mountain, sets up his batteries and fires his first cannon shot against Putnam, cannot require more than four or five days (since the batteries can be constructed even while the cannon are being brought up) it would be indispensable, then, to occupy this mountain; this is what we have done by the two works S, T. . . . I don't think it any longer possible for the enemy to select it as his debarkation point; it is true that from there to the first battery . . . is more than a mile; but one must consider that it is not a question of firing on a work, on a small space, but on a multitude of boats, ships, horses, carriages, men; everything conceivable assembled in one spot where all the apparatus of an army munitions of all types being unloaded. It is clear that at a distance of more than a mile each cannon round Is almost sure and it must always strike something; that consequently one cannot select such a point to establish himself; moreover the enemy, getting off of his ships, will not expose himself by camping on the plain under the fire of these same batteries, he must then withdraw to the rear of this point. We can conclude that he will prefer to disembark at the other place. . . . This is already an advantage, to move further away the enemy's disembarkation point; this stretches still more his communications, gives greater facility to attacking him, renders more difficult the transportation of artillery and munitions.

Let us suppose now that the enemy established on the plain at the required distance and on the mountain (U) opposite our redoubts, what decision will he make then? Will this be to advance on our left under the fires of [two of our] batteries . . . and those that can be set up on the same mountain for the attack on the redoubt Willys, then on Webbs, from there to Putnam or Clinton? The absurdity of such a plan is too palpable for there to be a need to show its effect. The enemy can do only one of these two things. He can advance by the mountain, . . . attack redoubt R in order to march against Rockhill, and from Rockhill against Putnam; but it must be noticed that redoubt R, can only be attacked in strength because it is perhaps impossible for the enemy to bring up large cannon against it as long as he does not control Redoubts S and T, secondly because it would be covered by [a] Battery, . . . against that which one might set up opposite . . . after having taken redoubt R by strong attack he must likewise take Rockhill and then Putnam for . . . the enemy cannot find (neither at the Redoubt R nor at Rockhill) cannon suitable for firing on the works.

The other route that the enemy can take to get to Putnam (which is still the central point to which he must come) is by the mountain . . . as we have already pointed out. He must then capture Redoubts S and T. If he captures only Redoubt T, he can easily establish his troops on the mountain, but he could only bring his cannon up there with an extraordinary, laborious and long toil, by the eastern slope; if he captures only Redoubt S he must bring his cannon along the Furnace [?] road, which can be regarded as almost impracticable, because it cannot be supposed in advance that he will bring his cannon through the valley under fire from Redoubts T and S and of their batteries. As to the difficulty itself of capturing the works, one can only set up batteries against them on the slope of the mountain opposite at more than 500 Toises, too great a distance to destroy them with cannon. There will be, moreover, in each of these redoubts an underground bomb-proof shelter to protect the garrison. The enemy must then always come to an attack in force and they are in such condition that the undertaking would certainly be very dangerous.

It seems to me that we have assured the defense of this mountain, as much as it is necessary to do it, in view of the number of troops the enemy can sacrifice to the attack of West Point. . . .

Munitions. We have supposed up to the present the post of West Point left to its own forces, that is, defended by its own fortifications with their garrisons. We will say a word on how to use the additional troops that should be on hand when the enemy appears or who should come in the course of the attack. First, as we have said, the first posts to be occupied are the points of debarkation. Since we think that the enemy cannot come from King's Ferry by land, one might question that we do not advise stringing out troops in quantity on the roads and paths which lead from this area to West Point. Patrols only are necessary to warn that the fort at Montgomery not be surprised from the rear.

After that, the mountains opposite the redoubts R, S, T, being the first posts where the enemy must establish himself in order to push his operations against West Point, it is thus also one of the first that we must garrison. Some hundred men on these mountains making the approaches difficult by abatis will stop the enemy for a long time. We must reconnoiter, look for ways to attack them, to dislodge them. In areas of difficult access, covered with woods and rocks, this is quite long.

I will note here in passing that in a mountainous country if troops are placed on a mountain which has another one on its flank, . . . it is appropriate to put some men (as small a number as it might be) on this other mountain. This would prevent the enemy, who does not know their strength, from descending in the valley in order to turn the troops on the first mountain for fear of finding himself between two, or cut. There is place to apply this principle in the locations of which I am speaking here.

After occupying the mountains of which it was just a question, the location of the troops which we have more of as well as the natural retreat of those forward, if they were dislodged and on the mountain M, O, then they would place themselves in the rear of the abatis constructed between the redoubts S. T. and along the eastern and western slopes within range of defending these redoubts and to oppose themselves everywhere to the passage of the enemy. These troops, depending on their number, would construct in their rear, fortifications in the most favorable locations, leading to the type of works they can execute; in a word, they must use everything to defend this mountain for as long a time as possible for on it depends principally the defense of West Point, it cannot be repeated too much.[17]

Plans for the defense of West Point were complete by fall 1779 and only required improvements and maintenance. The complex now consisted of a mutually supporting system of forts, redoubts, and batteries designed to close the Hudson to enemy vessels.

The French military engineer Marshal Sébastien Le Prestre de Vauban stressed the use of single massive fortresses, so Duportail viewed West Point's scattered defenses with misgivings. However, Vauban noted that defenses ought to utilize and augment the surrounding natural terrain.

The Crown forces did not attack West Point that fall. Duportail proposed to reconnoiter Verplanck Point on the morning of September 30. A covering party of three hundred men alarmed the British, who opened fire on them with their artillery and sent a reinforcement from Stony Point to Verplanck Point.[18] After the British abandoned Stony and Verplanck Points, Gouvion led a large detachment of soldiers to level the enemy works at Verplanck Point.

WINTER QUARTERS

Washington wrote General Duportail on September 22, 1779, about making preparation for winter quarters. He decided on the Highlands, and it became necessary to increase the accommodations at the different forts:

> Head Quarters, West Point, Sept. 22nd 1779
>
> Sir,
>
> I am to request you will give instruction to your attendants attached to the different works—to turn their attention to the different barracks necessary at each to cover the men required to be constantly stationed for the immediate security of the respective posts—and the places at which it will be most proper to erect them—Were it not for the difficulty of transporting material to those high mountains to build barracks at each sufficient to cover the whole number of men required for its complete defence, I should give a preference to this; but the difficulty of transportation inclines me to desire only strong guards during the winter at each post, to put them out of the reach of a surprise and coup de main by a small detachment and consequently barracks proportioned to these.—I

leave it to your judgment, what guards will be sufficient to answer this purpose and to regulate the arrangements for barracks accordingly—and I shall be obliged to you to make a report as speedily as possible.

I have the honor to be etc.

P.S. These barracks ought to be in the works where they will admit them—and where they will be so near as to always be sure of a communication on any sudden emergency and effectively protected by the fire from the works. How far can the bomb-proofs be made to answer the purpose?

General Duportail sent in a lengthy report two days later, covering the works.[19] He was still in camp with Washington on October 3 when Washington wrote to General Wayne that General Duportail planned to reconnoiter the post of Stony Point the following day "to ascertain the distances from the enemy's works to the places proper for the establishing of batteries."[20] He requested an escort to meet him and a reconnoitering party consisting of a regiment.

ARNOLD'S TREASON

Duportail was ordered south in 1780, leaving Lieutenant Colonel Gouvion in command of the defenses of the Highlands. When Gouvion left West Point to replace Duportail at Washington's side, Major Villefranche replaced him in the Highlands. In August 1780, Washington sent Gouvion to examine the fortifications with Villefranche to correct any deficiencies. They found some matters needed urgent attention.

Gouvion's report to the commander in chief, dated August 22, 1780, began as follows:

Sir,

I received last night the letter your Excellency has honored me with; your orders concerning the safety of this post shall be exactly complied with.

Villefranche soon directed more than four hundred men to repair the works, while a band of ten musicians eased their labor. Although the newly formed companies of sappers and miners should have assisted Villefranche, they were stationed instead at Dobb's Ferry with the artillery until the end of October, when they moved to West Point for the winter. Construction and repairs lagged, and West Point became weaker.

General Benedict Arnold had been put in command of the post early that year, replacing General Robert Howe. While the work of strengthening the weaknesses in the fortifications was progressing, Arnold was secretly communicating with the enemy, plotting to deliver the whole into their hands. British spy master Major John André was captured on September 26, and Arnold fled, making his complicity evident. Washington arrived and immediately took possession of West Point. Surprise, terror, and consternation spread like wildfire, but Arnold's treachery had some beneficial effects on the country at large. It rekindled the fires of patriotism, which were in danger of being extinguished.[21]

The situation of American affairs was extremely distressing. The allies had no decisive victory since Saratoga, and they progressively lost territory since General William Howe evacuated Philadelphia in 1778.[22] D'Estaing's fleet returned to the West Indies after the repulse at Savannah in the fall of 1779, leaving the entire Atlantic coastline exposed. The small fleet that had brought Rochambeau and his army had been anchored at Newport since July 1780, but both fleet and the army were too small for their respective commanders to attack the enemy safely until reinforcements arrived from France. The whole southern army remained prisoners at Charleston.

Little else happened in the Highlands throughout the harsh winter of 1779–1780, except the construction of barracks and the customary repairs to the great chain. Kosciusko attempted to build some fortifications, but the lack of artificers and laborers, a recurring problem at West Point, stymied him, as did the difficulty of transporting materials to the mountains.[23]

JOINT CAMPAIGN

The real campaign of the year, however, had been arranged in May with the French minister plenipotentiary Gérard, who visited Washington's headquarters at Middlebrook. They planned a combined action of the American army and the French fleet under Admiral d'Estaing, preferably against New York. Washington had requested that the French fleet

> proceed with all despatch directly from Martinique to New York, so as to arrive there before the return to the harbor of Admiral Byron's squadron, which had wintered in the Caribbean. Washington considered it

essential to any extensive combined operations, that France maintain
a clear superiority over the British naval force in America. If this
plan should not meet with favorable consideration he suggested that
d'Estaing sail for the South Atlantic coast and give aid to General Lincoln in driving the enemy from the province of Georgia, which had
been invaded by the British the preceding November.[24]

The season was nearly over to accomplish much of anything for
that year. Meanwhile, illness forced Mr. Gérard to leave his post. He was
replaced by the Chevalier de la Luzerne, who had visited Washington at
camp in the Highlands in September. He landed in New England and
made a detour on his way to Philadelphia. As the new minister knew nothing more than Washington about the location of the French fleet, they
reviewed the plans agreed upon with Gérard but could make no definite
arrangements.[25] Luzerne continued on his route to Philadelphia, and Washington continued to strengthen the defenses of the Hudson.

A messenger from Congress arrived at 12:30 p.m. on October 3 with
news of the French alliance. One dispatch contained two letters Congress
received from the French minister, the Chevalier de la Luzerne, sent from
Charleston, South Carolina, with the dates of September 5 and 8, that
told of the arrival of the Comte d'Estaing's fleet off the shores of Georgia. Another dispatch was a resolution from Congress "authorizing and
directing" Washington "to concert and execute such plans of cooperation
with the Minister of France or the Count as he may think proper." The
resolution said,

> Whereas, Congress have received authentick information of the arrival
> of Count D'Estaing with a powerful fleet within these United States;
> and whereas by the vigorous exertions of the said states, the allied forces
> may be able to strike an important blow against the enemy,
> Resolved that it be most earnestly recommended to the several states
> to furnish General Washington with such aid as he may require of them
> respectively, as well as detachments from their militia as by providing
> that the allied armaments in the United States be speedily and effectively
> furnished with ample provisions; and that the most vigorous exertions
> be made for that purpose.[26]

The commander in chief immediately sent his aides to notify the
several states and the commanders of troops concerned. Massachusetts was
asked to send 2,000 militiamen at once; New York, 2,500; and Pennsylvania, to provide transportation and all kinds of supplies, so her militia quota

was only 1,500. General Sullivan was ordered to return from his Indian expedition in a hurry, and General Gates was to hold the continental troops under his command in readiness to direct them against New York if the cooperation with d'Estaing could be effected.

General Washington sent a letter to Admiral d'Estaing describing the situation. He gave it to Major Lee, who was sent to wait for the arrival of the French fleet at Sandy Hook. He gave a second letter to General Duportail and sent him to Philadelphia with Colonel Alexander Hamilton to confer with the French minister regarding further plans. He was given orders to select some spot on the coast to the southward where the fleet could be seen as it approached. When all this was accomplished and before retiring the night of October 4, thirty-six hours after receiving the resolution of Congress, General Washington wrote a report of what he had done and sent it to the president of Congress by special messenger: "New York is the first and capital object upon which every other is to depend."[27]

It was decided that Duportail and Hamilton should wait for the French fleet at the Delaware capes. They chose Lewes, near Cape Henlopen, as their stopping place. The letter they carried to the count was merely a note of introduction, leaving it to them to explain the situation of the American army and the intentions of its chief. The letter said in part,

Head Quarters, West Point, 7 October 1779

I have appointed Brigadier General Duportail and Colonel Hamilton to wait upon your Excellency . . . and explain to you fully my ideas of the proposed cooperation. . . . I have instructed them to disclose to you every circumstance and every consideration with which it is necessary you should be acquainted. . . . [Y]ou may repose the most implicit confidence Duportail and Colonel Hamilton, and accordingly I recommend them to your kind civilities and attention.[28]

General Washington's first letter to his officers instructed them as follows:

I have been favored with Col. Hamilton's letter, mentioning your arrival early on the 11th at Philad.a and your being about to set off for Lewistown the morning on which it was written.

I have attentively considered the object to which you particularly refer, and am now to authorize you, (provided the Count will not determine on a co-operation to the full extent of my instructions), to engage the whole force described in my letters to him, comprehending the continental troops and militia, in such an enterprise against the enemy's shipping as the Count and you may agree to undertake—In a word I will aid him in any plan of operations against the enemy at New York or Rhode Island in the most effective manner that our strength and resources will admit. He has nothing more to do therefore than to propose his own plan if time will not permit him to accede to ours, weighing thoroughly the consequences of expence and disappointment.

Enclosed is some intelligence received from Elizabethtown since your departure. You will observe the preparations of the enemy for throwing every possible obstruction in the Count's passage.

A chain of alarm ships are stationed in the sound to communicate the first approaches of the Count's fleet to the garrison at Rhode Island. they can propagate in a few minutes by signal guns.—In a letter from Gen. Gates of the 13th inst. he advises me of the arrival of the fleet which some time ago sailed from New York. It amounts, to 56 sail, and appeared to be only in a set of ballast. This was confirmed by one of the vessels which fell into our hands for a few hours. The opinion is that it is designed to take off the garrison.

Genl. Gates makes the marine force at New Port, one fifty and a thirty-two gun frigate. The refugee fleet and wood fleet about thirty-seven sail mostly armed, at the head of which is the *Restoration*, late the *Oliver Cromwell* of 22 guns. One frigate is also taken notice of in the fleet from New York.

Should the operations against New York in either case be undertaken, it will be of the utmost consequence to block up the garrison at Rhode Island. You will consider the propriety of suggesting to the Count the detatching of a superior sea force for this purpose previous to his approaching the Hook. For should the measures be deferred till his arrival there, it may not then be possible to prevent their junction with the army at New York as the notice can be so very suddenly transmitted by means of the signals which they have established.

Every proper attention has been given to preparing the necessary number of fascines, and such other materials as may be required in this quarter.

Fascines Gabions etc. are also held in readiness at Providence in case of an operation against New-port. I had thought of the fire ships and have taken order in this matter. I do not however choose to go to the great expence they must run us into until something is decided with his Excellency Count d'Estaing, but every thing relative shall be provided, so as to occasion no delay when such matters become necessary.[29]

STONY POINT AND VERPLANCK POINT

General Washington announced to General Duportail and Colonel Alexander Hamilton on October 21 that the British evacuated Newport. Before sending the letter, he also received news that the Crown forces had withdrawn from Stony Point and Verplanck Point, leaving the passage of the Hudson free at King's Ferry. He immediately sent General Gates to take possession of Newport and sent Colonel Gouvion to "throw up some small works at Stony Point to protect communication" there.

He wrote the following letter on October 21 to Duportail and Hamilton on the coast:

> In my letters of the 10th and 18th I transmitted all the intelligence I had obtained respecting the Enemy from the time of your departure . . . and by the present conveyance I enclose you an extract of a letter from Major General Gates of the 15th. By this you will perceive he was fully persuaded that the Enemy were preparing to evacuate Rhode Island . . . there is no room to doubt they have all things in a condition to do it on the shortest notice whenever they shall think the exigency of their affairs shall require it. It is also equally certain that they continue to carry on their Fortifications for the defence of New York with the utmost industry and perseverance and appear to be providing for the most obstinate resistance. Indeed, as their reduction would be attended with the most alarming and fatal consequences to their nation nothing else can be reasonably expected. . . .
>
> The Garrisons of Verplank's & Stony points still remain . . . but . . . all matters are putting in train for an evacuation in case events make it necessary. . . .
>
> I am led from the vast magnitude of the object which carried you from Head-Quarters and the very interesting consequences it may involve, all of which I am persuaded will occur to your consideration, to remark that the Count's entering New York Bay with his fleet must be the basis and ground work of any cooperation that can be undertaken by us, either for the reduction of the Enemy's whole force or for the destruction of their shipping only. Every thing will absolutely depend upon it in either case; as without it and a free and open communication up and down the Rivers and in the Sound, which cannot be effected or maintained in any other way, we could not possibly undertake any operations on Long Island, as our supplies of provisions and stores could only be obtained by water. This point I am certain would have your due consideration, but it appearing to me the Hinge, the One thing upon which all Others must rest, I could not forbear mentioning it.

. . . I have only to add, from a desire of preventing a misconception by either side, if any Cooperation is agreed on, that the terms and conditions may be explicitly understood. And whether it shall extend to an attempt to reduce the Enemy's whole force or only to the destruction of their Shipping, your engagements will provide in it for the continuance of the Count's fleet to secure our retreat & the removal of our stores from Long Island & York Island, if unhappily it should be found on experiment, that neither is practical and we should be obliged to abandon the Enterprise.

I am. etc.

P.S. ¼ after 3 P.M. Three Deserters have just come in who left Verplank's point last night. They all corroborate the accounts, by a detail of circumstances, of the preparations to evacuate both that and Stony point. I have no doubt that things will at least be held in readiness.

After dispatching the above, I received a letter from Major General Heath of the following is a copy; "I now have the pleasure to acquaint your Excellency that the Enemy have both points, having burnt and destroyed their Works."[30]

Before receiving this letter from General Washington, both observers on the coast had become uneasy. They had transferred their base from Lewes on the Delaware side of the bay to Little Egg Harbor, "forty-four miles from the extremity of Cape May, a hundred and ten from Sandy Hook and about fifty from Philadelphia."[31] Hamilton wrote to General Washington,

We have stationed expresses at the pitch of the Cape and have established regular communication with Major Lee [at Sandy Hook] and with the city. If the fleet should appear off the Delaware, we can be there in twelve hours after its first appearance; and if at the Hook, in less than four days. . . . By recent information from Philadelphia . . . we find that so late as the 4th of this month, the Count, as yet, was to open his batteries against the enemy at Savannah. The time that will probably intervene between this and the probable reduction, the reembarkation of the Count's troops, the dispositions for sailing, and his arrival on this coast, may, we fear, exhaust the season too much to permit the cooperation to which our mission relates.

We do not, however, despair, for if the Count has been fully successful to the southward, and should shortly arrive . . . the enterprise may possibly go on.[32]

As November arrived with no sign of d'Estaing or his fleet, General Duportail and Colonel Hamilton felt that the expense attendant upon their further stay and the slight probability of accomplishing anything that fall did not warrant maintaining their observation post much longer. They wrote to Washington, asking for further instructions. The commander in chief replied on November 11,

> Being absent from head-quarters on a visit to several outposts of the army, when your favor of the 2nd instant arrived, and not returning till last night, it was not in my power to answer it before.
>
> I am precisely in the predicament you are, with respect to the Count, his intentions and ultimate operations. I have not heard a single syllable about either since your departure, except what was transmitted in my letter of the 30th ultimo,[33] a similar account to which you will have seen in the public prints. From this circumstance and the lateness of the season, I do not expect that he will arrive in this quarter, or if he should, that the Enterprise which he proposed could now be prosecuted. It is too late to begin it. However, as I received my advices from Congress, of the Count's intentions to cooperate, and considered myself as bound by their direction to prepare for it, I have not thought myself at liberty to desist from my preparations, or to fix upon a day for them to cease. I have written to them today upon the subject, stating the uncertainty I am under with respect to His Excellency's coming, the great expense which must necessarily attend the continuing of our measures for a cooperation, and the difficulties supposing it undertaken, from the advanced season; and I requested their earliest decision as to the part I am to pursue. . . .
>
> When you have received the determination of Congress, if it be against a cooperation, it will be necessary for you to recall the pilots, except such a number as may be thought material for general purposes in case of the Count's arrival, for the security of his Fleet and such as were employed here or immediately in consequence of My Letters, you will desire to send in their Accounts.[34]

Washington heard of the disaster at Savannah between November 11 and 16 when he wrote to Major General Gates from headquarters at West Point, in part as follows:

> Much more time having been spent in the seige of Savannah . . . than was at first expected, and there being no certainty of reducing them in a short time by regular approaches, it was agreed to attempt the place by storm on the 9th ultimo; the attack was accordingly made by the allied troops, who were repulsed; in consequence the seige was raised, the cannon and stores having all been previously brought off.[35]

Reconstructed Spring Hill redoubt. This area was the focal point of the fighting during the Battle of Savannah. *Photo courtesy of the author.*

The Count has been obliged, I imagine, from his engagements in another quarter, . . . to leave the coast of Georgia. It remains now to put the army in such a chain of winter cantonments as will give security to these posts, and with the remainder to take a position, which will afford forage and subsistence, and will at the same time preserve us from the insults of the collected force of the enemy.[36]

Washington wrote General Schuyler from West Point on November 24 that Duportail had returned to camp; Alexander Hamilton, however, was detained by a slight indisposition. Headquarters were moved to Morristown, New Jersey, early in December. Here, Washington wrote to General Lincoln, who had been in command at Savannah,

I had the pleasure of receiving yours of the 22d of October, by Colonel Laurens, to whose information I am indebted for a very particular account of the situation of affairs to the southward. . . . While I regret the misfortune [of Savannah] I feel a very sensible pleasure in contemplating the gallant behavior of the officers and men of the French and American army; and it adds not a little to my consolation to learn, that instead of the mutual reproaches which too often follow the failure of enterprises depending upon the cooperation of troops of different nations, their confidence in and esteem for each other are increased. I am happy in believing, that the delicacy and propriety of your conduct upon every occasion have contributed much to this agreeable circumstance.[37]

Despite the loss at Savannah, the allies began to cooperate. Washington might have feared at first that the evacuation of Newport was intended as a trap and that the British would return when least expected. The passage across the Hudson at King's Ferry also remained open, permitting the allied armies to cross safely on their way to Philadelphia and Yorktown in 1781. D'Estaing's fleet and his attack on Savannah prepared the way for the subsequent allied successes at Yorktown two years later.

COLONEL RADIÈRE'S DEATH

Colonel Radière died suddenly of some illness at West Point on October 30. Washington briefly announced it from West Point to the watchers on the coast in a note dated November 1, 1779, where he says, "I am sorry to inform you of the death of Col. de la Radiere, who died on Saturday. He is to be buried this day with the honors due his rank."[38]

To all appearances, Colonel Radière was with General Duportail in the Highlands during part of the summer of 1779 and probably was left in command of the engineering work during the latter's absence in the search for d'Estaing. Colonel Laumoy was at Charleston in the South, so the only member of the Royal Corps nearby was Lieutenant Colonel Gouvion. This officer's letter to General Duportail announcing the death of their companion is not among the documents, but there is one written by Gouvion to Marbois, secretary to the French minister, which mentions his death and certain facts that throw an interesting light on the evacuation of the advanced posts on the Hudson by the British:

King's Ferry November 5, 1779

Sir,

I have not been able to send you the details of the evacuation of Stony Point and Verplank's Point as soon as I wished because I was absent from the army when the English abandoned the posts; I had been sent by General Washington to see to having some preparations made further down than White Plaines and in case some operations were undertaken against New York. The reports were so different in the place where I was that I did not wish to send any thing from there not knowing what to believe. I had not been here but one day when I learned of the death of Monsieur de la Radiere and I was obliged to go instantly to New Windsor (from which place I returned only yesterday) to put his affairs in order. So this sad event retarded a few more days the news which I send. I join also, Monsieur, a plan of the position of the English. I shall be very happy if this sketch of a point whose possession was the unique end of the operations of General Clinton during this campaign, interests you.

I am at present engaged in destroying the works of the English on both sides of the river, and in repairing two that we made last spring to prevent the English ships from interrupting the communication which is constant and very necessary for the subsistence of our army. If you know where Mr. Duportail is dare I beg you, Monsieur, inform him of the death of Mr. de la Radiere. I have written him on the subject but as there is nothing so liable to get lost as letters in this country, it is possible that he has not received it. You will be so good as to have Monsieur de la Luzerne accept the assurance of my respect.

I have the honor to be with Respect, Monsieur, etc.

Gouvion.[39]

General Duportail returned to camp near the end of November. His first care was to look after the affairs of his friend. He wrote the French minister,

Morristown 12 Xbre 1779

Monsieur,

I take the liberty of sending you, Monsieur, as you have very kindly permitted me, the papers concerning the late M. de la Radiere. Since a death certificate is lacking because we could not have the Church having no part whatever in his burial, I have had two certificates drawn, one for Colonel Baldwin, engineer Colonel who cared for him up to the very last moment, the other for the adjutant general of the army who ordered military honors and conducted *la pompe funèbre* [funeral]. Besides I have joined one for myself as Commandant of the Corps in which M. de la Radiere served in this country. I think that these certificates, signed also by your Excellency, will be sufficient to prove legally the death of this officer. Indeed I am informed that nothing more is permitted in this country where every one makes his entry into the world and his exit from it the most often, without any written proof of either the one or the other.[40]

The following note from Marbois was found among the Washington Papers:

A Philadelphie the 1 March 1781

Monsieur,

I have received a letter from the relatives of M. de la Radiere who are distressed at the loss of that officer. They desire that Your Excellency will be so good as to express in a personal letter to me, or in any other way, your opinion regarding services and his zeal: I know how much his family will prize such a testimonial. If anything could lessen the regret which they feel for this loss it will be to know that he merited your esteem. I eagerly seize this occasion, Monsieur, to assure you of the profound respect with which I am etc.

DE MARBOIS.[41]

Washington replied,

Head Quarters 23rd March 1781

Sir,

I had the pleasure of receiving your favor of the 1st. while at New Port, upon a most agreeable visit to Count de Rochambeau and the Gentlemen of the French Army. I shall most readily grant the Certificate which the friends of the late Colo. La Radiere desire, but as it will be necessary for me to see General duportail to ascertain some particulars relative to the different ranks which he bore in the American service, I must defer transmitting the Certificate until the General returns from R. Island.

Washington forwarded the requested certificate on May 16, 1781, but no copy was preserved among his papers. The testimony to the character and merits of the deceased must have satisfied the family.

General Washington directed General Duportail and General Greene to meet the morning of December 16, 1779, to "examine all the grounds in the environs [of the encampment at Morristown] and make a written report to me without delay of the different spots which appear most proper to be occupied in case of any movement of the enemy towards us, pointing out the comparative advantages and disadvantages of each." They were to "consider the several positions as relative to an army of ten thousand men in two lines, three divisions in the first and two divisions in the second."[42]

Duportail wrote to Marbois about the situation of the army on taking up winter quarters,

Morristown, 11th Xbre 1779

Sir, I have not had the honor of writing you since I returned to camp from Boston because nothing of importance had happened either on our side or that of the enemy. You have learned, doubtless, that we have left West Point and have come to take up our winter quarters in the outskirts of this town. Perhaps some persons will be surprised that we did not go farther down in New Jersey to be in a position to prevent the excursions of the English. It is certain that the force of our army, since the troops of Gates and Sullivan have joined us, would have permitted us to do something at this moment without danger, but we have to think of the future. It is well to realize that our army is obliged to remain in winter quarters long after the season permits entering on a campaign; that this year in particular the army will have melted away by half before the month of april, because at least a third of our soldiers belong to a group that will have two or three months leave and there is very little hope that they will reinlist; the small value of continental paper does not permit one to believe that others can be induced by that means to engage themselves. The country people will not even sell us their poultry, or their butter for this money therefore it is not at all likely they will be willing to sell themselves.[43]

The Washington Papers contain numerous notes and memoranda in the hand of General Duportail and others in that of Colonel Gouvion during the winter of 1779. They relate to defenses, plans of operations, and so on and show how much the commander in chief relied on these men for their accurate knowledge and trained minds.

When Washington sent Duportail to help Major General Benjamin Lincoln at Charleston, South Carolina, Gouvion left West Point to replace Duportail at headquarters. Another change occurred in August 1780, when Colonel Kosciusko departed West Point to serve as an engineer in the South with General Gates. Major Jean-Louis-Ambroise de Genton, the Chevalier de Villefranche, succeeded Kosciusko as West Point's engineer.

5

THE CAMPAIGN OF 1780

Charleston

General Washington ordered General Greene on December 15, 1779, to cooperate with General Duportail in determining what position the army should take in case of an enemy attack and to make a report to him. They submitted their report on January 16, 1780, but the sketch map accompanying the report seems to have been lost:

> To locate the army to any particular spots, may facilitate the Enemi's getting possession of advantageous grounds, either upon one or the other of our flanks—It appears to us more proper therefore, that we move the troops upon the high and advantageous grounds, according as the motions of the enemy may indicate an intention to make an impression at particular places.
>
> Having examined the ground in and about camp, agreeable to your Excellency's order of the 15th of December, We are of opinion, that the range of hills marked P. O. N. is that upon which the troops may be most advantageously posted, to receive the enemy should they present themselves in front of the mountains from Morristown to Kembles. Should the enemy approach us by Baskinridge and that quarter, we must occupy the grounds from the hill P. to the hill R; but if they approach us by Pluckemin, Black River and Mendham, we must draw up in the form of two sides of a square, from the hill R. to the hill S. and from the hill F. the last of which lies a little in front of the Pennsylvania line. Should the enemy attempt to penetrate our line by the way of the York Brigade, we must take post from the hill U. to the hill N.
>
> Some of the positions are weaker than others, and some parts of each weaker than the rest; such are the intervals between the mountain Q. to the mountain R. and between the mountain R. and the mountain S. Therefore to be safe in those positions (should we be greatly inferior

to the Enemy) it will be necessary to strengthen these places by art; and for this purpose it would be well to preserve as much of the wood as possible standing, on the ground.

The several positions we have marked, being composed of a chain of hills, have the advantage, that we never can be brought to a general action; the hills being divided by deep valleys, which form each, in a manner, a distinct post.

We must govern our retreat according to the enemies approach. If they approach us by the way of Morris, we can retreat by the way of Mendham, but if they approach by the way of Baskinridge, or Mendham, we may retreat by the way of Morris. However the position of the army is at such a remove from the enemy and so difficult of access, that there is little probability of their attempting any thing against us, without a greater diminution of our force, then we have reason to expect.

The suffering of the Continental Army at Morristown during the winter of 1780 was as great as, if not more than, that at Valley Forge in 1778. Not only was there lack of clothing and provision of all kinds, but also the general depression and widespread lack of enthusiasm throughout the country threatened the very existence of the army itself. General Washington's January 8 circular to the magistrates of New Jersey urged them to send immediate aid:

> The present situation of the army with the respect to provisions is the most distressing of any we have experienced since the beginning of the war. For a Fortnight past, the troops, both officers and men, have been almost perishing for want. They have been alternately without bread and meat, the whole time, with a very scanty allowance of either, and frequently destitute of both. They have borne their sufferings with a patience that merits the approbation & ought to excite the sympathy of their countrymen. But they are now reduced to an extremity no longer to be supported. . . .
>
> The distress we feel is chiefly owing to the early commencement and uncommon rigor of the winter, which have greatly obstructed the transportation of our supplies. . . . From present appearances it must be more than five weeks before we can have the benefit of any material supplies beyond the limits of this state. . . .
>
> Influenced by those considerations my duty to the Public and my affection to the virtuous inhabitants of this state . . . have determined me to call upon the respective Counties for a proportion of grain and cattle to satisfy the present emergency.[1]

RETAINING THE SERVICES OF THE ENGINEERS

Washington wrote to the president of Congress on January 2, expressing his desire to retain Brigadier General Duportail, Colonels Radière and Laumoy, and Lieutenant Colonel Gouvion in the service of the United States for another campaign because "their conduct has more than justified the opinion expressed in my letter. . . . They have been particularly useful in the course of this last period, and have acquired general esteem and confidence. I cannot forbear adding that the better the gentleman at the head of the corps is known the more he is found to be a man of abilities, and of distinguished military merit."[2]

Congress agreed to Washington's request on January 14 that they

> be retained in the service during the war or so long as is consistent with their duty to their King and agreeable to their inclinations.
>
> Resolved, That Congress have a very favourable opinion of the conduct and capacity of General Du Portail and Messrs. Laumaoy and Gouvion and lament the untimely death of Col La Radiere who during his services in America had by his zeal and exertions highly recommended himself as an officer and a gentleman.
>
> Whereas Brigadier General du Portail and Colonel Laumoy, and Lieutenant Colonel de Gouvion, have continued in the service of the United States pursuant to a resolution of Congress of the 1st day of January, 1779, and under a permission from the Minister Plenipotentiary of his most Christian Majesty, and have obtained from the Commander-in-Chief ample testimonials of honorable and useful services rendered during the last campaign:
>
> Resolved, That Brigadier General du Portail and Messieurs Laumoy and Gouvion be retained in the service of the United States (if permission can be obtained for that purpose from his most Christian Majesty or his Minister Plenipotentiary) so long, during the present war, as shall be consistent with their inclinations and duty as officers to their King:
>
> That the Board of War be directed to confer with the Minister of France on the subject, and inform General du Portail and Messieurs Laumoy and Gouvion of the result of such conference.[3]

Washington notified Colonel Moses Hazen on January 21 that General Duportail would leave for Newark the following day and proceed to reconnoiter Paulus Hook. He ordered Colonel Hazen to have two hundred men at Newark to take his orders, and they would return to camp the following day.[4]

DUPORTAIL WANTS TO GO TO THE CAROLINAS

Earlier in the season, in a letter dated simply "*Samedi matin 1779*" but probably written very soon after Duportail and Hamilton's return to camp following the fruitless wait for the French fleet on the Jersey coast, Duportail asked Hamilton's assistance to get authorization to go to the Carolinas. He seems to have had a persistent idea that it might be exceedingly useful to the allied cause if he were to spend the winter in the Carolinas to make preparations for the ensuing campaign. He noted several reasons that made it unwise for him to ask on his own behalf to be sent down. The request or order must come from the commander in chief or from Congress. He wanted Hamilton to direct matters tactfully to successful completion. He ended by saying, "However the affair turns, let this letter be a secret between us; but I absolutely desire to be gratified in this respect. Adieu."[5]

It cannot be verified whether it was because of Colonel Hamilton's assistance, but Congress resolved on March 6 "That Genl. Du Portail be directed to repair to the State of South Carolina with all possible expedition, and join the southern army, and *act either With the main army or in the immediate defence of Charlestown, as shall appear to him to be conducive to the public service.*"[6] The resolution, however, was postponed.

Meanwhile, Washington took up the matter directly with Congress and wrote the following letter to General Duportail on March 27:

> Notwithstanding the occasion we should have of your services in this quarter should any active operations [be] commenced, the critical situation of Charles Town and the importance of that place induce me to wish you were there.
>
> I am doubtful whether you can arrive in time; but I have submitted the matter to Congress to determine according to the advices they have received. The letter to them is inclosed, which after reading you will be pleased to deliver to the President. Should you go to the Southward I request you will favour me with a detail as frequently as circumstances will permit, of the military operations in that quarter; and I entreat you to believe that I shall at all times take great pleasure in hearing of your success and glory.[7]

His letter to the president of Congress is as follows:

Head Quarters, Morristown, 27 March 1780

Sir,

In the present situation of Southern affairs much will depend on having an able Engineer in that quarter. I have a very good opinion of the Gentleman there in this line [Colonel Laumoy], but the confidence I have in General Duportail's abilities makes me think his presence would be of the greatest utility. Though we may sensibly feel the want of him here should any active operation commence; yet upon the whole I would be willing to spare him were there a probability of his arriving in time. I have no doubt from the season and from every other circumstance that General Clinton will press the enterprise with all the vigor and dispatch in his power; but the loss of his horses may necessarily retard his progress. I beg leave to submit to Congress the propriety of sending General Duportail, which they will be best able to determine from the general complexion of the advices they have received. As he is in Philadelphia their orders immediately to him will prevent delay. In case of his going it will be of course necessary to bear his expenses and furnish him with the means of expedition, and it were to be wished he may receive his orders as soon as possible.

> I have the honor to be etc.
> Go. WASHINGTON.[8]

General Washington was under intense pressure at this time. Things were going badly in the South, and the country was gradually becoming disillusioned with the war. The commander in chief's will to succeed sustained the patriots during this long and difficult time. In this case, his desire to have General Duportail render what service was still possible at Charleston coincided with the wishes of Congress, so that the order was immediately given following the reading of the letter from the commander in chief. Two days later, on March 31, he was voted to receive $20,000, and a further sum of $8,000 was added on April 5 "in consequence of a letter from the Board of War" that Duportail took with him to General Lincoln, along with the following letter of introduction:

Morristown, March 30, 1780

Dear Sir,

This will be delivered to you by Brigadier-General Duportail, chief engineer; a gentleman of whose abilities and merit I have the highest opinion, and who, if he arrives in time will be of essential utility to you. The delay that will probably attend General Clinton's operations, in consequence of the losses that he has suffered on the voyage, makes me hope his assistance may not come too late; and the critical situation of your affairs induces me to part with him, though in case of any active operations here, I should sensibly feel the want of him. From the experience I have had of this gentleman, I recommend him to your particular confidence. You will find him able in the branch he professes; of a clear and comprehensive judgment; of extensive military science; and of great zeal, assiduity and bravery; in short, I am persuaded you will find him a most valuable acquisition, and will avail yourself effectually of his services. You cannot employ him too much on every important occasion.[9]

REINFORCEMENTS

General Washington wrote to the Board of War on March 30, notifying them that he had received information that the enemy was preparing to send reinforcements to the South and that he was sending Major Lee's corps there as quickly as possible. As they would need many items for the long march, he directed the officers to go to Philadelphia and apply to the Board of War. He requested a liberal supply, as the items could not be procured in the South.[10]

Duportail was undoubtedly moved by these testimonials of his ability, character, and zeal, coming as they did from a man as reticent as General Washington. His reply of April 2, 1780, says,

I have received the letter with which your Excellency has been good enough to honor me as also the one addressed to the President of Congress, I saw to it that it was immediately handed to him. This very evening I received a resolution of the Congress that I should go to Charlestown. Later I received by M. de Castaing the letter for General Lincoln. I cannot allow the opportunity to pass without expressing to Your Excellency how touched I am by the manner in which you have spoken of me in these letters. It is the greatest reward which I could possibly receive for my efforts in serving the United States. As nothing else could arouse me to efforts that would justify the good opinion your Excellency has wished to give of me, may I in this circumstance fulfill your expectations: and may it be possible for me to arrive before it is too late!

Conformable to your orders I will render to your Excellency as often as possible an account of our operations.

Although in the present circumstances I go South with pleasure, because I wish to be where I can be most useful, still I wish to express to your Excellency that in case Charlestown is taken or delivered from danger, in a word if the Carolinas do not become the principal scene of the war, I desire to return to this part of the country. My place, my veneration, my devotion to your person, binds me to the army which you command and it is only in such circumstances and the actual circumstances in which the Carolinas are placed that would permit me to leave you except with the greatest regret; and it is a very great pleasure for me to think that I can [manuscript faded] and open the campaign in that place.

During my absence I have the honor to propose to your Excellency to have M. de Gouvion replace me in the army here; and as you know we have to form companies of sappers and miners I propose that he be charged with those companies. The Board of War has assured me that the men we need have been included in those required of the different states; therefore it will only be question of taking them as they arrive.

I have sketched out a plan of instruction for the officers and soldiers of the company, but it is not in a state to be presentable. I shall have the honor of sending it to your Excellency from Carolina.

Colonel Gouvion wrote me recently that General Howe who commands at West Point asked for a plan of the place. It seems to me very proper that he should have one but I think that when the plan is made [illegible] who commands at that place without its being possible for it to be taken away. It seems to me very improper that copies should be multiplied.

> I have the honor to be, with the most profound respect
> of Your Excellency etc.
> Duportail.[11]

Duportail was appointed to lieutenant colonel in France, attached to the infantry, on April 5, 1780, and General Washington acted on Duportail's suggestion to replace him with Colonel Gouvion in the Army of the North on April 28. Gouvion was still in the Highlands, and Washington sent the following order to Major General Howe: "General Duportail being gone to the southward, it is necessary that Colonel Gouvion should repair to this army. If there are any previous arrangements you wish him to make, you will be pleased to direct him to make them, and to set out for head-quarters as speedily as he can."[12]

In the meantime, General Duportail had proceeded with all speed to Charleston, arriving at 7:00 a.m. on April 25, only a few days before the question of terms of surrender of the city was discussed in a general council of the officers present. As soon as he arrived, he observed the enemy, their positions, and their strength, then inspected the defenses. He concluded that the British could have captured Charleston ten days before he got there. Having determined the positions were untenable, he requested to depart the city, but General Lincoln refused to let him go.

General Benjamin Lincoln surrendered the city on May 12, and General Duportail was among the captives. He wrote a lengthy account of the surrender on May 17, and one of his letters was read before Congress on the same day.[13]

DUPORTAIL'S REPORT

He sent the report to the president of Congress, with a copy forwarded to General Washington and another to the French minister, the Chevalier de la Luzerne. The following translation is from the *Papers of the Continental Congress*:

> You will probably have heard of the surrender of Charlestown by the time you will receive this letter. I arrived here the 25th of April at seven the morning, after having passed during the Night in the Midst of the Enemies, through the Woods with the assistance of good guides. I found the Town in a desperate State almost entirely invested by the British Army and Fleet which has passed the Bar and Fort Moultrie. They had surmounted difficulties which were generally looked upon as insuperable without experiencing scarce any resistence. The Enemy had brought their trenches upon the neck within about 120 or 130 yards from the Fortifications; in a word the fall of the Town was unavoidable unless an Army come to her assistance which then did not appear likely. After having examined the situation of things I thought an evacuation highly advisable and I proposed it—but the Council found an impracticability in the measure although for my part, it only appeared difficult and hazardous and such as we ought to risk in our present situation.
>
> That Plan being rejected the only object was to protract the term of our Capitulation. I have done on my part every thing that was in my power to fulfill that object in the same manner that Colonel Laumoy had before my arrival, but time brought us to lose sight of the term of our resistance. The Enemy succeeded in draining part of the Ditch was in front of our intrenchments and raised nine Batteries in their third Parallel. The day they opened them they sent a flag with a Letter to summon General Lincoln to Surrender. Upon this a Council of Generals and field officers was called and after having asked whether terms ought to be proposed to the Enemy and it was carried in the affirmative by great majority, myself was of that number. As the first propositions

were from the Enemy we might expect advantageous Conditions, I
have even some hope that we might have saved the Garrison; besides
a positive refusal to treat with an Enemy who within a few days could
have been in a condition of giving us the law appeared imprudent and
unreasonable. It was then determined in Council that propositions
should be made, but afterwards by an extraordinary oversight they left
to the General officers the care of determining what was to be proposed.
This is the moment where I left off taking any part in what has been
done being of a contrary opinion to that of the other Genl. officers.
They agreed to propose that the Continental Troops should be prisoners
of war. I opposed that measure with all my might. I represented that if
even our situation required it, it was not our business to propose it &
that we showed an ignorance of what is practised in those cases which
would make us appear in a ridicule light. I represented that if I had been
of opinion with the greatest number to propose terms to the Enemy,
I mean that they should be honorable terms, both advantageous to the
Army and Continent; as for instance to surrender the Town alone with
the artillery store and Ships; but to save the Troops; that if the army
must be prisoners of war it was more eligible to hold out in order to
justify such unfavorable Conditions by a longer resistance and more
distressing situation. My representations had not the desired effect the
propositions were made such as you will see them. Fortunately, such as
they were the Enemy would not grant them and proposed others less
advantageous which General Lincoln did not however think proper to
accept. The Truce was broken and the operations of the Siege vigorously continued. But the second day after the militia refused to do duty
General Lincoln thought from this that the Capitulation was absolutely
necessary and called the Council who countenanced the Measure. For
my part I thought we ought to try before to bring the Militia to their
duty by every possible means, by acts of authority, and if necessary by
exemplary punishments; this was likely deemed impracticable; and the
Capitulation took place to my great regret; not that I think we could
have held out longer than three or four days, but that we should have
put the Enemy in such a situation to render a further resistence on our
part blamable to every body; then our defence would have done us
much more honor. It is true that in that case the Conditions would
not likely have been the same but I was for sacrificing that advantage
to a little more glory. Fortunately in all this the honor of the American
Arms is secure and the Enemy have not great subject to triumph. To
remain forty two days in open trenches before a Town of an immense
extent fortified by sandy intrenchments raised in two months without
covered way, without our works, open in several places on the water
side, exposed every where to attacks and defended by a Garrison which

was not sufficient by half of what was necessary, before such a place I say and display all the appearance of a regular seige, is nothing very glorious.

Perhaps the English General followed the rule of prudence in conducting himself so—but at best the troops that he commanded have assuredly no reason to boast of their ardor or enterprising spirit; while on the other hand the American troops gave certain proof of their firmness to support, for more than forty days, a terrible fire—and to remain so long exposed to the danger of surprises, or attacks *de vive force*, which were certain of success if the enemy took its measures carefully.

M. de Laumoy and the engineers whom he has under his orders, have been so busy constructing the fortifications of Charlestown, both before and during the seige that there was no time to make a design of the plans—this deprives me of the satisfaction of sending them to Congress—supposing indeed the enemy would permit it.[14]

General Duportail sent this note to the French minister the following day, enclosing a copy (in French) of the report given above:

I intended to give your Excellency a detailed account of all that has happened since my arrival, but I have not had the time. I asked Genl. Clinton to permit me to go to Philadelphia on parole. He refused. He seems to conduct himself towards every one in a manner *malhonnete et grossière*. We shall lack every thing here, and I in particular, who, to arrive more quickly, left behind the few articles I possess not wanting to be burdened.

If I have the courage to again expose myself to a refusal, I will ask to have my prison here changed to one in the north, Charlestown against New York. I am not yet fully decided. The voyage with the English and the sailors offers much discomfort. If I have the means of writing your Excellency I shall surely do so as often as possible. Not being able to give you a detailed account today of the principal events, I will send you a copy of the letter I wrote to the President of Congress.

I have the honor to be etc.
Thousand compliments to M. de Marbois.[15]

PRISONER OF WAR

Duportail found an opportunity to write letters on July 7, 1780. He sent two letters to the French legation in Philadelphia; one to the principal secretary, Marbois; and a longer description of his condition and surroundings to Luzerne. Translated parts of the two letters follow:

To Monsieur de Marbois:

You probably did not think, Monsieur, when you saw me hurrying to Charlestown that I was going to put myself in prison. Neither did I think so truly. I was very far from supposing that the American Commander would put himself in a position to allow himself to be taken with all his troops, the only resource of this whole region. How all this has been conducted. How many people have reproaches to hurl at Congress, at the state of Carolina, at Lincoln—I do not know who should consider themselves most to blame. As for myself I am persuaded that Charlestown could have been saved or if the enemy was absolutely determined to have it, at least they could have been made to evacuate New York which would have been some compensation. As it is, where will our losses end? It has been said at one time that General Gates is in North Carolina with ten thousand men; now they say it is only de Kalb with the Maryland division. May *[la] grace éternelle* inspire the Philadelphia senate with that spirit of vigor and resolution which will repair these losses and prevent others so the effect will be less considerable. . . .

We live here in complete ignorance of what is going on in America as well as in Europe. I have only learned that the Spaniards have gone to sleep and allowed themselves to be surprised at Gibraltar. They have experienced a terrible reverse which indirectly affects us. . . .

In the sad condition in which I find myself such things become the objects of my meditation and the indignation they give me prevents me from falling into lethargy.[16]

To Monsieur de la Luzerne:

M. de Plombard—former consul at Charlestown, will deliver the letter—he has done every thing possible to oblige me since I have been in captivity. Without him I would have been very much embarrassed to find some means of getting money—besides we needed it so as not to die from hunger. He performed the same service for M. de Laumoy who needed it all the more since he was taken down with small pox, which nevertheless he says he already has had but there are many examples to prove that it can be had twice—my brother, the one who had the honor of seeing you at Malesherbes—was one and certainly it is not difficult to believe.

We await news from Congress—our hope very much is that there will be an exchange between us and Burgoyne's army. For myself I fear very much because I doubt if there are many brigadier generals in that army. If I had been major-general I could have been exchanged for Major General Phillips commander of Charlestown—but it is hardly likely that Congress—all other means failing—would think of giving me that rank—the idea was given me by an American general. . . .

At this moment, M. le Chevalier, you are doubtless living in one of the pleasant country houses near Philadelphia. You are enjoying the beautiful season of July—a moderate climate with pleasing prospects. I am sure you walk daily in cool woods—whereas I am here in a flat country where green stagnant pools exhale corruption—there is no water fit to drink—the soil is nothing but sand which burns the flat of the foot and blinds one when the wind blows. Although we are surrounded with woods we are not allowed to walk in them and they are of a kind of pine that gives no shade and interrupts the little air one might enjoy. Corn and potatoes are the only products of the country. . . . [O]ne sees a few negroes—covered with a few miserable rags . . . and wretched peasants only a little less dark than their negroes—who go about barefooted and without education or politeness. . . . At night, if one does not have two mosquito nets there is no hope of closing the eyes. Even so the noise they make keeps one awake—any way, no matter what is done they manage to enter in an infinite number of places and the body is covered with bites which oblige one perpetually to scratch with both hands. I have had to stop this letter twenty times for that reason. You will see Monsieur, how we pass our time here, and you may judge how much I wish to leave this place.[17]

PRISONER EXCHANGE

Before this letter could reach its destination, Congress had passed the following resolution on July 13, 1780:

> The abilities and experience of Brigadier General du Portail, in the line of his department as an engineer, appearing to Congress essential to the effectual promotion of the operations of the ensuing campaign;
>
> Resolved, that General Washington immediately endeavor to obtain the exchange of Brigadier General du Portail, now a prisoner on parole.[18]

Washington, in consequence of this resolution of Congress, wrote to the commissary general of prisoners on July 24, 1780,

> In consequence of directions I have just received for the purpose you will propose to Mr. Loring to exchange any Brigadier General belonging to those in our hands for Brigadier Genl. du Portail who was taken at Charlestown, and if the proposition is agreed to, you will take immediate measures for releasing the officer given on our part and will give an order for releasing Genl. Portail for his safe conduct to Philadelphia or some part of Jersey, if Sir Henry Clinton will indulge him with a passage

by water, or if not till he may arrive at such place in North Carolina, as he may mention.[19]

He also wrote to the president of Congress on July 22, 1780, "I was honoured Yesterday with Your Excellency's Letter of the 14th, and with it's inclosure, directing me to endeavour to obtain the exchange of Brigadier General du Portail. A proposition to this effect will be made by the earliest opportunity; in compliance with the direction, but I do not think there is any prospect of it's being acceded to."[20]

General Washington here alludes to officers taken prisoners at Saratoga in October 1777. Negotiations began at once. He wrote to Abraham Skinner on September 17, 1782, to specify the general rules for him to follow in negotiating the release of officers and mentioned that Congress specifically directed the release of General Duportail. He wrote a second letter more than three months later, on October 31, 1780: "It is my wish that you exchange the Gentleman of the Convention above mentioned—but I make it a condition to the exchange of the general officers that General Du Portail and the other characters particularly mentioned to you by Congress and the Board of War be included."[21]

The following communications tell the final steps of the exchange. The first is to the president of Congress, in which Washington says,

> I have the pleasure to inform Congress that at the late meeting of the respective commissaries, the exchanges of about one hundred and forty of our officers, and all our privates in New York, amounting to four hundred and seventy-six, were effected. Among the former are Major General Lincoln, Brigadier-General Thompson, Waterbury, and Duportail, and Lieutenant Colonel Laurens.

Washington was pessimistic that the British would accept the proposal, but Duportail's exchange was effected on October 17, 1780.[22]

In a letter to General Greene, commander of the Army in the South, dated November 7, 1780, he sent the following message, with a letter to General Duportail enclosed: "I have to request that you will be pleased to send by a flag of truce the enclosed letter to Brigadier-General Duportail, who is exchanged."[23]

Washington wrote to General Duportail the next day, "I have the pleasure to announce to you your exchange for Brigadier General de Gaull the Convention troops. Inclosed you have a Certificate of the same, and Sir Henry Clinton's passport for your return to Philadelphia. I need not tell you how happy I shall be to see you again with the army."[24]

One can better imagine than describe the joy with which this message was received. Duportail regretted that he could not take his subalterns with him. Colonels Laumoy and Cambray and Captain L'Enfant were not exchanged until nearly a year after the surrender of Yorktown, although they had been previously released on parole for some time.[25]

General Duportail had been a prisoner in Charleston since May 1780. His certificate of release was dated November 1780, but some time elapsed before it reached him at Charleston. Before leaving the South, he visited General Greene at his camp on the Pee Dee River in early January 1781. Greene had been put in command of the Army of the South after its defeat under General Gates at Camden. Duportail was traveling under a British "passport" to Philadelphia, where his exchange was to be finalized. Colonel Nisbet Balfour, the British commander at Charleston, angrily complained that by visiting Nathanael Greene's camp, Duportail had committed a "direct breach of that passport."[26]

Duportail may have seen Lafayette, for he speaks of bringing letters from him to Washington as he was on his way to join the Northern Army and to inform General Washington about conditions in the Southern Department. He stopped at Petersburg, Virginia, on January 23, 1781. Baron von Steuben was away, so he gave Greene's letters (January 11 and two dated January 13) with all the news to von Steuben's aide, who would "send them immediately."[27]

6

THE CORPS OF ENGINEERS

Congress created the Continental Army on June 14, 1775, and two days later, the day before the Battle of Bunker Hill, it authorized one chief engineer and two assistants, as well as one chief engineer and two assistants "in a separate department," commissioned in the grades of colonel and captain, respectively. Congress also resolved on January 16, 1776, "That if General Washington think proper Col. R. Gridley be continued chief engineer in the army at Cambridge."[1]

It soon became apparent that the army needed experienced engineers, and they looked to France, where the Corps of Engineers was very honorable and from which different European powers sought officers. Congress instructed its ministers to France, Silas Deane and Benjamin Franklin, to "secure skilled engineers, not exceeding four," who might serve in the Continental Army, and to solicit material assistance. The commissioners made an agreement with the four selected men to advance them one degree from the rank they held at home, but when they arrived in America, they found their situation was very different with respect to officers in all other corps. They saw, for example, a major of artillery exalted four ranks, as a chief. They reported these circumstances and appealed to the equity of Congress, but Congress was too busy to consider creating a Corps of Engineers.

1777

Washington's plans for 1777 included a request for an organized Corps of Engineers. On December 27, 1776, Congress authorized him "to raise and collect a corps of engineers and to establish their pay" for a period of six months, but the shortage of proficient engineers prevented him from taking any action on this resolution. Congress resolved on July 8, 1777, "That the treaty made by the Commissioners in France on the 13th day of February last, be confirmed as far as it respects the chevalier du Portail, monsieur de la Radière, and monsieur du Gouvion; the first to be a colonel, the second a lieutenant-colonel, and the third a major of engineers."[2] These officers were from the Royal Corps of Engineers in the French army. The war attracted them and other educated military engineers to this country. As no regulations had yet been made regarding cavalry or engineers, these French engineers received five months' pay as infantrymen, which did not even cover the expenses of their voyage.

Around January 18, 1778, Duportail submitted a proposal to the commander in chief to supplement the engineer officers with companies of combat engineers and called them companies of sappers and miners, according to European custom. The sappers dug the entrenchments (saps) for a formal siege; the miners constructed underground tunnels. These companies, which Duportail felt should become a permanent part of the Continental Army, could execute small projects or supervise infantry details in more extensive undertakings:

> I would desire to have three Companies of Sappers formed—they should be instructed in every thing that relates to the construction of Field works—how to dispose of the Earth to cut the Slopes—face with Turf or Sods—make fascines—arrange them properly—cut and fix Palisades &ct.
>
> The Sappers should be distributed in the different works, and a sufficient number of fatigue men drawn from the line should be joined to them to work under their direction, by which means the work would be executed with a perfection and celerity which otherwise will ever be unknown in this army—it is, I believe, altogether useless to enlarge upon a matter so obvious—I proceed therefore immediately to the principal Conditions on which the Corps should be formed.
>
> The corps should be formed on the following principles:
>
> 1. The pay ought to be greater than that of the ordinary foot soldier, as is the practice in Europe, because the service is exceedingly hard. They should also receive extraordinary pay, when they work and vigorous soldiers should be selected with preference given to Carpenters and Masons.
>
> 2. The non-commissioned officers should all be able to read and write and be intelligent persons of good characters.

3. The companies of sappers should be under the command of the head engineer.

4. The captains of sappers will be charged with the detail of their companies and each of them will be accountable to the commanding officer of the engineers, in order that he may always know the state of the companies, their strength etc.

5. Each company should always have its tools with it, carried in a wagon provided for the purpose. The company should be answerable for all tools lost and, in case any should be broken, the pieces are to be produced to the officer to whom the detail of the company is committed.

The camp of the sappers is to be assigned by the commanding officer of the engineers adjacent to the place where they are to be employed.

Of the Officers.

If it is important to choose the Privates in these Companies, it is much more so to choose the Officers. The Congress ought in my opinion to think of forming Engineers in this Country to replace us when we shall be call'd home—The Companies of Sappers now proposed might serve as a School to them—they might there acquire at once the practical part of the Construction of Works—and if choice be made of young men well bred, intelligent and fond of Instruction, we shall take pleasure in giving them principles upon the choice of Situations, and the method of adapting works to the ground.[3]

Duportail recommended speedy execution of the plan, if approved, so the companies could serve their apprenticeship before the opening of the campaign. He also noted that four engineers were not sufficient because one, and sometimes two, is always detached.

1778

Duportail made further recommendations to General Washington in an undated letter docketed "Feby 1778":

1° in all europa the pay of engineers is higher than that of all other officers, besides a particular traitement is allowed to them in time of war; in france it is more Considerable than their appointements. that is founded on several reasons and between them on the hardship of their service wich obliges them to be perpetually running about, in Consequence of it they Cannot often live with the same means wich may be found in Camp. therefore they are put to Charge of a good deal of expense.

2° each engineer even being only Capitaine wants two horses one for him and another for a servant who attends him where he may be detached. but every body Knows that the Continental horses are extremely bad, Consequenty unfit for our service; therefore we must provide with, but they are so dear that our appointments whatever may be Cannot afford for that purchase.

i ask sr pleases to the honourable Congres to grant us the necessary money, according the account here after.

to Lieut. Col. [Jean-Baptiste de] gouvion and major villefranche two horses for every one.

to Colonels La radiere et laumoy for three horses.[4]

Duportail did not await a response to this memorial, as he was aware of the responsibilities that would be required of the engineers in future combat. He created a school of engineering to start the next campaign on a good footing. Gouvion undertook the administration and could instruct the corps in a rigorous and homogeneous manner.

Duportail frequently broached Congress about creating a Corps of Engineers, and Washington continued to exert pressure, but the topic never received serious consideration. Congress approved the formation of three companies on May 27, 1778, but the army moved slowly, and Washington appointed officers only on August 2, 1779, after Duportail personally interviewed the candidates. Washington transferred the carefully selected enlisted men from infantry regiments a year later.

1779

Corps of Engineers Established

Congress resolved to formally establish a Corps of Engineers on March 11, 1779:

> that the engineers in the service of the United States shall be formed into a corps, styled the "corps of engineers," and shall take rank and enjoy the same rights, honours, and privileges, with the other troops on continental establishment. That a Commandant of the Corps of Engineers shall be appointed by Congress, to whom their orders or those of the Commander-in-Chief shall be addressed, and such Commandant shall render to the Commander-in-Chief, and to the Board of War, an account of every matter relative to his department.[5]

This legislation gave the engineers the status of a branch of the Continental Army with the same pay and prerogatives as artillerymen to prevent any jealousy between the technical branches. It also formed three companies, each with a captain, three lieutenants, four sergeants, four corporals, and sixty privates.

After preparing the plan to rearrange the engineer corps, the Board of War recommended Congress promote Jean-Bernard Gauthier de Murnan to the rank of major in the corps. Congress took no action until January 13, 1779, when it appointed Murnan a major in the Corps of Engineers "to take rank as such from the 1st day of March last, and to receive pay and subsistence from the 1st day of February last, the latter being the time he was employed by Brigadier du Portail, and the former the time he was directed by the Commander-in-Chief to act as major."[6]

Commandant

Brigadier General Duportail was appointed commandant of the Corps of Engineers the following May 11. The corps would also include companies of sappers and miners. Congress brevetted several of its officers, and its chief was promoted to the grade of major general on November 16, 1781, "in consideration of his meritorious services, and particularly of his distinguished conduct in the siege of York, in the State of Virginia."[7] The records include the names of one brigadier general, six colonels, eight lieutenant colonels, three majors, and ten captains, but the list is most likely incomplete.

The officers of the Corps of Engineers were very dissatisfied with Congress's September 2, 1776, decision of limiting command of engineer officers, in contravention of the then Articles of War. They also complained that officers of equal rank refused to take orders from them and that many of the men and some of the officers used foul language in their regard and abused their servants. As their memorial to Mr. Thomas Jefferson, the president of Congress, received no reply, the whole corps determined to resign their commissions, but Colonel Williams and Major Wadsworth were the only field officers then in the corps who actually resigned.

Corps of Sappers and Miners

General Washington wrote to the Board of War on February 26, 1779, to notify them that General Duportail would revise his plan for the Corps of Sappers and Miners to include amendments that Washington thought proper. He forwarded the revised plan to the Board of War the following day, along with his remarks, after speaking with General Duportail about them. The Board of War approved the plan and sent it back to Washington on April 1 with remarks from Congress for his approval before printing the plan.[8]

Congress approved an Act for the Pay and Subsistence of Engineers, Sappers, and Miners on May 11, 1779, and General Duportail's title was changed to commandant of the Corps of Engineers and Sappers and Miners to reflect his additional responsibilities.[9] Officers (three captains, three first lieutenants, and three second lieutenants) interested in taking commissions in the Company of Sappers and Miners were urged to apply to Duportail; post the necessary qualifications, such as their knowledge of practical geometry and drawing; and give their names at the adjutant general's office.[10]

Washington wrote to Duportail on July 27, 1779, ordering him to "make an arrangement of the officers who have presented themselves for appointments in the companies of Sappers and Miners, which I will transmit to the Board of war to obtain their commissions."[11] Until more men could be recruited, he suspended the formation of companies of sappers and miners because the numerous drafts from the line for different purposes would make it inconvenient to take out others to form these companies. He also offered a "bounty of two hundred dollars is to be given to each man who shall enlist during the war, and twenty dollars to the officer as a gratuity for every man so enlisted."[12]

Recruiting

Consequently, Congress authorized the recruiting of engineers from the various colonies. General Duportail then proceeded to prepare for their recruitment, as can be seen in his letter to Joseph Reed, president of the Supreme Executive Council of Pennsylvania, on September 10, 1779:

> Congress some time since ordered the formation of three Companies of sappers and miners, of which they were pleased to honor me with the Command. The soldiers for these Companies were originally to be drafted from the line, but his excellency, general washington, finding some inconveniency in doing it at this time prefers their being raised. In Consequence he has written to Congress praying them to recommend it to the different states, to permit this levy, which Recommendation your excellency will probably receive. I therefore send Captain Mc Murray into your state to recruit for these Companies and I intreat that you will be pleased to give the business all the aid of which it may stand in need.

Cap. McMurray has the regulations made by Congress for these Companies. I dare pray you to have the goodness to run them over and you will see what is to be their service and their instruction; you will see that the officers are to have the means of acquiring all the knowledge necessary to engineers, and that the soldiers will learn to Construct all the works relative to fortifications. May I therefore be permitted to observe that it would be very advantageous to the state of pensilvania to furnish a number of these soldiers who, returning into their own Country after being instructed, may be of the greatest utility to it. As I flatter myself your excellency will judge of it in the same manner, and your eagerness to form every kind of establishment useful to the state which you govern is well known, I take the liberty to propose to you the formation of one of these Companies of sappers and miners, to belong to the state itself. This plan has been mentioned to general washington and met his approbation in that case. As there are two vacancies in the Company of Mr. McMurray they Could be granted to two gentlemen of the state of pensilvania for this purpose; if your excellency should be acquainted with any gentlemen disposed to embrace this profession and proper for it, I should esteem it a favor you would send them to me for examination. The qualities necessary for the officers of sappers and miners are in the first place a good education in general, which will be a security for the integrity of their sentiments.

It must be Considered that these officers becoming Engineers and so in a situation to have in their hands the plans of the frontiers of the fortifications, the memorials concerning them, in a word all that has relation to the defence of the state, they ought to be qualified to inspire great Confidence in their fidelity and in their attachment to their Country; in the next place it is proper they should have some mathematical Knowledge—the more they have the better; but we may not exact a great deal from young men who do not exceed the age of twenty, who besides have had a good education, possess a fund of intelligence and show an inclination to instruct themselves, they may be the easier dispensed with, as there will be a master of mathematics attached to the Companies, and they will be furnished with regard to this object with all the means to supply the defects of their education.[13]

The companies of sappers and miners still lacked a full complement of officers and enlisted men by the summer of 1780. In fact, despite the influx of foreign volunteers, the Continental Army never had as many engineers as it needed. Washington's compelling need for technical assistance also forced him to seek the creation of a separate geographer's department to supplement the work of the engineers. The officers complained that the problem resulted in part because they had never "been put upon a proper footing for the recruiting business."[14] Meanwhile, the officers already on active duty were "acquiring a knowledge of the service to which they . . . were destined,"[15] but they waited impatiently to perform some worthwhile service for their country.

Washington reinstituted drafts from the line in an effort to get the troops he still needed. He proposed to take one man from each regiment. Joseph Plumb Martin was drafted into the Company of Sappers and Miners as a corporal. General Duportail recommended Captain Daniel Nevin to General Washington, who wrote to the president of Congress on January 26, 1780,

> Sir: I have the honor to inclose the copy of a letter from Brigadier General Du Portail. From the character he gives and which I have otherwise received of Capt Neven, I shall be happy it may please Congress to make the appointment solicited. As the Engineers we now have are only for a temporary service and it will always be essential to have men skilled in that branch of military science in this country, it appears to me to be a necessary policy to have men who reside among us forming themselves during the war under the present Gentlemen. Capt Neven has a turn to this profession which joined to his past services induce me to wish he may become a member of the corps; and it seems but reasonable that he should have the rank and from the time mentioned in General Du Portail's letter.
>
> I request also the directions of Congress to the Board of War on the subject of Commissions for the officers of Sappers and miners. These Gentlemen in consequence of the resolution of Congress for establishing these companies, underwent an examination by General Du Portail and were found the best qualified among a number of candidates. Considering their appointment as a thing of course they were nominated in General orders [of August 2, 1779] and an arrangement of them sent soon after to the Board of War for the purpose of obtaining commissions. These I now learn they have not yet received. As probably the Board do not think themselves authorized to grant the Commissions, without the instructions of Congress, I take the liberty to trouble them upon the subject. The Gentlemen in question, several of whom left Regiments in the line to come into these companies begin to be anxious about the delay. By the establishment of the Corps of Engineers the men for these companies were to be drafted from the line; but the weakness of the batalions has hitherto suspended it. An attempt has been made to recruit but without success. The officers 'till the companies can be formed are engaged in acquiring a knowledge of the service to which they are destined against the next campaign. These

companies if any active operations are to be carried on will be very important; we feel the want of something of the kind whenever we have works to construct; but, at any rate, the officers will be useful in the Engineering line to which their studies are relative and preparatory. The present number of Engineers is not adequate to the exigencies of the service. I have the honor etc.

The Board of War resolved on February 5, 1780,

That the officers attached to the companies of sappers and miners be commissioned, and rank as follows:
Mr. Nevin, captain, April 25, 1779. Mr. Bebee, Mr. Murray, Mr. Du Veil, captains; Mr. Gilleland, Mr. Bushnell, Mr. Cleveland, captain lieutenants; Mr. Welsh, lieutenant; August 2, 1779.[16]

The Chevalier de La Luzerne notified General Washington on March 8 that the Comte de Vergennes and King Louis XVI also approved the "Request respecting the Officers in the Department of Engineers."[17] Washington was very pleased.

The first recruits joined the Corps of Sappers and Miners on May 28, 1781, and General Duportail was ordered to send an engineer to direct and superintend the fortifications to be erected at or near Fort Herkimer. Three days later, Duportail was at Wethersfield, Connecticut, with General Washington to meet with the Comte de Rochambeau and Admiral de Barras, but the British fleet appeared off Block Island, and they (Rochambeau and Barras) did not think it prudent to leave Newport.[18]

Congress did not immediately address Duportail's concerns about the future arrangement of the artillery and engineering departments. He submitted proposals on September 30, 1781, and appealed on October 6 for permission to return to France with General Laumoy and Colonel Gouvion. Congress approved the leave on October 10. As the superintendent of finance subsequently announced that he had no funds for paying Duportail and his officers, the general again appealed to Congress for relief on October 29.[19]

1782

Major Villefranche became the chief of the Corps of Engineers in 1782 during the absence of General Duportail and Colonel Gouvion and pending the release of Colonel Laumoy and Lieutenant Colonel Cambray, the commanding officer of engineers at West Point, both of whom were captured at Charlestown, South Carolina, and were still prisoners of war. Villefranche's April 1782 report identifies the situation of the different members of the corps:

RETURN OF THE CORPS OF ENGINEERS FOR
THE MONTH OF APRIL 1782

Name	Rank	here employed
Messieurs du portail	M. Genl.	on furlough
Koskiusko	Colonel	Southern army
laumoy	"	prisoner
gouvion	"	on furlough
Wuibert	Lt. Col.	fort pitt
Cambray	"	prisoner
de Brahm	Major	on furlough
Villefranche	"	"
Rochefontaine	"	"
de laren	Capt.	southern army
l'enfant	"	on furlough
Niven	"	main army
Shreibur	"	prisoner

West Point, april 12, 1782
MAJR. VILLEFRANCHE Commanding engineer

Thaddeus Kosciusko, as ranking colonel of engineers, should have had the post of commandant in the absence of General Duportail; however, he had never been willing to serve under the chief of the Royal Engineers. General Washington had definitely chosen Duportail because the good of the service demanded that there should be but one head, and he had been sent by the French king in 1777. Kosciusko was also friends with General Gates. They had served well together in the Northern Campaign, which ended with General Burgoyne's surrender at Saratoga. While Kosciusko may not have played a role in the Conway cabal that attempted to replace the commander in chief with Gates in the winter of 1778, he was Gates's friend, and Washington seemed deliberately to avoid contact with this Polish officer.

After Gates's defeat at the Battle of Camden, Kosciusko served faithfully under General Greene until the end of the war. When he left America, Congress, at Washington's request, made him a brigadier general by brevet, but no special honor was accorded him. However, posterity has more than recompensed Kosciusko for this neglect. His memory is particularly honored at West Point, and historians have recognized his services more than any other engineer of the Revolution.

Promotions

Duportail returned to America from his furlough in the middle of December 1782. He began an energetic and persistent demand to both the commander in chief and to the president of Congress for advancement in rank for every engineer who had served the United States as members of the corps. He was not thwarted by any excuses, delays, or difficulties. The *Papers of the Continental Congress* contain many petitions that were read before that body, and General Washington supported every case.

The Washington Papers contain the appeals sent directly to the commander in chief. Duportail always pointed out that the requests would not render the position of Congress difficult in any way. He also noted that none asked for more than commission by brevet, so there would be no change in pay. Because all the men were returning to France, their rank on leaving America would not affect the service in this country. When they came to America, they all received promotions to a rank above the one they had in France. Now that they were returning to France, their rank would be lowered by one grade, so a promotion would benefit them upon their return.

Neither Congress nor Washington had any objections. The problem was due to the number of things that Congress had to attend to and the tendency to put off decisions that did not require immediate attention. Duportail understood this and tactfully bided his time without ever giving up the determination to see these men promoted. His efforts failed in just one case, that of his aide-de-camp, Castaing, addressed later.

The congressional committee appointed to examine Major Ville-franche's and Captain L'Enfant's cases reported on May 2, 1783,

> The long and meritorious services of these two officers in the important department of the army in which they have acted, and of the proofs which they have produced of the Commander-in-Chief's entire approbation of their conduct, as well from his own observation of their conduct as the testimonials of other Genl. officers under whom they have more immediately served with distinguished skill and bravery, entitle them to the notice of Congress and to the promotion which they have requested as the most important reward of their services, and strongest proof Congress can give of their approbation.[20]

Major Villefranche received the rank of lieutenant colonel, and Captain L'Enfant, that of major by brevet. Cambray was made colonel at the same time.

Positions in the French Army

After getting promotions for the officers of his corps, Duportail turned his attention to getting them positions in the French service according to their merits. He begged Washington to write favorably to the French minister about the services of Villefranche and Rochefontaine and sent a very cordial letter to Luzerne on November 6. The French minister replied on November 21, in part, "It gives me the greatest pleasure to receive testimonials from Congress and from Your Excellency of the satisfaction the French officers have given in the service of the United States."[21] The minister then congratulated General Washington on the evacuation of New York and said he expected to attend the celebration on the twenty-eighth.

In a note left with the Comte de Rochambeau, Duportail also pleaded with the French minister to do what he could to secure a "company in the Royal Grenadiers or in a Provincial Regiment" in France for Lieutenant Colonel Villefranche.[22] He asked a similar favor for Major Bichet de Rochefontaine.

The only American belonging to the Corps of Engineers, as listed by Villefranche in April 1782, seems to have been Captain Nevin (also written *Niven* and *Neven*). He was probably of Huguenot descent and came from the region around New York. He had first served as an engineer under Kosciusko, who recommended him for character and qualifications. Later, he was associated with Gouvion, when the latter officer was sent to rebuild the fortifications on the lower Hudson after the destruction by the British when they evacuated in 1779. Duportail wrote to Washington, asking him to intercede with Congress to make Captain Nevin a major. The commander in chief forwarded the request, adding a recommendation of his own: "As the Engineers we now have are only for a temporary service and it will always be necessary to have men skilled in that branch of military science in this country, it appears to me to be a necessary policy to have men who reside among us forming themselves during the war under these Gentlemen." Congress granted the request, dating Nevin's commission as major from April 23, 1779.[23]

Villefranche's list mentions Captain de Lauren, but no other information about him can be been found.

Major Ferdinand J. S. de Brahm joined the Corps of Engineers on February 11, 1778. He was taken prisoner at Charlestown and exchanged on April 22, 1781. Congress appointed him to brevet lieutenant colonel on February 6, 1784. He also asked for money to pay his passage home, which Congress granted, and he retired from the service.

Peter de Castaing

General Duportail assiduously recommended Peter de Castaing, his aide-de-camp, to both General Washington and to the president of Congress for promotion. The first appeal was presented after the siege of Yorktown and before Duportail left for France on furlough. He said Castaing was a Frenchman born in Martinique, one of the "oldest lieutenants in the army." He came over at the very first and always "conducted himself in a way to merit the esteem of French and Americans alike," but he had never received any particular favor for "extraordinary services."[24] He was appointed Duportail's aide-de-camp in June 1779 and served loyally and well through the siege of Charlestown and later at Yorktown. The first request for a commission of brevet captain was denied at that time because of the jealousies it would arouse and other difficulties that would result from the promotion.

Castaing obtained the rank of captain in a Massachusetts regiment after Duportail returned to France. When he returned to America, Duportail renewed his efforts to secure the rank of major for his former aide-de-camp. Shortly before sailing for home, Duportail wrote a letter to General Washington on November 6, 1783, begging for this special favor from Congress and hoping Washington would endorse his request. He said he would take it as a "new proof of that goodness towards me which has attached me till now to America."[25]

Washington forwarded the letter to the president of Congress, which considered the case twice. The committee that reported on it the second time very warmly recommended the promotion, but the motion lost. The *Journals of the Continental Congress* give detailed proceedings under February 24, 1784.

Pierre L'Enfant

Pierre L'Enfant was the only foreign officer of engineers listed by Villefranche in April to remain in America. This young man, who was only twenty-two years old when he was one of the first to enlist on du Coudray's staff in Paris in the summer of 1776, sailed with that officer from Le Havre on the *Amphitrite* in December 1776. He returned when the vessel was ordered back, landing at l'Orient in January 1777. Beaumarchais's letter of February 10, 1777, to his secretary, Francy, at Nantes mentions him:

> I should like to be very sure whether M. du Coudray has taken or left with someone, the commissions of the officers and their money. . . . In any case find out exactly the position of every one and especially that of M. l'Enfant because he has been very highly recommended to me. He has written and seems to be in great need; you might let him have a few louis if there is no way of finding out what has become of his gratifications and appointments on condition they be returned if the latter can be discovered.[26]

L'Enfant later joined du Coudray in America. After du Coudray's death, he was among those volunteers who preferred to serve in the American army without pay until a place could be made for them rather than accept the money from Congress to pay their passage home. Along with Colonel Fleury, Captain Walker, and Duponceau, L'Enfant served under Baron von Steuben for a time when the latter was appointed inspector general of the army. On April 3, 1779, Congress considered the baron's report setting forth the "great diligence and attention these men had displayed in his service."[27] He also requested a sum of money from Congress for each man according to his rank and expenditures up to that time. L'Enfant was appointed a captain of engineers the same day to have rank, February 18, 1778. Congress voted him the sum of $500 on April 16, 1779.

Soon after his promotion in the Continental Army, L'Enfant went south and joined Colonel John Laurens's light infantry. He was wounded at Savannah, taken prisoner at Charlestown, and not exchanged until the beginning of 1782. It seems that Duportail first observed him while a prisoner at Charlestown and remembered him after his (Duportail's) release. The Rochambeau Papers include the following note:

> M. L'Enfant came to America with M. du Coudray furnished with a brevet of Lieutenant in the Colonial troops. He served in the American army and obtained in 1778 a commission of Captain of Engineers. Later he attached himself to the light Infantry in the Army of the South. He was at the Seige of Savannah and in the assault of that place he commanded an American column. He was wounded *a coup de feu* and remained on the field of battle. He was at Charlestown during the seige and was made a prisoner. He owed his exchange to the Comte

de Rochambeau; since that time he joined the Army of General Washington where he has been employed as Engineer. M. Duportail intends immediately to request Congress to raise him to the rank of Major. He desires strongly to obtain for M. L'Enfant a company in the Royal Grenadiers or in the provincial Regiments with a pension as for M. Villefranche; those two officers have been obliged to spend the greater part of their fortune in the service of the United States.[28]

In the meantime, L'Enfant personally addressed Washington in connection with the question of rank after having learned that Captain Rochefontaine, his ranking inferior, had been made major after Yorktown. He deplored the fact that his nineteen-months' imprisonment prevented him from the privilege of serving at that siege. The letter dated February 18, 1782, said, "I do not complain nor pretend to any preference to my brother officers, when I say that in five years I have served the United States, I have sought every opportunity and neglected none that offered, to distinguish myself by love of their service."[29] He gave the following detail of his service in America:

> In 1778 I was honored with the commission of Capt. Engineer. By leave of Congress attached to the inspector general from this moment I have made every possible effort to employ for the public benefit the little theoretic knowledge I had acquired by study—having finished that campaign by working five months successively during the winter of 1778 and 79, and seeing no appearance of an active campaign to the northward—my whole ambition was to obtain leave to attend the southern army where it was likely the seat of war would be transferred. I arrived at Charlestown at the moment when General prevot [Major General Augustine Prevost] retired from before it—and hastened to join the army but finding very little to do in the corps I belonged to and I obtained leave to join the light infantry *under lt. col. laurens* his friendship offered me many opportunities of seeing the enemie to advantage. . . . I remained attached to the corps of engineers seizing every opportunity to follow the light infantry when any thing offered,—and in this manner I passed the campaign of *in georgia.*
>
> the affair of savannah was I thought a glorious opportunity of distinguishing myself. . . . my disappointment was compleat, I had however this satisfaction to have been among troops, who among the distresses of that unfortunate day, acquired as much glory as if they had been crowned with success—it is without partiality I say that never were greater proofs of true valour exhibited than at the assault at Savannah. . . .

there my military career was stopped for a time by a wound I received that day which detained me in bed till january 1780—my weak state of health did not permit me to work at the fortification of charlestown, and when the enemy debarked I still was obliged to use a crutch. . . . the 30th march . . . the major who commanded the light infantry being wounded by the fire, I supplied his place. . . . I successfully opposed the parties sent by the enemy to reconnoitre the works . . . from this moment to the reduction of the place. . . . I attached myself wherever I could render the least service.

. . . sensible of the duty of an officer and jealous of my personal honor I have done nothing with a lucrative view, my ambition was to gain the general esteem of the army and perticularly to merit the approbation of your Excellency deprived (by my captivity) in sharing in the reduction of Yorktown I dare, however . . . compare the merit of several unfortunate campaigns with the good fortune of those who happened to be at York. . . .

I have etc. L'ENFANT, capt. of the corps of engineers.[30]

The commander in chief wrote a personal reply on March 1, 1782, expressing his sympathy at seeing "inferior officers promoted over one's head."[31] He explained that he had no part in the promotion of Rochefontaine, that it was done solely on the recommendation of Duportail to Congress and according to the custom in Europe. The letter ended with the following complimentary observations regarding L'Enfant's record: "Your zeal & active services are such as reflect the highest honor on yourself and are extremely pleasing to me and I have no doubt they will have their due weight with Congress in any future promotion in your corps."[32]

The French minister wrote General Washington about this time, asking that L'Enfant be permitted to remain a month at Philadelphia and adding, "[H]is presence will be very helpful in constructing a hall which I am making in order to give to Congress and the inhabitants of Philadelphia a festival to celebrate the birth of Monseigneur the Dauphin."[33] Washington replied, begging his excellency to be assured that he is most happy to have the opportunity of doing him a favor "but especially on the present occasion," which he viewed as "diffusing the most sensible joy to the allied nations of France and America."[34]

L'Enfant received his long-desired promotion of major by brevet, as did Major Villefranche and Lieutenant Colonel Cambray on May 2, 1783. This was shortly after Congress ratified the Preliminaries of Peace on April 15, 1783, and Washington's announcement to the army of the cessation of hostilities.

L'Enfant's most signal honor, however, was having his design chosen for the insignia of the Order of the Society of the Cincinnati, which was organized May 10–13, 1783, at Newburg on the Hudson, where the army was encamped. Washington, as the first president, had written to the major, asking him to suggest a design. L'Enfant replied in a lengthy letter on June 10, published many times since by the society in their records, in which he says in part,

Dear General:

Immediately on receiving your letter of the 20th May . . . I set about the plan of the medal: I send you the design with both faces made very large so that you may better judge of them. . . . I have not complied with your desire to make it oval, as such a form for a medal is not proper. . . . A medal is a monument to be transmitted to posterity and consequently it is necessary that it be executed to the highest degree of perfection possible in the age in which it is struck.[35]

The society approved his design at the next meeting:

Cantonment of the American Army, 18 June, 1783

Resolved that the bald Eagle, carrying the Emblem on its breast be established as the Order of the Society, and that the Ideas of Major L'Enfant respecting it and the Manner of its being worn by the Members be adopted. . . .

   Resolved That the thanks of this convention be transmitted by the President to Major L'Enfant for his care and ingenuity in preparing the aforementioned designs, and that he be acquainted that they cheerfully embrace his offer of Assistance, and request a continuance of his Attentions in carrying the Design into Execution, for which purpose the President is desired to correspond with him.[36]

L'Enfant was given leave of absence from the army in October until May of the following year for the purpose of going to France on his own private affairs.[37] Duportail, Gouvion, Laumoy, Cambrai, Villefranche, and others joined the Order of the Cincinnati before leaving America.[38] Later, L'Enfant planned the national capital in Washington, DC.

Jean-Bernard Gauthier de Murnan

Jean-Bernard Gauthier de Murnan joined the Corps of Engineers while the Continental Army was at Valley Forge in 1778. He served as major to the end of the war and received honorable testimonials from his superior officers, Generals Sullivan, Lafayette, Hand, and Howe, and later from the Chevalier de Choisy, under whom he served before and at Yorktown. There was one unfortunate incident while he was in Connecticut that called forth a letter from the governor. He was said to have stabbed a sergeant in a quarrel, but the case seems to have been amicably settled, as he remained in the army there. When the French army joined that under Washington at Philipsburg before marching south to Yorktown, he stayed at Newport under the orders of Choisy, who was left to guard the port with a detachment of four hundred men. This detachment later followed Barras's fleet and took up its post at Gloucester on the opposite bank of the York River.

Congress granted Murnan a certificate on May 24, 1783, attesting to his "activity, intelligence and bravery on all occasions."[39] There is no evidence that General Duportail attempted to secure a raise in rank for this officer at any time after Yorktown, probably because Murnan temporarily left the corps and joined the French army.

Jean-Louis-Ambroise de Genton de Villefranche

Major Villefranche's painstaking, plodding part in the Revolution deserves special attention. He never failed in his duty, though he regretfully saw the opportunity of taking part in an active, energetic campaign pass him by more than once. The commanding engineer at West Point might have been called into active service had Washington's favorite plan of attacking the British in New York become reality. But though the British soon lost control of the approaches to the defense of the Highlands and though there was no attempt to capture West Point after Arnold's treason, the significance of the post on the Hudson remained unimpaired until the close of the war, and its superintending engineer was a person of outstanding importance.

Villefranche was ordered to West Point during the summer of 1780 to replace Colonel Kosciusko. Washington wrote to General Arnold, then in command,

Head Quarters, Peekskill 6th Augt. 1780

Sir,

Col. Kosciusko having permission to join the southern army—Major Villefranche has directions to repair to West Point and take upon him the superintendence of the Works. You will, I am persuaded, find this Gentleman fully acquainted with his Business, and I doubt not but he will give general satisfaction to those with whom he will be immediately concerned in the execution of the Works.

I am etc.
Go. WASHINGTON.

There are many letters, reports, and so on in the handwriting of Major Villefranche in the Washington Papers and from the generals immediately over him that show the painstaking attention to detail that characterizes his work. Finely drawn maps of the region (published by Justin Winsor in his history) also remain, testifying to his skill and knowledge of technique.

When the army moved south at the end of August 1781, Villefranche hoped to be allowed to go also. Instead, he was sent west into the Indian country to rebuild the defenses near Fort Herkimer. When he learned that the officers who took part in the siege of Yorktown were getting promotions in rank, he must also have expected a promotion. General Heath wrote to the commander in chief about him on February 21, 1782,

His faithful services, unremitting zeal and exertions for the public, exhibited on all occasions, constrane me to represent them useful. He wished to go South. The Northern frontier being then threatened by the Enemy, he was sent back. He went with the greatest expedition. . . . On every occasion he discovered abilities, warm attachment to the cause, and ardent desires to promote the public service.[40]

General McDougall wrote even more warmly on February 24,

intelligent, excellent, careful officer, especially of the public stores. . . . His manners are well adapted to our kind of government and besides, his general exterior corresponds to it. He possesses great calmness of temper. He however feels himself chagrined when his countrymen in the same line with him were promoted, from an apprehension of its lessening his character in the eyes of his Master and his national countrymen. I wish that so deserving an officer may be given a grade which his long services and singular qualifications merit.[41]

Washington avoided promotion issues as much as possible because rank in the army was fraught with so many complexities that gave rise to jealousy and bickering. He had great respect for Major Villefranche, who was later promoted due to the untiring exertions of the commandant of engineers, who busied himself with matters of promotions in his corps as soon as he had returned to America at the end of 1782. In the meantime, Washington wrote a soothing letter to Villefranche on March 4, 1782, that said,

> I beg you to accept my thanks for your services in constructing the several works on the Mohawk River. . . . I am very sensible of the zeal, professional knowledge, and activity you have shown during your services in this country, and should be happy in contributing to your advancement.
>
> . . . That you had not the good fortune to share in that success [Yorktown] was not your fault. . . . Your character in the army will always command such testimonies . . . as will give that just value to your services which they merit.[42]

Washington learned of the birth of the dauphin in France in April 1782 and directed Major Villefranche to plan the celebration at West Point. The celebration took place on May 31 and was such a success that Washington wrote to congratulate him on June 4:

> Sir,
>
> I take the early opportunity of expressing to you the high satisfaction I felt at the taste and elegance displayed in the preparations you made for the celebration of the birth of the Dauphin—the very great part you had in contributing to the pleasures of that day deserves my warmest acknowledgements and I beg you to receive this testimony of my thanks for your exertions on that occasion.[43]

It seemed that Villefranche would have the opportunity of active service once during the summer. He wrote to ask permission to march with the army but was again disappointed. Washington sent the major a note through one of his aides, which read in part,

> Newburg August 28, 1782
>
> Sir,
>
> . . . His Excellency was pleased to inform me . . . that he would have you at present continue to superintend . . . the work now carrying on at West Point, but in case we should come to serious operations in the field, he will not be unmindful, in making his arrangements, of employing your Talents in such a manner as will be useful to the public and reputable to yourself. In the mean time, the General proposes that all

the Engineers (except Col. Lomoy & one other who will be named by him), be employed under your orders in carrying the works now in hand into execution.[44]

Structuring the Corps of Engineers

Colonel Gouvion sent General Washington his "Opinion on Post-War Army" on April 16, 1783. His memorial is very interesting because he specifies a single organization and a course of instruction based on his experience in France. He considers the scientific and technical subjects but does not specify all those taught at Mézières. Duportail might also have been consulted on the program of study. The following is Gouvion's memorial:

> How large must be the continental army to be kept after this war is not an easy matter to determine in the present moment, it depends from two different and distinct objects which comprehend a very extensive plan, the first is the number of forts absolutely wanting garrison for the protection of the frontiers, and opposing the Indians in case they would keep up their hostile invasions or renew it at any time. The second is the garrison of the harbours for the continental navy, which being destined to contain stores of great value and importance are not to lay open to an invasion in case the united states should happen to be at war with any power. I shall not enter into any discussion about these two great objects, but lay here only a few remarks concerning alterations which I think are necessary in the continental army for its future establishment.
>
> Each regiment to be kept or to be raised ought not to belong to any particular state, but to the continent at large, the officers and men to be taken indifferently from any part, it is to be feared that if the contrary did exist the officers would alwais use all their influence to be alwais stationed in the state they should belong to, and in a short time be like inhabitants to the great detriment of discipline and military spirit.
>
> a regiment or part of it ought never to keep garrison more than eighteen months in the same place, in a longer length of time they get too many acquaintances injurious to the service, and being in a manner settled neglect their duty to employ themselves about their own conveniences
>
> promotion by seniority is the destruction of emulation, because every officer is sure to be promoted according to his rank, also many worthy officers are fit to be captains but not to be field officers, so that sistem ought to be left aside, merit, activity and attention constantly pay'd to instruction, duty and discipline must be the only recommendation for

promotion above the rank of captain, a board of superior officers be the judge of it, and the necessary precautions to be taken to hinder private interest from prevailing.

as the number of troops keept on foot during the time of peace shall be inadequate to that necessary in time of war, they must be alwais in the best and most regular order, so that being distributed among the regiments raised for a war they should bring with them discipline, instruction and enable the other men to perform in a short space of time every part of a soldier's duty with propriety.

the young officers who should be willing to acquire some military knowledge ought to be permitted to follow the after mentioned military academy and proper encouragement given to them, those to be admitted in the quarter master department ought to be obliged to it, because it is not only to perform their duty in all its different parts chiefly when an army of some extent has to move in a difficult country.

It is not very difficult to form an officer of foot, or of horse, it does not require a long space of time, but an officer of Artillery and an Engineer want a great application to be perfectly instructed in all the different branches of their service. being more acquainted with the duty of these two corps than of any other I will particularize as much as in my power the different methods to be follow'd for the instruction of their officers, and the regulations to be established to attain it. Their service is of so important a nature, and of such a consequence in the field that no pains ought to be spared to have them fully acquainted with the theorical and practical parts of it

the military operations of these two corps have such a connection that it is not possible to be a good officer of Artillery without having a pretty extensive knowledge of the service of an Engineer and this one to serve with some reputation must be acquainted with the principal parts of the artillery service, then I think that it should be advantageous to the good of the service to have these two corps united, to form one only, and that each officer should acquire the necessary knowledge to be able to perform with propriety what belong to one or the other of these two duties, according to what circumstances should require from him.

A well-established military academy and kept up with great care, is the basis which is to serve to raise that corps to the pitch of instruction necessary to it. officers of knowledge, carefull, and attentive must be put at the head of it, they must consider that the pains they shall take are to form officers who are to have charge afterwards of important operations, which require sometimes great military talents. there must be attached to it a good professor of mathematicks and another of drawing. every young gentleman to be admitted in the said academy must have had a liberal education, and be previously instructed in arithmetick, geometry including trigonometry, at his coming in, his knowledge of mathematicks must be carry'd to perfection, he shall receive instruction about the different machines employed by the artillery or the engineers, their construction, the forces to be employed to put them in motion, and their effect. he shall be taught to survey by every method, and to draw exactly the ground surveyed by him, to make plans and profils of works and buildings in the greatest detail, the above mentioned parts belong entirely to the professors, what follows must be thought [taught] by the commanding officers

The young gentlemen shall be instructed how to chuse positions for an army in consequence of the part of the country to be covered and the communications to be kept open, they will learn to fortify them by field works depending from the nature of the ground, the number of troops supposed to be employed to defend them, and the strength of the ennemy. They shall be taught to determine the most advantageous batteries on a field of battle, and their construction in the most expeditious manner; they are to be instruits in the greatest detail of all what relates to the fortify'd towns including the maritime places, their training, construction, and the estimate of the quantity of work and expences, those parts can not be attended to with too much care, because the least blunder is often attended with infinite bad consequences. They shall receive instruction concerning the subterraneous fortification, the attack and defense of works by the means of mines. They shall be taught how to reconnoitre an ennemy's fortification, lay it on the paper, and determine exactly the different distances from it. every year the commanding officer of the academy should make choice of a piece of ground fit to lay out a front of fortifications, the directions in the heighth of the works should be mark'd with poles, he should explain to the young gentlemen the use of each part of it, and the reasons which have determined the direction of it; that part being finished they will proceed to the attack of it, all the batteries and works necessary from the opening of the trenches to the reduction of the place are to be laid out and some parts of it to be done to give them an idea of the different construction made use of in those occasions, they will pay a particular attention to the advantages afforded by the nature of the ground, also to the means the besieged could employ to oppose the approaches with success. that being performed every young gentleman is to survey that front and its attack and make a copy of it, also a memorial on its construction its attack and defense, adding to it an estimate of the artillery stores, and ammunitions necessary for the besieged and besiegers in consequence of the strength of the fortification, and of the supposition of the time the siege could last. when perfectly instructed in all the different parts here above mentioned, of which the general commanding the corps, and the officers at the head of the academy are to be the judges he is to be admitted into one of the regiments of artillery, the continent cannot keep less than two, and are to be composed as follows, light companies of gunners, two companies of bombardiers, one of sappers and miners and one of artificers.

The regiments are to be exercised twice a week to the firing of canon, Mortars, then [?] a field officer to be always present and report to the commanding officer of the regiment when absent from the field of exercise.

The subalterns ought to receive twice a week a lesson about the theorical parts of the artillery and a captain to be present to it, to maintain the good order and preside to the instructions and from time to time they should be exercised again about what they have learned in the Academy

The Captains and field officers are to have two times a week a conference where they should treat of all the parts concerning artillery, fortifications, manufactures of arms, powder mills, castings of canons, shells, balls, the best dimensions to be given to the pieces and carriages, in short their object should be to carry the instruction and service of that corps to the greatest perfection, the commanding officer should ask a memorial from every officer on the interesting points he would have proposed for discussion.

besides the officer on duty with the regiments there should be a certain number to perform the duty on Engineers where necessary, but none should be sent for that purpose unless he had been employ'd successively in the four distinct sorts of companies forming a regiment and should be perfectly acquainted with their service. He could not be on that command for more than three years, after which time he should join a regiment and be relieved by another officer sent to the same effect.

a company ought not to be detached from the regiment for more than two years, because it is to be feared that (in a longer space of time) the men would loose the greatest part of the instruction acquired with the regiment if too a long time absent from it.

The companies of sappers and miners should have a particular exercise relative to their duty in the field, but their officers should also partake of the general instruction of the corps of artillery. it is absolutely necessary that the officers of the companies of artificers should be intelligent, attentive, and industrious, they ought not only take rank with those of the others companies but their places should be considered as places of trust and confidence.

there ought to be some officers (extra of the number of those with the regiments) detached in the different manufactories of arms, places for casting canons, and powder mills, to superintend the works, they should be relieved from time to time by others coming from the regiments, those stations are to be looked upon as of great importance.

a field officer should be in every district at the head of fortifications, and judge of every thing to be proposed, he could not remain there when promoted but join a regiment.

it is of the utmost consequence that an officer of artillery attached to a brigade with some field pieces should be perfectly acquainted with the different maneuvers of the troops, so it is a part which is not to be neglected.

the plan I propose here to form but one corps of those of artillery and Engineers was put in execution in france, but as it was in time of war some Engineers were sent to the army to do the duty of the Artillery, and some officers of artillery to serve as Engineers, but having not had time to be perfectly acquainted with the details of a service of which they had but a general knowledge it was found proper after a little while to let every of these officers serve in the line they did formerly belong to, and the two corps were desunited but I am confident that if the reunion had taken place in another circumstance, so that the officers of each corps should have had time to acquire what knowledge was wanting to them of the service they did not at first belong to; that plan would have succeeded and found afterwards very advantageous.

Newburg april the 16th, 1783
Gouvion[45]

Washington quickly synthesized the works submitted to him on May 2, 1783. He insisted on the importance of preserving the experience acquired over the course of a long and difficult time of service and the need to have a standing army to preserve the military knowledge acquired and not have to depend on the benevolent aid of foreigners to defend the country if ever faced by new hostilities. It must be understood that a corps of competent engineers and expert artillerymen cannot be created overnight or as quickly as training militiamen into an infantry.

After getting his officers promoted and securing positions for them in the French army, Duportail turned his attention to structuring the Corps of Engineers and the American army. He reported on September 30, 1783,

To answer the Confidence I am honored with, I will at once say what I think best for the United States to do in that Respect. It is to unite the Department of the Artillery with that of the Engineers so that after the union every officer should be without any Distinction an Artillery Officer and an Engineer. There are many reasons for the operation which I propose; the following are the principal ones.

1st. The preliminary Knowledge necessary for an Artillery Officer or an Engineer, as the different branches of Mathematics, the Natural philosophy etc. are the same.

2ndly. The very great Relation between the professions themselves. The most important use of Cannon, that one which requires most skill and Knowledge of the Art is for the Defense of Fortified Places or the Attack of them. When an Engineer combines the different lines and Angles of a fortification between themselves and the Surrounding Ground to make that Fortification of the most advantageous Defense; when to the Contrary he frames the Plan of the Attack of it, and lays out his trenches and other works, he has principally in view to prepare the use of the Artillery, facilitate its effects and make them as great as possible. So he must be personally acquainted with the Nature of that Arm and have really on that Point all the Knowledge of the Artillery Officer. It is true the thing is not reciprocal and that the Artillery Officer when he is not Engineer at the same time and is confined to the execution of his Cannon does not want to have the Knowledge of the Engineer; but why not make him acquire it since he has already all the Preliminary Knowledge and the practise of the Artillery; and so he wants only to add the Study of the Art of fortification. Do we not see clearly that to do otherwise is to make two Professions of what ought to be the object of one only.

3rdly. The great economy which results from that union. Wherever there is any fortification there is an Engineer to have the charge of it, and there is an Artillery Officer for the Artillery. But very often each of those Officers has not a Sufficient Employment in his Department and if the Departments were united one Officer could do the Duty of the two with the greatest ease. I think one third of Officers might be Spared upon the whole without the least inconveniency for the Service.

4thly. That great Relation which we said to take place between the two Professions of the Artillery and the Engineers is the Cause of frequent Disputes and Dissentions among them because the line of Separation cannot be drawn exactly, principally for the most delicate circumstance in War, and the more Knowledge and Talent each Corps possesses, the more Difficulties arise between the individuals, because they have more pretensions. So that reciprocal Envy and Enmity make the very qualities which should be conducive to the good of the Service turn against it.

For those Reasons and many less important the Departments of the Artillery and of the Engineers are united in some European States, and in those where they are not Plans for uniting them are proposed every Day. In France that union has been executed once and if it did not last it was because the time was not proper (in the midst of the war), and the Operation was formed upon a bad Scheme. Besides the private Interests of many Individuals principally of the first Officers were much hurted by it. Add to this that as those Corps in France exist a long while ago, each of them has acquired a particular esprit which makes it very adverse to such Union. However every Officer of experience almost, is persuaded of the advantage of it, and that it will take Place one Day or another. But here where there is not yet private interests or passions of the Corps to combat, the Congress must avail themselves of a happy circumstance which may never return to make at once their Establishment upon the Plan that Experience show to the old Peoples of Europe to be the best, although they cannot always follow their Notions.

ESTABLISHMENT OF THE CORPS OF ARTILLERY AND THE ENGINEERS

I suppose here, according to the letter which his Excellency Genl. Washington has honored me with, the present Establishment must be calculated only for the wants of the Frontier against the British for if the United States intended to have fortified Harbours what I am going to propose should be insufficient.

I propose two Regiments each to be composed of five Companies of Gunners one of Bombardiers, one Sappers & Miners, one of Artificers, each Company in time of peace shall be composed of 3 Sergeants, 6 Corporals, 24 privates commanded by a first Capt. a second Capt. a first Lieut. and Second Lieutenant. (in time of war the number of privates may be doubled).

The Regiment shall be commanded by one Colonel, one Lt. Colonel, one Major adding to this one pay master adjutant, one Qt. Mr., two Surgeons, one Sergent Major, the Drum Major, 6 Drums and fifes, which would make the whole of the Regiment altogether of 327 Men and the two Regiments of 654.

I propose four Officers in each Company because it is necessary to have some to detach without Troops to different Places for the erection or care of Fortifications sunderies etc. Thus one of the Captains or Lieutenants, may be detached that makes 16 Officers for the two Regiments. one of the field Officers, the Lt. Col. or the Major may be detached also, so in all there will be eighteen which will be sufficient in this Moment.

I propose to divide the whole extent of the frontiers in three Parts at the Head of which there should be an Officer of the Rank of Brigadier or Colonel to have the Direction of all what concerns the Artillery or the fortifications erected or to be erected and generally of all the Establishments relative to that Department.

Above all there must be a Commandant Director of all the fortifications of the United States. To the Director General the three Directors of the Districts mentioned shall be accountable for every thing as the Colonels of the Regiment and every Person employed in that Department.

Through him shall the Orders of the Board of War or the Congress be transmitted to the Corps. Such an Officer appears to me absolutely necessary, to have that important Branch of the Administration governed upon the same Plan and constant Principles. Let us remember that a great many things tend to break the union between the American States. All the Continental Establishments ought to be calculated to reinforce that union. Thus, if in this instance there were at the head of the Department of the Artillery and fortifications many Officers independent one from another, great inconveniences might result from it. These Officers would differ in opinion and soon be jealous and enemies of one another. Some might acquire more influence with Congress than others. So in the Establishment of fortifications in the Distribution of the Means of Defense, each State might be treated, not according to what its situation, its importance requires, but according to the Credit of the Officer who has the Direction of that Department.

Some persons will perhaps imagine that the three Directors of Districts proposed are not necessary, that for the sake of economy the Colonels and the Lt. Cols. of the Regiments may be charged with the functions attributed to those Directors. but if they observe those functions shall be to make under the Direction of the Director General an exact Reconnoitre of all the frontier, to search for the most proper places for the Forts and for all the Establishments relative to War, after that to plan those Establishments, preside over their erection, they will confess probably, that the Director of the District shall have enough to do without clogging them with the particular command and care of a Regiment, which they could never attend to. But, as I have mentioned, a field Officer of each Regiment shall be detached with the Directors of the District to assist them and have under them the command of the Captains and Subalterns employed in the Busyness above mentioned.

I do not think it necessary here to expatiate myself upon Talents and Knowledge which the Duty attributed to the Director of the District requires of them as well as of the Director General. I take the Liberty to refer on that Head to the Memorial, wherein I endeavored to sketch what is to be done. A Vauban [Marshall Vauban] is the greatest engineer France and europe had; he lived under the reign of Louis XIV it is he who framed the general plan of defense of the kingdom and gave the situations and designs of almost all the fortified places [Duportail's note in his hand] would be necessary in this Moment to the United States and nobody unless he thinks himself as able a Man as that famous Marshall, can undertake, without the greatest diffidence, that difficult work. And he who would undertake it without any fear proves that he has not the least idea of it.

ACADEMY

The necessity of an Academy, to be the Nursery of the Corps, is too obvious to be insisted upon. The Academy must be commanded under the Director General by a field Officer, assisted by a Captain. It requires a Master of Mathematics and of Natural Philosophy, one of Chemistry and one of drawing; as for Military Matters, it belongs to the Officers of the Head of the Academy to give those kind of Instructions. This is not the Place of enlarging upon this Subject. The Student ought to spend three years at least at the Academy. According to the total number of Officers of the Corps, ten or twelve Students should be sufficient to keep the Corps compleat. But as it is very advantageous to introduce in it the soonest possible, Men of Theory and Knowledge, I will propose here to leave in each Company the place of Second Lieutenant vacant, to fill those vacancies with the first Students which will receive their instruction at the Academy. So the number of Students in this Moment might be of twenty, and I do not doubt that it shall remain such afterwards, because if the union of the states is durable the Establishment proposed here will certainly be found too Inconsiderable and if I propose it so it is only to fall in with the present Circumstances and Dispositions.

[Note by Duportail in his hand]—it is not improper perhaps, to observe here that according to the calculations i make the total establishment such as i propose it including the academy the rations and clothing will not cost much more than two hundred thousand dollars only i lessen a little the pay of the soldiers which is a little too high.

DUPORTAIL.
philad. Sept. 30[46]

The Corps of Engineers was disbanded in November 1783, but Duportail's model was adopted when the army was revived. (See appendix B for a list of the chiefs of the Corps of Engineers, 1774 to 1893.)

7

PRISONERS OF WAR

Several of the engineers were taken prisoner after the surrender of Charles-town on May 12, 1781. General Duportail was now cut off from news of the outside world during these long and dreary months. He concluded that France must be roused to greater vigor in the prosecution of the war. He wrote a lengthy memorial to the French minister, the Chevalier de la Luzerne, but he could not send it to him until several months later. He wrote in great detail about the part he thought France would have to play to achieve a victory, beginning,

> If France wishes to see the end of this present war it seems to me nec-essary for her to bend her efforts more directly toward the cause and object of this war; that object is the establishment of the independence of the United States and to oblige England to recognize it. The way to succeed in this appears to be to establish the independence by the fact of driving the English from all the points where they remain. Now if we will consider the actual state of things we shall see with regret that the English, very far from having lost ground since France signed the Alliance with the States, have gained considerably.[1]

The memorial is developed under the headings "Fleets," "Land Troops," "Siege of Charlestown," "Siege of New York," "Finance," "Clothing," and "Military Equipment." He begins with general principles, then treats each division of the subject from personal knowledge of the American situation. Thus, regarding the fleet, he says in the beginning, "The necessity of constantly having a superior fleet to that of the English is so generally recognized as to need no comment."[2] He goes into great detail, showing ways and means by which successful sieges of the two most important points in the possession of the British, Charlestown and New

139

York, can be effected. He then describes the depressed condition of the country, the depreciated currency, and the lack of clothing and supplies: "It is undoubtedly unfortunate that France must bother herself with such questions, but it is necessary that she do so." He concludes forcefully,

> [I]n recapitulating all that I ask of France for America, it may seem exhorbitant—but is it not true that it is only so because we have accustomed ourselves from the beginning to think that the Americans could carry on the war with only slight help from us and so drive out the English? Moreover it is not a question of whether or not America is doing all she can on her side—if it is thought France should not be obliged to make such great efforts we must start from the actual state of things. It is here a question of finishing with honor a thing which is as much ours as the Americans. I do not go far enough; it is more so from certain points of view. The Americans with less shame than we, can yield and return to the domination of the British. They will always be received with open arms. They [the English] are preparing now to receive them as brothers who with good will become reconciled—but for France—who in the face of the Universe has recognized the independence of America—she has irrevocably attached her honor to that independence and its annihilation would be for the nation an affront that could never be effaced.[3]

Some of the prisoners were exchanged for British prisoners of equal rank. Others took longer for a variety of reasons. Laumoy and Cambray were in this latter category. The delay in the exchange of these men was not due to neglect either on the part of Congress or of their friends in America. Special efforts were made during the summer of 1781 to exchange all the prisoners and to secure, while waiting, the release on parole of those whose exchange could not be procured immediately. Many prisoners of war taken at Charlestown and elsewhere reached Philadelphia in July 1781. Congress recognized their pitiable condition and passed several resolutions regarding them:

> [C]onsiderable numbers lately relieved from loathsome confinement of prison-ships and dungeons . . . are arrived in this city . . . having been subjected to every evil which their faithful adherence to our righteous cause could prompt a vindictive and disappointed enemy to inflict upon them. . . . Resolved that, for the purpose of administering a suitable relief . . . a recommendation [be made] to promote a loan of money . . . of which Congress will guaranty the repayment. . . . Your committee further recommends . . . the encouragement of benevolent contributions by way of free gifts.[4]

LAUMOY AND CAMBRAY

General Duportail heard of the arrival of the members of his corps from the prison camps of the South. On his way to meet Grasse in the Chesapeake in late August 1781, he took occasion, in his busy passage through Philadelphia, to confer with the Chevalier de La Luzerne, the French minister, regarding measures to be taken for the release of the prisoners. It was decided to make a special appeal to the commander in chief. The Chevalier de La Luzerne wrote a note to Washington and forwarded three letters given to him by General Duportail, Laumoy, and Cambray. The French minister wrote,

> Philadelphia, 24 August 1781,
>
> Monsieur
>
> I have the honor of sending you three letters which have been given me by Genl Duportail, Mrs. de Laumoy and de Cambray. These officers desire infinitely to be exchanged and they have hardly any other hope than the goodness of your Excellency. I implore your Excellency to consider that their services in the Southern States might be useful in the present circumstances; their knowledge of the country which they have acquired during the three last campaigns gives them some right to expect to be preferred. At least this is what the South Carolina delegation expressed, who seemed disposed to for their exchange if it met with the approval of your Excellency.
>
> LA LUZERNE

Duportail wrote,

> philadelphia 22 august 1781
>
> Dear general
>
> i have seen just now a resolve of Congress about the exchange of prisoners by which the matter is referred to your Excellency. in this circumstance i take the liberty to recall to your mind Colonel Laumoy and Lt. Col. Cambray. as my countrymen, my friends, i wish extremely to see them at liberty, but in this moment i may add that the public advantage is joined to their private and my own satisfaction. the acquaintance they have with the southern states may render them very useful. i shall have, dear general, the greatest gratitude of what your Excellency will be pleased to do for them in this opportunity and i shall consider it as a great favor for myself.

there are besides in my department Captaine schreiber and Captaine l'enfant who are also prisoners. but if the exchange is a general one they shall probably be exchanged of course. nothinstanding i recommend them to your excellency's goodness.

i have the honor to be with the greatest respect and attachment your etc.

DuPORTAIL.[5]

Colonel Laumoy wrote,

philadelphia august the (?) 1781

Sir.

I have the honor to forward to your Excellency a letter from Genl. Du Portail by which he shows his Desire of my being exchanged. Your Excellency can easily imagine how extremely anxious I am to be in activity; how painful it is to me to be a prisoner, when I could show, at least by my good will, my strong attachment at the Cause of America.

The particular situation I am in gives me the greatest uneasiness; the British having none or a very few Colonels, we, of that rank, have no Hopes but either in an exchange settled by Tariff or in a partial one. As to the first, your Excellency knows what terms of an exchange are more advantageous to the United States and will certainly regulate his conduct upon that consideration alone. Happy those that so wise a plan will favor. But if I could not be one of that Number I should ardently wish and beg that your Excellency would, if practicable, propose a partial one for me, or recommend it to Congress. It would be presuming too much of my own talents to think them equal to so great a favor; but your Excellency may be sure that, what little I have, will be exerted to the utmost of my power to promote the good of the Country and convince your Excellency that I was not unworthy of his kindness. And my gratitude for it will be equally Boundless.

I am with the greatest Respect
Your Excellency's etc.
LAUMOY, Col. of Engres.

Although I was taken to the southern I hope that will not be an impediment to my being exchanged here.[6]

Lieutenant Colonel Cambray appealed,

Philad. 23 August 1781

Sir

Having heard of a resolution of the Hon. Congress for exchanging the officers of the Convention [of Saratoga], I take this opportunity to recommend myself to your Excellency, being extremely anxious to go into the field and to show my good will in being useful.

I would even [?] the invasion of Gl. Prevost in the southern department—the different events of which [I was in] that part of the continent gave me an opportunity of acquiring some knowledge of the southern states, which induces me to believe my services may be of some utility.

As I apprehend that the delays of a negotiation and the length of the journey, should make me take the southern army too late, I beg your Excellency be so good as to have my certificate of exchange sent to me without delay, with an order for being furnished with horses that I may repair to the army with the utmost speediness.

I am your Excellency's etc.

CAMBRAY, Lt. Col. Eng. taken prisoner at Charlestown.[7]

Washington wrote to the president of Congress on September 1, reporting that General Duportail had "very earnestly solicited the exchange of Colos. Laumois and Cambray," but Washington could not give those men preference to others of the same rank who had been longer in captivity without deviating from an order of Congress and an established rule of exchange, so he asked Congress for advice on the matter.[8]

Although Washington was hurrying southward to join in the Yorktown campaign, he wrote to Abraham Skinner, the commissary general of prisoners, who replied,

Elizabethtown, Sept. 3rd 1781

Sir

In obedience to your Excellency's commands I have obtained the release of all our Privates in the hands of the Enemy. I am this day to confer with the British Commissary on the subject of your letter of the 28th ulto. relative to the exchange of General Burgoyne for our officers, and shall immediately report to you my proceedings on my return from Staten Island, the place appointed for our meeting. I am, with the highest respect your Excellency's etc.

Abm. SKINNER, Commisy. Genl of Pris.[9]

The privates were all exchanged, but it was not easy to satisfy both sides regarding the officers. The Board of War received and considered General Washington's letter on September 24, 1781, addressing the exchange of Colonel Laumoy and Lieutenant Colonel Cambray. They observed that

> the same obstacles which have occurred to the Commander-in-Chief create difficulties with us of so important a nature that unless we were pointedly ascertained that the services of these gentlemen are so absolutely necessary for the operations of the war, that they could not be dispensed with, we could not undertake to recommend a measure which deranges the system of exchanges and causes infinite jealousies in the minds of the officers who conceive themselves retained in captivity by any preferences. On this consideration we beg leave to return the letter of Colonel Pinckney as connected with this subject, leaving Congress to judge of the reasons he has mentioned, which will at least serve to show the grounds we have to believe much uneasiness will be created by the exchange of Colonel Laumoy and Lieutenant Colonel Cambray would derange the system of exchanges and cause infinite jealousies. . . . Preferences have been given heretofore to foreign officers on principles of policy and if Congress should be of opinion that such principles should prevail on this occasion, they will be pleased to direct General Duportail's request in favor of these gentlemen to be complied with. We cannot but add in favor of these Gentlemen, that we are convinced of their abilities, and join with General Duportail in opinion that their abilities, with the local experience they have added to their professional knowledge cannot be more usefully employed than in a Southern enterprise.[10]

The impatience of these officers to find themselves free to take part in the siege of Yorktown, then underway, had to be controlled. There were long, dreary months of inaction still before them. Finding himself unable to be of any service to the American cause, Lieutenant Colonel Cambray petitioned Congress early in October for leave to go to France on a short furlough in order to arrange his affairs that had been seriously compromised by his captivity and the fact that he had not received any pay from Congress. He also asked that his account be settled. The following resolution was submitted on October 26, 1781: "Lt. Col. Cambray desires to go to Europe on account of his destitute situation in regard to money, and as he is a very deserving officer—that his accounts be settled by the comptroller."[11]

JACOB SCHREIBER

Captain Schreiber also petitioned for permission to return to Europe awaiting exchange but on condition that Congress would settle his account "in specie" because American paper had no value in Europe. He said, "[T]he same principle that made me enter the service still pushes me through all the hardships and dangers of its continuance, and nothing but the mere impossibility of continuing it would make me leave it."[12]

Captain Schreiber's petition was submitted on August 6, 1781. The Board of War reported on his case on November 12:

> [F]rom General Lincoln's warrant it will appear that Mr. Schreiber resigned his commission of a Lieutenant of artillery in order to undertake the duties of an engineer with the rank of Captain. It appears to the Board to be but just that Mr. S. should receive the pay, having done the duty of an engineer, and therefore we give him a warrant for six months pay as a prisoner captivated at Charlestown.[13]

The report then goes on to say that because he desires it, there is no reason preventing him from going to Europe, especially as his services are not really necessary to the corps; therefore, it was ordered that the comptroller cause accounts forthwith to be settled.

Captain Schreiber had not expected such a result from his petition. He had not wished to resign from the corps. It seems also that General Duportail, to whom he appealed for advice and who was then preparing to sail for Europe, regretted very much the action of Congress. Duportail, therefore, wrote a letter, in which he said, "[H]aving had in Charlestown the opportunity of knowing the zeal and intelligence of Capt. Schreiber I think it my duty to inform Congress that I should be very sorry to loose this officer. . . . it would be very advantageous if Congress would give him the assistance he asks at this moment and keep him in the service of the United States."[14]

Captain Schreiber sent Duportail's letter with an appeal from the recent decision of Congress. The matter was taken up November 23, 1781, and a resolution proposed that the request be granted and that he be allowed to retain his "rank and appointments."[15] It was "negatived," however, by Congress. Captain Schreiber's position remained that of a prisoner with no further opportunity of serving in the army of the United States. He seems not to have been exchanged until near the end of the war, in 1782.

The accounts of Cambray were likewise ordered settled by the comptroller, as he is comprehended in the resolve of Congress prescribing the "mode of settling accounts of officers not belonging to any state. . . . He is entitled to three months pay as an officer captivated at Charlestown and this will put him on a footing with other officers captivated there so far as present exigencies will permit. It is sad to contemplate the hard lot of these prisoners, especially of the foreign officers, so far removed from any help from home."[16]

The names of Laumoy, Cambray, and Schreiber, with those of fourteen American officers, were attached to a petition addressed to the president of Congress, dated March 6, 1782:

> [A]fter our arrival here from Carolina in July last, Congress ordered . . . that we should be supplied with wood until further orders—The end of December [it was] ordered that no wood should be given us but at the end of every month money to pay for some. End of January given only half allowance—end of February both wood and money refused. Now we are told the Sec. of Finance refuses both. This is "punishing us for our misfortunes," and as the resolutions of July and August have not been repealed, and as such unjust regulations cannot be approved by Congress, we have presumed Sir, through you to state the matter.

The records of Congress show that the petition was read in Congress on March 6 and "ordered to lie," which means no further notice was taken of the appeal.[17]

Finally, in August, through the instrumentality of the Comte de Rochambeau, Colonel Laumoy was exchanged, as documented in the following letter:

> New York August 1st 1782
>
> Sir,
>
> Your Excellency's proposal in your letter of the 17th July last, to make up the ballance of Forty four in the exchange of Colonel de Laumoy for Majors Green and Timpany, out of the remaining convalescent prisoners sent from Gloster to New York in February last, I think reasonable and readily consent to it, and the more freely, as it will finish, to your Excellency's observation, the exchange of our land officers by the Count de Grasse's fleet.[18]

COLONEL LAUMOY'S EXCHANGE

Colonel Laumoy received the happy news of his release through the French minister. He immediately wrote to General Washington,

philadelphia August the 14th 1782 10 o'clock A.M.

Dear General

His Excellency the Minister of France has just informed me that the Count de Rochambeau had effected my Exchange, and that he was sending to your Excellency the papers relative to it. I should upon their intelligence only have set off immediately to join your Excellency's Head Quarters, but as the Count's aid is going to you in an hour hence and is to be back again in a very few days I'll wait till his return and for your Excellency's orders, upon receiving of which I'll set off without delay. I have to assure your Excellency that my gratitude for the share you had in this is equal to the very Respectful Consideration with which I have the Honor to be

Your Excellency's etc.
LAUMOY.[19]

Two weeks later, the commander in chief sent for Colonel Laumoy to join the army at Newburg:

Head Quarters, Newburg Aug. 28th 1782

Sir,

The army is about to take a position in the field; it is my wish you would attend it yourself as Chief Engineer, and take one other officer of that Corps with you—The remainder of the Gentlemen belonging to it, in this Department, you will be pleased to order to West Point, to assist Major Villefranche in superintending and carrying into execution the works now erecting at that Garrison and its dependencies.[20]

Lieutenant Colonel Cambray had not the good fortune to be included in the exchange. He wrote to General Washington on August 12, asking whether, because it was out of his power to be serviceable to the army, he could not employ the time in being serviceable to himself. He included in his letter some testimonials in his possession and asked for one from Washington, who replied,

Head Quarters [Newburg] 21st Augt. 1782

Sir,

I have received your favor of the twelfth instant. Were it reduced to a certainty that your exchange would not be effected for a considerable time to come, I should have no objection to recommending your request for liberty to visit France, to Congress—But as the offer which I have just made to Sir Guy Carleton of appointing another meeting of Commissioners may possibly be productive of an exchange of a number of officers, I think your application had better stand suspended till we see the issue of the proposed meeting. I return your Certificates for the present, without adding my name to them, not because I have any doubt of your abilities and merit, but because I would wish to do more than barely signify that due credit ought to be given to the honorable testimonials already in your possession, which is all I could do having never had the pleasure of commanding you personally—I hope before you return to France to be able to speak from my own knowledge.[21]

ENDLESS NEGOTIATIONS

Negotiations seemed to drag endlessly. Cambray renewed his discreet appeals in October to have his present distressing situation mended. Congress responded with assurances that they entertained a "high sense of his merit and military talents and of his zeal and activity in the cause of the United States."[22] He was granted a leave of absence for twelve months but received no money. Alexander Hamilton chaired the committee to consider the financial settlement. The committee reported on December 4, 1782, that it renewed their sense of the peculiarly distressing situation of foreigners, "remote from any resources they may have in their own (country) and destitute of any competent provision here."[23] Nevertheless, the embarrassment of the present financial situation made it impossible for them to advise any measure of relief. They were obliged, therefore, to turn the matter over to the superintendent of finance, whose discretion would enable him to decide what was proper to be done.

Cambray undoubtedly owed his exchange to the efforts of Rochambeau and the French minister, but the date or nature of the transactions remain unknown. His letter asking for a brevet commission as colonel was read in Congress in April 1783. His request was granted on May 2, along with a raise in rank for Major Villefranche and Captain L'Enfant.

Cambray returned to France soon after this date, as is evident by a letter from him to Franklin, asking that letters he was sending be forwarded to friends in America and that mail for him be readdressed to "No. 1 rue St. Pierre, qr. Montmartre." He wrote again in August, asking Franklin's aid in securing an interview with the Comte de Vergennes as part of a plan of advancement in the French army, which had the support of the Marquis de Ségur, the minister of war, and other prominent men. In this letter he speaks of the testimonials from Washington, Lincoln, and Congress, which he brought with him from America, as well as those from the states of North and South Carolina, and of the medal given him from the latter state in reward for very exceptional services rendered at the siege of Charleston.

The Rochambeau Papers in the Manuscript Division of the Library of Congress include a testimonial from General Duportail regarding several members of the Corps of Engineers and requesting places for them in the French service. Regarding Colonel Cambray, Duportail says,

> M. du Cambray entered the French Artillery in 1770. Passing to the service of America in 1778 he had the happiness to obtain without effort the rank of Lt. Colonel in the corps of engineers. Since that time he has justified the favor so prematurely accorded him by Congress, through the distinguished manner in which he served in the South where he merited the most flattering testimonials from the Generals who commanded him. He asks to be made Major in the Royal Grenadiers or in a provincial regiment.[24]

Colonel Cambray's efforts and those of his friends do not seem to have secured the desired results. A letter from his sister to Franklin, supposed date 1784, speaks of her brother being in a destitute condition and asks for an advance on the debt still owed him from the United States. Franklin must have written home, as a letter from the comptroller's office in New York reached him in 1785. It stated the sum due Cambray with interest prior to 1784.

After the passage of Alexander Hamilton's Assumption Bill, Congress caused a list of claims with amount and interest still due French volunteers in the American service to be advertised in Europe in 1794. The sum due Colonel Cambray was stated as $6,977.72 (the interest on these debts stopped by 1792). The list continued to be advertised in Europe for the next nine years and was definitely closed in 1803. Cambray's name, with the unclaimed sum due him, was still there, along with those of Lieutenant

Colonel Villefranche and Colonel Gouvion and an unclaimed sum of $637.76 (interest on principal of $2,657.33, paid to the heirs in 1796) belonging to the estate of Colonel Radière. Colonel Gouvion died in 1792 but apparently had no heirs.[25]

8

THE CAMPAIGN OF 1781

Yorktown

Congress appointed Colonel John Laurens its minister extraordinary to the Court of France in December 1780. He stopped at headquarters on the Hudson, where Washington and the army were spending the winter, and spent three days there, conferring with the commander in chief about the assistance he should request from their ally. Washington's instructions to Laurens were almost identical to those expressed in the memoir of his commandant of engineers to the French minister, even though the two had had no opportunity of meeting, much less discussing the situation since the latter's release from prison. Washington's instructions said in part,

> January 15, 1781.
>
> . . . inexperience in affairs, necessarily incident to a nation in its commencement, the want of sufficient stock of wealth, the depreciation of the currency, the general difference that has taken place among the people, the calamitous distress to which the army has been exposed by the mode which, for want of money, has been resorted to for supplying it . . . have brought the country to a crisis which renders immediate and efficacious succors from abroad indispensable to its safety. . . .
>
> . . . the patience of the army, from an almost uninterrupted series of complicated distress, is now nearly exhausted, and their discontents matured to an extremity . . . which demonstrates, the absolute necessity of speedy relief.
>
> . . . There is danger that a commercial and free people, little accustomed to heavy burdens, pressed by impositions of a new and odious kind, may not make a proper allowance for the necessity of the conjuncture, and may imagine they have only exchanged one tyranny for another. . . .

In consideration of which [we need] an immediate, ample & effica-
cious succor in money, large enough to be a foundation for a substantial
arrangement of finance, revive fallen credit and give vigor to future
operations . . . a constant naval superiority, additional . . . troops. . . . it
were however better to diminish the aid in men . . . than diminish the
pecuniary succor. . . .

 . . . no nation will have it more in its power to repay what it bor-
rows than this. . . . its independence being established [it will be able] to
redeem in a short term of years the comparatively inconsiderable debts
it may have occasion to contract.

[Finally] . . . the people are discontented, but it is with the feeble
and oppressive mode of conducting the war, not with the war itself.
. . . a large majority are still firmly attached to the independence of
these states, abhor reunion with Great Britain and are affectionate to
the Alliance.[1]

Washington also wrote various other documents showing the hope-
lessness of the situation without greatly increased aid from France during
this trying period. He wrote in a letter to Benjamin Franklin, introduc-
ing Colonel Laurens, "[T]he period of our opposition will very shortly
arrive if our allies cannot afford us that effectual aid—money and naval
superiority."[2] After visiting Rochambeau at Newport, in March 1781,
Washington made a more emphatic statement in another letter to Laurens:
"Day does not follow night more certainly than it brings with it some additional proof of the impracticability of carrying on the war without the aids
you were directed to solicit."[3]

Franklin, together with the Comte de Vergennes, had been working
toward the same end in Paris: substantial aid in money, supplies, and naval
superiority on the American coast. Less than two weeks after Colonel Laurens's arrival, the Comte de Grasse set out from the port of Brest with his
fleet. Vergennes assured Franklin that the king would send a free gift of six
million livres.[4]

Meanwhile, Duportail was on the road to New York, where he was
to rejoin the commander in chief, on January 11, 1781. He left Nathanael
Greene's camp in South Carolina on or about January 13. A few days
before February 5, he was in Maryland, on his way to Philadelphia to
inform Congress that "our Friends in Carolina . . . are suffering much, &
anxious for an Exchange."[5]

On February 8, Duportail was in Philadelphia, where he wrote to
Washington, thanking him for his exchange, expressing his impatience to
return to headquarters under his command, but asking at the same time to

have leave to stay until he could renew his depleted possessions, as he lost everything during his captivity. He closed by begging to be permitted to send his regards to Mrs. Washington and to his friends at camp.

General Washington replied on February 13,

> I received with much pleasure your letter of the 8th from Philadelphia, & sincerely congratulate you on your liberation from captivity, and safe arrival at that place.
>
> I shall set out the day after tomorrow for New Port.—Had you not so lately come of a long tiresome journey, I should have been glad of your company thither—but this being impracticable, and there being no immediate occasion for your presence at this Post, you have my free consent to remain in Philadelphia till the business you had in contemplation is accomplished, after which I shall be impatient to welcome you to Head Qrs.
>
> Col. Gouvion (if he has not already done it) is about setting out for New Port—Majr. Villefranche went thither a month ago.[6]

General Washington wrote Duportail again on February 21,

> My trip to Rhode Island has been delayed. . . . important considerations make me wish to have you with me this trip. . . . If not inconvenient you will leave Philadelphia immediately. Let me know by express if you can come and what day I may expect you at Head quarters. . . . You will forward your reply with all possible despatch as I shall await your answer and be governed in my departure by it.[7]

Matters were rapidly beginning to take shape. Before receiving General Duportail's reply, the commander in chief wrote him again on March 1, "Some unexpected events have determined me suddenly to set out for Rhode Island. I depart tomorrow—and dispatch you this to request you will join me there as soon as possible, Your information and advice will be very important to our plans."[8]

Washington's two letters arrived at the same time. Duportail complied with the orders and wrote the following hasty note on March 5,

> i receive this afternoon your two letters, one of the 21 of february the second of the first of march. i have not time enough to enquire how it happened so, but i am exceedingly sorry of that accident. i will do all my endeavors for repairing it as much as it is possible. i will set off tomorrow morning and i will go as fast as my horse will be able to do; i will go by new windsor and fiskill although i believe it is not the shortest road. but

i have not time enough to enquire and i must now agree with Colonel pickering about the road i will take on account of the horses.

i am exceedingly afraid not to joint your excellency—at a time—but i take the liberty to beg (if you leave rhodisland before I arrive there, and you have other orders to give me) to send them by the different roads I may take. this is principally necessary if you do not come by the same road you went.

i dont thinck i shall arrive at newport before the 14th.[9]

Duportail traveled quickly, passing through New Windsor and reaching Newport, as expected, on March 14, only to find that he had passed Washington on the way. Washington had left the day before but took a different route. Duportail remained with the Comte de Rochambeau for three weeks, discussing the American situation with him from every point of view and going over the plans and suggestions that had been brought out during the visit of the American commander in chief. Rochambeau wrote General Washington from Newport on March 31.

DUPORTAIL'S MEMORIAL

Duportail's lengthy memorial, written undoubtedly while at Newport and undated but classed as belonging to the end of March 1781, is titled "General Observations upon the different operations which can be undertaken according to the different cases at the arrival of the Comte de Grasse at the Hook." He begins by confronting the problem of taking New York, supposing that Admiral de Ternay could force Sandy Hook. He then considers alternatives if they could not attack New York. He notes, "The enemy either will have evacuated or they will have left a Garrison at Portmouth." After discussing all the possibilities and having exposed the situation at Charleston, he determines that the possession of the port of Portsmouth was the most important action to undertake in the South because possession of the harbor there would make it easy to capture the few Crown positions left in Virginia:

> If it is determined that Count De Grasse cannot force the Hook [Sandy Hook], but if he is master of those Seas, I suppose 'till November when he must go to the West Indies, it is asked in what case we may attack New York.
>
> I think that if the British at New York have not received any Reinforcement from Virginia and if Count De Grasse brings 4000 men with

him we may undertake to attack New York, to speak more generally, to attack New York in the case mentioned here, I would have no less than thrice the number of Men which we suppose that the Enemy have, because the time for the siege is determined and if we don't succeed, we lose all our advantages we could get in other quarters. . . .

Let us suppose now, that the circumstances do not permit to attempt any thing against New York, then we must consider these two cases.

Either the Enemy shall have evacuated Virginia entirely or they shall have left a Garrison in Portsmouth.

If the Enemy have evacuated Virginia entirely, I suppose they have made this distribution of their Troops, they have sent 3000 Men to New York and 12,000 to Charlestown. I suppose besides, that Lord Rawdon has now 3500 and that in case of an Attack, the British may collect 1500 Militia that will make 8000 Men in all. Is it advisable to undertake something against Charlestown so Garrisoned?

I answer that we have here a circumstance like that at New York. I mean that the harbour may be forced, and that by the local circumstances, after you have forced it, you may Stay in it as long as you please. Although not in possession of the Town, so that with a moderate number of Troops you can reduce it by Famine, if not by force.

I cannot say what difficulty we could meet now in the attempt for forcing the bar; but I observe we must observe it cannot be defended by land Batteries, it must be defended only by Armed Ships, Frigates, floating Batteries; Gallies, etc. When I was Prisoner near Charlestown, I heard the British had only sometimes one two or three small frigates at most, with one or two Gallies for that purpose; if it is the case now, I think that it should be very easy to force the bar with four or five large Frigates, or better, one or two 44 Gun Ships. Admiral Arbuthnot, in one of his Letters to Lord Germaine, says there are 19 feet of Water upon the bar at high tide. I think this is enough for a 40 Gun Ship. After you have forced the bar and entrance of the Harbour, you may introduce two or three fifty Gun Ships in it and then I believe you could brave all the attempts of the Enemy to get in again, so the whole fleet of Ships of the line may go where they are more necessary.

When we are perfectly Master of the Harbour of Charlestown, we then may choose either to attack it, or to block it up according to our means and strength.

To block it up, I think 7000 Men are enough on the Land side between James and Ashley Rivers, because we may fortify them if necessary. The quantity of Troops we must have on James's Island, and on the other sides of Cooper and Ashley, either for the greater security of our Fleet or from hindering the Enemy from getting Provisions, it depends upon this how far up the Ships have been able to penetrate into the Harbour and the Rivers (because the Enemy can make obstructions in some places, but in the most advantageous case, I think 4000 Men part of which may be Militia shall fill our object.

So I think that with 1100 [11,000?] Men we can block Charlestown up entirely.

To attack it I would have at least 4000 More.

A difficulty occurs, is it possible to supply with Provisions, so large a number of Men in that Quarter.

I believe it is, if the Expedition takes place, it will be before the Rice is cut, so that we can get plenty either in Carolina or Georgia, where we may send a body of Troops for that purpose.

Besides, I observed already that after we are in possession of the Harbour, the Fleet may go away. I suppose it will go to Chesapeak; so far they shall cover perfectly well the Transportation of our Supplies. If Count De Grasse is obliged, in the beginning of November to return to the West Indies, I do not doubt he will leave a fleet Superior or at least equal to that of the Enemy, so that our Convoys shall be safe; besides, we know that from Chesapeak to Charlestown, there is between the Main and some Islands an interior Navigation which may render the transportation very easy. It is only necessary to have for that purpose some small Armed Vessels to protect them against Privateers. So I think that on account of the importance of the Capture of Charlestown this year, as soon as it is determined that we cannot undertake any thing against New York, we must embark all the French Troops and as many of the Americans as can be spared with plenty Provisions, etc., and go, under the protection of the whole fleet, directly to Charlestown. . . .

. . . Mr. Duportail with whom I have had conferences upon all these objects, is quite of my opinion, he goes away on the 1st of April, and proposes being at New Windsor on the 5th; he will give your Excellency a more ample relation of the discussion of the different objects which were the subjects of the conferences with your Excellency here.[10]

LAFAYETTE SENT TO VIRGINIA

Washington sent the Marquis de Lafayette to Virginia in April 1781 with a force, including some of the sappers and miners, to stop Arnold's raids. The chief engineer was a valuable asset because Washington valued Duportail's knowledge of the enemy position in New York, his proven ability to evaluate the rebels' strength, and his camaraderie with fellow French officers like Rochambeau.[11]

Washington's headquarters, New Windsor, New York. *Photo courtesy of the author.*

Duportail set out for New Windsor on the Hudson after taking leave of the Comte de Rochambeau and the officers of his army. He arrived on April 6, and General Washington wrote to General Lafayette two days later, countermanding the permission he had given Lafayette to increase his staff by the addition of Lieutenant Colonel Gouvion: "It is General du portail's desire that Col. Gouvion may return to him. Independant of the occasion which there may be for him here, there is another reason which operates against his going with you; it is that he would interfere with Col. Kosciusko who has been considered as the commanding engineer with the southern army."[12] Moreover, Kosciusko never wanted to serve under the French commandant of the Corps of Engineers.

The Marquis replied on April 13 that he would have liked to keep Colonel Gouvion, and he forwarded Washington's orders to Philadelphia, where Colonel Gouvion was located. Meanwhile, Washington wrote to the Comte de Rochambeau on April 7,

> As genl. du portail did not arrive till yesterday, I had no opportunity
> of conversing with him before this day. After relating to me what has

passed between your Excellency and himself, and being informed by me
of the resolution I had taken to let your troops remain at Newport for
the present and with the reason which induced me to take that resolution, he fully acquiesced with me in the propriety of it.[13]

Washington received a letter from the Comte de Barras on May 11,
announcing his safe arrival at Newport to command the fleet of the Chevalier Destouches, who assumed command after the death of Admiral Ternay.
Washington immediately replied, congratulating him and announcing the
date of the interview that was to take place between the French and American commanders on May 21 at Wethersfield, Connecticut.

WETHERSFIELD MEETING

The Comte de Barras's flagship, *Concorde*, also brought the Vicomte
de Rochambeau with the latest instructions from the Court of France.
Duportail accompanied Washington at the historic Wethersfield meeting
and was present at all the discussions. They returned to New Windsor on
the twenty-fourth, and the French delegation went back to Newport. The
Concorde was then dispatched to the Comte de Grasse in the West Indies
with the report of the deliberations held at Wethersfield.

A letter from Colonel Laurens in Paris informed Washington on the
twenty-sixth that the king had announced the free gift of six million livres
to the United States. Two days after receiving Colonel Laurens's letter,
Washington wrote to General Duportail,

> You are perfectly acquainted with the plan, which has been concerted
> with his Excellency Count de Rochambeau at Wethersfield, I need not
> enter into a detail of particulars. I have only to request, therefore, that
> you will be pleased to make the estimates of the articles in your depart-
> ment necessary for the operation and that the previous arrangements for
> the siege as far as they are within the limits of our ability, be put in the
> best train, which the circumstances will admit. In the mean time, it has
> become necessary, from decay of the works . . . to abandon the post of
> Fort Schuyler, and erect new fortifications, at or near Fort Herkimer; I
> have to request that you will send an engineer to superintend the works
> in that department.[14]

PREPARATIONS FOR AN ATTACK ON NEW YORK

General Duportail sent Major Villefranche to superintend the erection of any defenses as would be necessary at Fort Herkimer and vicinity. He then turned his attention to preparing for an attack on New York, as tentatively determined at Wethersfield.

Washington instructed Duportail on May 28 to estimate the engineering department's needs for conducting a siege. The chief engineer responded in a matter of days. His evaluation included a rare calculation of the manpower and time required to make some of the principal instruments of siege craft: gabions, saucissons, and fascines:

DUPORTAIL'S ESTIMATE OF REQUIREMENTS
FOR A NEW YORK SIEGE
New Windsor, June 2, 1781

Plancks for platteformes about 12 inches broad and 2 inches thick.

I make amount to 150 the number of Cannons of different Caliber and mortars which we Can get and which are necessary whether to batter the ennemy's lines on new york island or long island or to secure the Communications and some other things.

Gabions and fascines. Gabions are the basket-like objects in the background. Fascines are the bundles of sticks in the foreground. Together, they are used to strengthen the walls of earthworks and fortifications. *Photo courtesy of the author.*

We must observe that the French army must be provided by us with the following articles.

Each piece Requires about 200 feet of plancks; for 150—30,000 feet. Saucissons (large fascines) for the batteries—72,000 feet. Gabions for batteries or trenches—4000 gabions. Fascines for the same—10,000 fascines.

The proportions of these things will be given to the officer appointed to superintend their Construction.

A man Can make a gabion in one day, so 500 men will make the 4000 gabions in 8 days.

A man Can make 36 feet of saucisson in one day, so 500 men will make the number Required in 3 days.

500 men will make the 10,000 fascines in 6 days.

Sand bags—30,000. We shall probably want some more but I have been told the French army have 60 thousand.

Tools: Shovels—5000; Pick axes—2500; Axes—1200; Bill hooks—800. If the french army had no[t] enough for them, we must have more than it is Required here.[15]

The sappers and miners were busy making fascines and gabions and frequently helped the engineers with reconnaissance. Washington moved the main body of his army from New Windsor between June 21 and 24. They moved farther down the Hudson and established headquarters at Peekskill on the other side of the river. Dr. James Thatcher, in his *Military Journal of the American Revolution*, says on June 23, "The army is now concentrated to a point in this place [Peekskill] and encamped in two lines, and in the same regular order that the troops usually form in a line of battle. . . . The campaign is now about to be opened, and we expect in a few days that the French Army will form a junction with us to cooperate with our troops."[16]

The two armies joined at Phillipsburg on July 6, still farther down the river and nearer New York. Washington, in his *Orderly Book* for this date, took occasion to thank "his Excellency the Count de Rochambeau, for the unremitting zeal with which he has prosecuted his march, in order to form the long wished for junction between the French and American forces . . . and from which the happiest consequences are to be expected."[17]

COMBINED OPERATION AT NEW YORK

A few days before, a combined operation had taken place against the Crown forces when the Duke de Lauzun brought his own legion to support a detachment under General Lincoln, who had dropped down the

Hudson at night and taken possession of ground a few miles back of Kingsbridge. As a result, the Crown forces retired to the other side of the Harlem River and took up their position behind Fort Washington on New York Island (Manhattan). In a letter to the president of Congress written the same day but before the arrival of Rochambeau and his army, Washington says of the retirement, "This afforded General Duportail and myself the most favorable opportunity of perfectly reconnoitering the works upon the north end of the island, and of making observations which may be of very great advantage in the future."[18]

The commandant of the engineers immediately put these observations to practical use. He began making a plan of attack to put into operation as soon as positive news arrived regarding the movements of Grasse and his fleet. The general officers assumed that the attack on New York would still be the wisest move. The combined armies continued to hold possession of the approaches to the north of the island of New York while awaiting news of Grasse and his fleet. The French command had always preferred a united effort in the region of the Chesapeake, however, but they had positive instructions to not influence Washington's decision in any way or to withstand his wishes.[19] Washington's and Duportail's preference centered around New York as the place for the first attack, especially after General Clinton had begun sending reinforcements to Lord Cornwallis in Virginia.

The reinforcements stopped during June, and the allies had no way of knowing what the Crown forces intended. Judging by Cornwallis's position, they thought that his army was to be transported to New York as soon as possible. While awaiting news from Grasse, the commander of the French fleet at Newport, Barras, wanted positive information regarding Washington's intentions, so he wrote the Comte de Rochambeau, who in turn addressed a letter to General Washington, asking for an interview the next day. In the letter, the Comte says, "I will bring with me the Chevalier de Chatellux and if Your Excellency will kindly advise M. Duportail so he may serve us respectively as interpreter and as approving of what your Excellency judges proper to propose to M. de Grasse under all supposable circumstances."[20]

The meeting occurred as proposed by the Comte de Rochambeau, and Washington's written reply on July 19 to the questionnaire presented to him ends with the following summary:

> Finally, every thing considered, I do not see that we can do more than
> follow the plan decided on at Wethersfield and recommend to the
> Comte de Grasse to come at once to Sandy-Hook and take immediate

possession if possible, of the post of New York and afterwards according
to the circumstances which arise to form a definitive plan of campaign
based on appearances which seem to appear the most sure.[21]

Washington sent the following note to the Comte de Rochambeau
a few days later (July 25) to be communicated to the Comte de Barras at
Newport:

> The officer by which I sent my dispatch for Count de Grasse has
> returned from Monmouth and has brought me an answer from General
> Forman. . . . the following is an extract from that Gentleman, which
> your Excellency will be pleased to communicate to Count de Barras, if
> you think proper.
>   Saturday the 21st of this month Adml. Graves with six or seven
> ships of the line sailed from his station off Sandy Hook, the wind at
> South West—the Fleet steered about South East—their destination not
> known, but conjectured to convoy Lord Cornwallis from Chesapeake
> to New York.
>   General Forman confirms the account of the *Royal Oak* having gone
> to Halifax to refit and adds that it is thought she will not be in condition
> for sea this season.[22]

The allies could not know the destination of the British fleet under
Graves at that time, but today it is possible to know what happened. A
sloop arrived at Sandy Hook the day of the meeting between Rochambeau
and General Washington. It bore the very important news that Colonel
John Laurens would sail from France with "money, clothing and military
stores"[23] before the end of June. He would be in a convoy of merchantmen
escorted by "one ship of the line, another armed *en flute* and two frigates."[24]
The British Admiralty deemed it so important to seize these vessels that it
issued orders to the commander of the fleet in the North to that effect.
When Graves was seen setting off from his station at Sandy Hook on Saturday, July 21, he was complying with those orders. Dense fog forced him
to return to Sandy Hook, where he arrived on August 18. Colonel Laurens
came safely into the port of Boston with his precious cargo on the twenty-
fifth. The fogs that saved him from the British delayed him so much that
the passage required eighty-five days.[25]

    This movement of the largest British ships under Graves, leaving New
York harbor comparatively unprotected, seems to have perplexed Duportail, who wrote the following to Washington on July 27:

I am so much vexed since three days ago by a certain idea that I cannot but submit it to Your Excellency. I remember that in the last Conference Count de Rochambeau told that the Count de Barras and all the officers pretended that it was not possible to force the entrance to the harbour of New York when there are some ships to defend it—if so why would not Admiral Barras, in this absence of the British fleet render himself master of the harbour? He could render himself master, he could penetrate every where.

I am surprised that the British left so the harbour and this makes me believe that there is something in their plan which we do not penetrate—maybe a junction with Rodney somewhere. But if the harbour cannot be fired Admiral Graves should not be in danger in it.[26]

General Washington replied immediately, "The subject you have written upon is equally perplexing and incomprehensible to my understanding—I will talk more freely to you thereon when we meet at two o'clock."[27]

DUPORTAIL'S PLAN TO ATTACK NEW YORK

There is nothing in Washington's papers to throw further light upon the subject discussed at the two o'clock meeting, but Duportail was preparing his plan in the meantime to be ready if and when the moment came to attack New York. He wrote on July 27,

General observations on the manner to pass over the island of New York.

If one considers the nature of the ground in the northern part of the island of New York it will be recognized I think, that it will not be a very difficult thing to take a position on the other side of devil's creek [Spuyten Duyvil]; batteries can be established on the mountain on that side strong enough to soon force the enemy to abandon Fort Charles and after that we will be masters of Kingsbridge. The works on Cox hill are of small account by themselves and can easily be taken sword in hand. If however the enemy were to remain, after the evacuation or the taking of Fort Charles, which I do not think likely, the feeble state in which they leave the fort on Cox hill shows they do not intend to defend that part of the island, and that their veritable defense front is from Laurel hill to fort Tryon.

Let us suppose that we are masters of Kingsbridge and have taken post on the other side, let us now see how we can progress. Considering the slope of the ground beyond forts Laurel hill and Tryon, its rocky nature, and the position between themselves . . . I do not think it practicable to attack them. . . . Doubtless, going at it properly it might succeed but it is hazardous, so I would prefer the following manner to establish ourselves—which is to go by boats across the Harlem river and boldly take a position between New York and Fort Washington at a place impossible to determine before arriving on the island.

. . . Two things must be considered—whether we will have a French fleet in the Sound, or whether we will not. In the first place we need not fear to be troubled in the Harlem by vessels, galleys or armed boats of the enemy; we will have a much greater number of boats to transport our men; we can choose the place of debarcation upon a very much wider extent of ground; we will have fewer troops to oppose us because the enemy will not be able to spare those on Long Island or even at New York. Success therefore seems to me very probable—it is much less so assuredly in the second case—that of not having a french fleet in the sound but it does not seem to me impossible even then, if we have many troops and much time.[28]

Duportail then discusses at length the possibilities in case of an attack without the support of the French fleet. He arrives at his conclusion: If a large number of boats can be brought secretly over land for the transportation of the troops over the Harlem River, and if they can command a force at least double that of the enemy, the taking of the island might be successfully attempted.

Duportail finished laying out the final plan for taking New York on July 27. He relied on support from the French fleet, but he deemed it possible to succeed without the fleet "if we have many troops and much time."[29] He thought that 20,000 men would suffice. This document is in the Washington Papers in French and does not appear to have been translated. Apparently, it was sent to Washington on the fifteenth with the following note:

Dear general

i send to your Excellency according to your orders the few general observations i have done after our reconnoiter of the island of New York, although the news we had yesterday made me afraid that they are now inutile. your other plans must probably be done but is it not advantageous to pursue the preparations for the attack of New yourk, to deceive our army et so the enemy—i am much afraid that we shall do nothing at all this campagne for want of secrecy—if the enemy perceive that we give up the idea of attacking New york they will reinforce portmouth Virginia, may be before we can get there.[30]

THE ARMY MOVES SOUTH

Before going south, Washington left Major General William Heath in the New York area to feign further siege preparations and to protect West Point. He then had his men march through New Jersey as if heading for Long Island. The sappers and miners stopped in Philadelphia for several days, "proving and packing off shells, shot, and other military stores."[31] They received shirts, overalls, and stockings, and each got a month's pay in specie. Sergeant Joseph Plumb Martin recalled the men's amazement: "This was the first that could be called money, which we had received as wages since the year '76, or that we ever did receive till the close of the war, or indeed, ever after, as wages."[32]

Washington wrote to Lafayette on August 14 with the news that had reached headquarters:

> The *Concorde* frigate has arrived at Newport from Count de Grasse. He was to leave St. Domingo the 3d. of this month, with a fleet of between twenty five and twenty-nine sail of the line, and a considerable body of land forces. His destination is immediately the Chesapeake; so he will either be there by the time this reaches you, or you may look for him every moment.[33]

He wrote in his diary the same day,

> Matters having now come to a crisis and a decisive plan to be determined on—I was obliged, from the Shortness of Count de Grasses promised stay on this Coast—the apparent disclination in their Naval Officers to force the harbour of New York . . . to give up all idea of attacking New York; & instead thereof to remove the French Troops & a detachment from the American Army to the Head of Elk to be transported to Virginia for the purpose of cooperating with the force from the West Indies against the Troops in that State.[34]

General Washington and the Comte de Rochambeau signed a letter to Grasse on the seventeenth and confided it to the care of General Duportail, who hastened south in hope of finding the French commander. He also brought dispatches to the Marquis de Lafayette. The letter to Grasse contains the following lines: "[W]e have determined to remove the whole of the French army, and as large a detachment of the American as can be spared, to the Chesapeake, to meet your Excellency there."[35]

ARRIVAL IN PHILADELPHIA

Washington and Rochambeau left a detachment behind to keep up the feint of the expected attack on New York and marched their respective armies up the river to King's Ferry. It took five days for them to cross with all their baggage and stores. The two commanders and their armies arrived in Philadelphia on Thursday, August 30, 1781. Robert Morris, superintendent of finance, being informed beforehand, had collected 30,000 "hard dollars" to be given as a surprise to the soldiers. Twenty thousand of these dollars had been borrowed from the Comte de Rochambeau. Morris promised to repay him by October 1. Colonel Laurens arrived at Boston from his mission to France on August 25 with 2.5 million livres, part of the donation of 6 million, enabling the superintendent of finance to fulfill his obligation.[36]

Before entering the city, the French troops were allowed time to dress in parade uniform. As they marched through the streets, Congress and the people were very joyful. The French minister, General Washington, and the Comte de Rochambeau then held conferences to plan the campaign. The troops who could not be transported to Yorktown by water would have to go on foot, so Lieutenant Colonel Gouvion was sent on September 2 to reconnoiter the roads they would have to travel. His orders:

> You will proceed with all convenient dispatch to the camp of the Marqs. de la Fayette in Virginia and receive further orders from Genl. Duportail or the Marquis. You will let your rout be by Christiana bridge—the head of Elk—the lower ferry on Susquehanna-Baltimore-Elkridge landing—Bladensburg & Georgetown—From Georgetown you will go by the best waggon road to Fredericksburg by Falmouth avoiding the Ferries of Occoghat and Rappahannock Rivers—and from thence you will take the road which leads most directly to the above camp.—From Baltimore—Georgetown—Fredericksburg and the Virginia camp you will report the state and condition of the interstate roads—and the measures proper to repair them—and if you could incite the inhabitants as you passed along to set about this necessary business it would facilitate the movement of our waggons etc. which must go by land greatly—I am persuaded, that it is unnecessary to add any thing, by way of prompting you to the preparation of fascines and other matters which can accelerate our operations & prevent the waste of a single moment.[37]

Meanwhile, General Duportail, after a long and difficult journey on horseback, found Admiral Grasse anchored off Cape Henry at the mouth of the Chesapeake and boarded the commander's flagship, the *Ville de Paris*. The Comte was surprised to receive an emissary from the commanders of the allied land forces and to learn that they were hastening on their way to join him before Yorktown. Grasse brought more than three thousand land troops from the West Indies under the command of the Marquis de Saint-Simon. Learning that General Cornwallis was fortifying himself on the York Peninsula, it seemed wise to attack immediately while the enemy was unprepared. He thought he could successfully accomplish that operation after the junction of Saint Simon's troops with those of Lafayette. Duportail's arrival changed his plans. He replied to General Washington's letter on September 2 in part,

> I received at the moment when I least expected it the letter which Your Excellency has had the kindness to transmit to me through M. duPortail, whose reputation has been known to me for many years. Therefore I have not hesitated to open my heart to him and acquaint him with all my resources and my orders. . . . I fear that the time at my disposal will not permit me to give all the aid to the united forces which I should wish to procure them. I had resolved to attack York with the Marquis de la Fayette's troops and those which I brought in my ships. But because of the letter which I received from Your Excellency, and on the advice of M. du Portail, I have suspended my plans until the arrival of the Generals, whose experience in the profession of arms, knowledge of the country and insight will greatly augment our resources.[38]

During their first conference, General Duportail and Admiral Grasse understood their respective situations. Grasse and Duportail both wrote to General Washington at the same time later the same day, September 2. Duportail wrote,

> Dear general: i arrived here this morning at five o'clock after a long and tedious journey on many accounts. but the pleasure I have to see at last a french fleet of 27 sail of line in your country makes me forget all the hardships i experienced. . . . count de grasse being obliged to it appears to be always determined to leave us in the time announced so we have only six weeks to operate. . . .
>
> i intend to join too morrow the marquis. the admiral has sent him already the troops he had on board which amount to more than 3000 men. now the situation of the marquis appear to me very nice, because on one side he must not according my opinion run any great risque till you arrive. that should be entirely improper unless the enemy gives a fine opportunity of an attacking against him which never must be

lost. [Duportail evidently alludes here to the attack as first proposed by Grasse.] but in another respect it should be very advantageous to confine the ennemy as much as possible that he could not obtain provisions because by what i heard of the advantages of his position at york, 6000 men well fortified shall be forced with difficulty. so if we could join famine to other means, we should have better chance of succeeding. but to determine to what degree it is convenient to aim at each of these different objects requires a very great judgment, fortunately the intelligence and good sense of the marquis must give us great confidence. i will put myself under his orders and second his views as much as i shall be able . . . but dear general come with the greatest expedition. let us make us[e] of the short stay of the count de grasse here. we have no choice left I thinck, when 27 of line are in Chesapeake, when great americain and french forces are joined we must take cornwallis or be all dishonored.[39]

DUPORTAIL JOINS THE MARQUIS DE LAFAYETTE

Duportail joined the Marquis de Lafayette the following day. Lafayette was aiding Saint-Simon to debark his men as quickly as possible. While the troops were disembarking, the Comte de Grasse sighted the British fleets under Graves and Hood and attacked them. The Battle of the Chesapeake has been characterized as the British navy's Waterloo and had much greater significance than Waterloo. It gave the allies mastery of the seas for a time, turning the tide of events completely in their favor. The ships were so disabled that the British were forced to abandon their project of relieving Cornwallis. They sailed back to Sandy Hook for repairs.[40]

In the meantime, Washington had received Grasse's and Duportail's letters. He wrote to Duportail on September 7,

> I am made happy by the receipt of your letter of the 2nd inst. and the other Dispatches announcing the arrival of the Count de Grasse. Nothing now gives me uneasiness but the two things you mention, not hearing from the Count de Barras who sailed the 24th of Augst. and the resolution for the departure of the fleet at a certain time.—Our measures must be forced, and every intermediate moment employed to the greatest advantage.
>
> The want of sufficient number of transports to carry our whole force and Apparatus from this place at once, is a great misfortune. We will however, hurry on the troops & preparations for the intended operation

as much as possible. The heavy Ordinance & necessary Stores will be forwarded immediately. & the Van of the American and French Armies consisting of 1000 men each will, I hope, be embarked tomorrow. The remainder of the Army will move by land to Baltimore without delay as you advise, and I shall come forward myself with all possible expedition.[41]

Washington seemed not to have noticed the Comte de Grasse's intention to immediately attack the British position. He replied to the Comte de Grasse's letter,

I Will only inform you, that the van of the Two Armies . . . will fall Down the Chesapeake to form a junction with the Troops under the Com'd of the Ct. de St. Simon, & the Marquis Lafayette, & to Cooperate in Blockg. up Ld. Cornwallis in York River, and in preventg. him to make his Retreat by Land, or collecting any Supplies from the Country.
    . . . In the Mean Time it will be of the greatest Importance to prevent the Escape of his Lordship from his present Position,—I am persuaded that every Measure which prudence can dictate, Will be improved for that Purpose untill the Arrival of our Compleat Force when I hope his Lordship will be compelled to yield his Ground to the superior Power of our Combined Forces.[42]

In a postscript to his letter to Lafayette of September 10, Washington said, "I hope you will keep Lord Cornwallis safe, without Provisions or Forage until we arrive. Adieu."[43]

Lafayette wrote to General Washington on September 8,

Lord Cornwallis will in a little time Render himself very Respectable I ardently wish Your whole Army may soon be brought down to operate. We will make it our business to reconnoiter the Enemy's Works and give you on your arrival the best description of it that is in our power—I expect the Governor this Evening and will again urge the necessity of providing what you have recommended.[44]

Before closing the letter, Lafayette made two requests: the first, that Washington, in answering Saint-Simon's letter that Lafayette forwarded, should make special mention of "your Admiration of the Celerity of the landing and your sense of their cheerfulness in submitting to the difficulties of the first Movement—indeed, I would be happy something might be said also to Congress on the Subject."[45] Lafayette concluded his letter with great modesty:

> Your approbation of my Conduct Emboldens me to request that, as
> General Lincoln will of course take command of the American part of
> your Army, the division I will have under him may be composed of the
> troops which have gone through the fatigues and dangers of the Virginia
> Campaign—This will be the greatest reward of the Services I may have
> rendered, as I confess the strongest attachment to those troops.[46]

Lafayette's letter to Washington of September 10 noted the arrival of
Colonel Gouvion at Lafayette's camp at Williamsburg. He did not mention
the report that Gouvion must have made or of what he had been able to
accomplish in improving the condition of the roads over which the heavy
army wagons would be forced to proceed. He certainly did the best he
could under the circumstances.

Duportail's October 29 letter to the commander in chief informed
him that Gouvion instantly threw himself, heart and soul, into all that
now presented itself to be done in relation to providing defenses for the
American part of the allied armies.[47] Those defenses were carried on under
Duportail's direction.

WASHINGTON AND ROCHAMBEAU
REST AT MOUNT VERNON

Washington and Rochambeau rested at Mount Vernon for two days, then
hastened to join Lafayette at Williamsburg. They arrived on September 14
and informed the Comte de Grasse the following day of their arrival. They
made arrangements for a conference onboard the *Ville de Paris* for the seventeenth. Washington recorded in his journal,

> 17th. In company with the Comte de Rochambeau, the Chev. Chas-
> tellux, Genls. Knox and Duportail I set out for the interview with the
> Admiral and arrived on board the *Ville de Paris* (off Cape Henry) the
> next day by noon and having settled most points with him to my sat-
> isfaction, not obtaining an assurance of sending ships above York and
> one that he could not continue his fleet on this Station than the first of
> November I embarked on board the *Queen Charlotte* (the vessel I went
> down in) but by hard blowing and by contrary Winds did not reach
> Williamsburg again till the 22nd.[48]

All the allied troops were assembled at a camp near Williamsburg by
September 27. Washington's orderly book for that day gave the "Order of

Artillery at the second parallel. *Photo courtesy of the author.*

Battle for the Army." They were to march to Yorktown, the Americans to form the right wing, and the French, the left. The "Park of Artillery and the Corps of Sappers and Miners" were to be located between them. Immediately after arriving the morning of the twenty-ninth, Duportail took command of the defenses of the American army; "Trees were felled, flèches were thrown up, and batteries were constructed at the points deemed most vulnerable."[49]

Cornwallis had withdrawn his men from the outer defenses before daybreak of the thirtieth and retired to those immediately about Yorktown. As soon as the allies learned of this retreat, they advanced and took possession of the abandoned ground, strengthening the old defenses and building new ones. Reconnoitering parties kept the armies informed of the strength and position of the enemy.

Washington wrote to the president of Congress on October 6, "[B]oth the Allied armies are assiduously employed in making fascines and gabions, and in transporting our heavy cannon, mortars and stores. . . . It being the opinion of the engineers that we now have a sufficient stock to commence operations, we shall this night open trenches."[50] Washington's diary for the seventh records, "The work was executed with so much swiftness

Reconstructed zigzag communication trench between the first and second parallels. The actual trenches would have been much deeper. *Photo courtesy of the author.*

Reconstructed redoubt 9, Yorktown, showing the fraise and embrasures
for gun emplacements. *Photo courtesy of the author.*

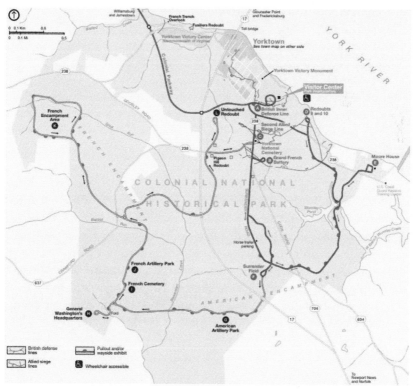

Map of Yorktown showing deployments and defense works.
Colonial National Historical Park Visitors Brochure.

and dispatch that the enemy were, I believe, totally ignorant of our labor till the light of Morning discovered it to them. Our loss . . . was extremely inconsiderable."[51]

Even though several of Duportail's engineer officers were still imprisoned following their capture at Charleston the previous year, the allies had more than a dozen engineers at Yorktown. Fifteen thousand fatigue men did the work, covered by "armed detachments numbering 2,800 men."[52] Duportail directed them with the assistance of only two of his officers, Lieutenant Colonel Gouvion and Captain Rochefontaine. Laumoy, Cambray, L'Enfant, and Schreiber were still detained prisoners.

The intense strain, constant activity, and responsibility involved undermined the health of the commandant of engineers. Duportail had dysentery at the end of the siege and was unable to take part in the final triumph. That did not matter much to him. It was more important to him that the united efforts of the allied armies succeeded. However, neither Duportail nor the commander in chief realized how badly the enemy had been beaten at Yorktown. They were too close to the conflict to realize the significance of what had happened.

SURRENDER AT YORKTOWN

After the surrender, Washington urged Grasse to help him drive the British from Charleston. Grasse thought that there was no need to waste time and treasure, not to mention human life, in wresting territory from the British. Failing in that request, he asked for assistance in transporting his army as far as Wilmington, North Carolina. The Comte de Grasse was willing and eager to gratify Washington, even though he himself realized that the effort was unnecessary. But he had already outstayed the time his orders permitted for the operations at Yorktown, so he and Washington expressed their good wishes and parted company. The British abandoned both New York and Charleston less than a year later without spilling a drop of blood. This was not due to the military power of the allies but to Great Britain's "temporary loss of maritime supremacy and political support."[53]

The day after the surrender, General Washington personally commended Duportail for his siege work in the attacks and commended him and Colonel Ethis de Corny in the general orders of the day "for the Vigor and Knowledge which were conspicuous in their Conduct of the Attacks."[54]

Reenactment of the surrender at Yorktown. *Photo courtesy of the author.*

REQUESTS FOR PROMOTIONS

Following the capitulation, General Duportail sought a leave of absence on October 24 to permit him to visit France for the approaching season, when little could be done in the field. He requested Washington's intervention to get him promoted to major general and an advancement in rank for Gouvion. He also asked for and renewed his entreaties that Colonels Laumoy and Cambray be exchanged. The letter ended with assurances of his attachment to the American cause in general but particularly to the person and glory of the commander in chief.

Washington replied two days later pointing out the very grave difficulties that stood in the way of asking Congress for a raise in rank for the Royal Engineers. It meant that all the foreign officers who had fought so bravely and so well would feel they had been slighted if some special promotion were not granted to each one. This, in turn, would set a precedent to American officers, and the troubles that surfaced at the beginning of the war would reassert themselves:

In answer to your letter of the 24th I beg leave to inform you, that as no immediate operation requires your presence in this country, I shall most cheerfully second your application to Congress for a six months furlough to yourself and Col. Gouvion for the purpose of arranging your private affairs in France.

The other request appears to me to involve difficulties that will deprive me of the pleasure which, from a sense of your merit I should feel on every possible occasion of promoting your views. In the present instance the infringement of the rights of seniority in so many individuals, and the pretentions of some who have particular claims upon their country, convince me that your desires could not be accomplished but at the expence of the tranquility of the Army—I cannot forebear adding at the same time that it will always afford me the greatest pleasure at all times, to give the most particular testimony of the real talents and distinguished services of yourself and Colonel Gouvion and entreat you to be persuaded my earnest wish that you may receive those rewards from Congress which you desire, at a more convenient opportunity.

Cols. Laumoy and de Cambray will probably be released in a short time under a general exchange.[55]

Duportail was insistent, at least under the then present circumstances, when he had definitely made up his mind that the rank in question was due himself and Gouvion and that Congress would be persuaded to grant the request if presented tactfully. He recognized at the same time the commander in chief's delicate situation, and he saw that the request should not come from that quarter. Duportail's real reason for the first letter to the commander in chief was to have some tangible proof in writing of his willingness that the requested grade should be granted. Washington's reply gave him all that was needed in this respect.

He addressed the commander in chief again on October 27,

When i am going to France it is so important for me to have here the rank of major general that i cannot easily give up the idea of getting it. it appears to be a plan of the french ministry to give to the officers who have served in this country a rank inferior to that they had here, accordingly being only a brigadier general they may very well leave me a lt. Colonel as i am now in the french army. i have many other reasons for believing that i shall not acquire any superior grade in france if i arrive there only brigadier general, yet it would be very hard for me to have lost five years, and it is for that reason that i take the liberty to write again to your Excellency about that matter. I beg leave to do as all my Countrymen have done till now, it is to try what i can myself with Congress, and i ask your Excellency to treat me as you did them not to oppose to what Congress should be disposed to do. When i do so, i do not intend to present a formal petition . . . because in case of no success i should be mortified to see their refusal inserted in the acts of Congress; but i may suggest to them what I desire. it is not improbable that the time of my services, the circumstances of my going to france, . . . the [case] of officers they asked officially to the french court . . . may dispose them to grant me and colonel gouvion what we desire. if so, then i shall see the effect of it in the army; if they do not appear dissatisfied then we shall come back; but if they appear dissatisfied we will stay in france. it will be certainly with great concern that i shall leave so an affair to which i am exceedingly attached and which i look upon as near the conclusion. but i could not bear to be disagreeable to the American army. so all what I beg of your Excellency is not to interfere in this affair. . . . if Congress requires your opinion about our demand, may not your Excellency be so good as to say something like this: that this promotion being not in the ordinary course, you have nothing to do with it, but you do not pretend to set any limits to the favours of Congress, and it should be easy for you not to compromise yourself.[56]

Duportail decided to write the French minister and suggest that he make the suitable intimation to some member of Congress. The letter, in French, was written near the end of October.[57] He sent the minister a plan of the attack on Yorktown and explained his intention to have kept the minister frequently informed of the progress of the siege, but the engrossing nature of his work and, later, his illness prevented him from doing so. He then explained to the Chevalier de La Luzerne, much as he had done to Washington, the importance for both himself and Gouvion to have the advanced ranks before returning to France. He stated that he relied upon the minister's kindness, of which he has had so many proofs, to say the necessary word that could not well come from himself. He planned to leave for Philadelphia in two days but would travel slowly because of his illness, and he hoped that the matter would be well underway or completed before he reached his destination. He planned to remain in Philadelphia for five or six days.

PROMOTIONS

While General Duportail felt hesitant to ask Congress for a raise in rank for himself, he had no qualms making requests for the members of his corps.

He was assiduous in seeking to have all the officers of engineers receive full credit for their efforts, whether they took part in the siege of York (York-town) or were equally faithful to duty in less conspicuous roles. He sent the following letter to the commander in chief about the same time as he wrote the minister:

> After the superb operation we have just terminated, i think it my duty in quality of Commandt. of the corps of the engineers to draw your Excellency's attention to the officers of the corps who have had the good fortune to be employed in it and who, having served well, appear to me, at least according to the usages established in the European service, to have an indisputable right to the favors of Congress and an immediate advancement.
>
> the first is lieut. colonel Gouvion; i cannot say enough of the bravery activity and intelligence which that officer has exhibited. all the most interesting parts of the seige having fallen to his share. he was superior engineer at the opening of the trenches, at the tracing of the second parallels, at the logement in the two redoubts that were carried etc. I think then that great marks of satisfaction can scarcely be denied this officer in the present circumstances. i regret that too great number of seniors in his line renders it impossible to sollicit for him the grade of brigadier but would it not be practical to give him that of Colonel. i know that the intention of Congress is to appoint no more of this grade. but perhaps they might make an exception in their general rule in favour of M. de Gouvion to whom it would be very important to have this grade for his advancement in france, if this however should be impossible I thinck it is just to indemnify him by the most brilliant certificate.
>
> i ask the grade of major for m. de Rochefontaine, who has served very well during the seige. this officer has in his line a sufficient seniority as captain and besides a circumstance so brilliant and by its nature so advantageous . . . ought to be a compensation in some degree to it.[58]

Washington forwarded the letter to Congress and wrote to the president at the same time, enclosing the following certificate:

> General Duportail, Commandant of the Corps of engineers, having specified his desire of obtaining leave to go to France for the arrangement of his domestic affairs, it is with the greatest satisfaction I embrace this opportunity of testifying the sense, which I entertain of his distinguished talents and services. His judgment in council, and well-conducted valor in the field claim the highest applause, and have secured to him the esteem and confidence of the army. His plan and conduct

of the late attacks in the late important and successful seige of York where he commanded the corps of engineers, afford brilliant proofs of his military genius, and set the seal to his reputation; while they entitle him to my warmest thanks.

Given at Head-Quarters, 31st October, 1781.[59]

Washington's letter to the president of Congress reads as follows,

Head Quarters near York 31st Octr. 1781

Sir,

I do myself the honor of transmitting to your Excellency, a letter from Genl. Duportail, in which he explains the motives of an intended application to Congress, for permission to go to France, & for the promotion of himself and the officers of his Corps.

I should conceal sentiments with which I am very strongly impressed, & do injustice to very conspicuous merit, if I did not upon the present occasion offer my Testimonies to the distinguished Abilities & services both of Genl. Duportail and of Lt. Col. Gouvion—their claim to the particular attention of Congress at this juncture, is founded upon the practise of Europe; a seige being considered as the particular province of the Corps of Engineers, and as entitling them, when attended with a success, important in itself and in its Consequences, to the greatest military Rewards—These officers besides are supported by a series of Conduct in the line of their Department, which makes them not depend merely upon the present Circumstances—For these reasons I am induced to recommend Genl. Duportail's Memorial to Congress for the grades which he specifies—and the leave of absence—the latter being by no means incompatable with the good of the service at the present period, as I am reduced, notwithstanding all my efforts, to the Necessity of retiring into Winter Quarters.

The same principles as those above mentioned, forbid me to be silent on the subject of Genl. Knox who is closely united with Genl. Duportail in the merits of the seige; being at the head of the Artillery, which is the other principle instrument in conducting attacks—The resources of his genius on this and many other interesting occasions have supplied the defect of means; His Distinguished talents and Services equally important and indefatiguable entitle him to the same marks of approbation from Congress, as they may be pleased to grant to the chief engineer.

With sentiments of Respect and Esteem, I am etc.
GEO. WASHINGTON[60]

General Duportail's efforts resulted in success for him and Colonel Gouvion. Congress promoted Duportail to the rank of major general on November 16, 1781. After the congressional delegates rejected a motion prohibiting promotions "on account of extraordinary merit or eminent services, contrary to the rule of succession," adopted by Congress on May 25, 1781, they approved a resolution promoting Duportail. President of Congress John Hanson wrote to Duportail the next day to convey the news:

> Sir, Philadelphia, 17th. Nov. 1781
>
> I have the honor of enclosing you a copy of an Act of Congress of the 16th instant, by which you will observe that you are promoted to the rank of a Major General in the Armies of the United States.
>
> This Act is so very explicit on the subject of your distinguished Merit, as to foreclose the Sentiments my feelings would prompt me to express. I will therefore only beg leave to congratulate you on the occasion, and to assure you that you have my best wishes for future prosperity and felicity.[61]

Hanson also wrote brief letters to Jean-Baptiste de Gouvion and the Chevalier de Rochefontaine of the Corps of Engineers, enclosing resolutions announcing their promotions by brevet to the ranks of colonel and major, respectively.[62] France awarded Duportail the Cross of St. Louis and a pension, as well a pledge of promotion to the rank of brigadier general in the French service.[63]

Duportail thanked General Washington for the part he played in procuring this important mark of appreciation from Congress for the work of the Royal Engineers, but his letter is prefaced by words of sympathy for the sad personal loss that the commander in chief experienced shortly after the surrender at Yorktown: the death of his aide-de-camp and beloved stepson John Park Custis from illness. Duportail's letter of November 24, 1781, says,

> i heard with great concern the domestique misfortune which your Excellency had lately, and in the apprehension that sad event will retard your arrival here, i take the resolution to write to you.
>
> i beg your Excellency to receive my most sincere thanks for the letters of recommendation which you have been so good as to give me for Congress. they have obtained to me the price of my demands. one thing yet is wanting to my satisfaction. i wish that your Excellency be pleased . . . to give me a letter to the marquis de Segur, Minister of war.
> . . . if you wish to see me again in this country it is perhaps necessary to

mention it, because the Court could claim my services at home or send me in another part of the world. if your Excellency is so good as to grant me the favour which I beg and the Chv. de la Luzerne has been pleased to permit, to send the letter immediately.[64]

Permit me, my dear general, in taking leave of you to present to you my wishes for your health during my absence. Would to God that I come back with fleet and troops for some important expedition under your orders and direction. We must all expect success and glory.

i have the honour to be with the greatest respect and attachment etc.

Duportail.

Permit me dear general to present the assurance of my respect to Mrs. Washington.[65]

Major General Duportail requested the brevet of captain for his aide, Castaing, in a letter of November 19, 1781. The Board of War reported on November 20,

That Mr De Castaing appears from the arrangement of the army to be at this time a Lieutenant in Colonel Jackson's Regiment and to take rank as such from the 24 day of April 1779. There is no doubt but that he is a deserving officer and has done his duty; but unless some very particular circumstance appear so as to distinguish him from the other officers of the army or the regiment in point of merit, uneasiness will be created by giving the Brevet requested, and the accidental circumstance of his having served in General Duportail's family will not be deemed sufficient by those who are affected by the promotion. It will too no doubt introduce similar claims from other officers who have served in the like capacity, and with equal merit with Mr De Castaing. Congress will be pleased to recollect that there are several valuable officers, who have served as Aids and have now the same Rank they had the Beginning of the War. True it is that in the early period of the War when rank was more easily obtained and duty not so clearly designated, those gentlemen procured commissions of higher grades than they were entitled to. But it is as true, that if many of them had continued in the line they would now have commanded regiments, and under this idea some of them complain that their promotion is stopped, and would be glad of a precedent whereupon to found their claims to advancement. I have troubled Congress so far on this subject as I would not wish to appear on slight grounds to contravene the recommendation of General Duportail, for which I have the greatest respect. If however Congress should not consider these observations as having any weight and that the recommendation of General Duportail should be attended to as sufficiently evidencing the particular merit of Mr De Castaing, they will please to resolve,

That Lieutenant De Castaing receive the Brevet of Captain in consideration of his services at the defence of Charlestown in South Carolina, and the siege of York in Virginia.[66]

Resolved, That the request respecting the promotion of Lieutenant de Castaing, cannot be complied with.[67]

Duportail had one more request for Congress. It probably would not have entered the mind of any delegate to propose such a request, considering the circumstances, but they were willing to grant it when made aware of the facts. Duportail understood the newness of that body and its limited experience in the use of the amenities of diplomatic communication, so he did not hesitate to instruct them regarding the proper procedure in his case. He wrote to the president of Congress on November 23,

> Considering that I am to appear in France under the character of an American general officer, it seems to me to be indispensable to be addressed and recommended to the Minister Plenipotentiary of the United States. . . . I and the two officers of the Corps of Engineers (Cols. de Laumoy and de Gouvion) who came to this country with me . . . [feel] it would be much more satisfactory to us if Doctor Franklin was particularly authorized and desired to express to our Court the sentiments they entertain of our services; this seems all the more proper as Dr. Franklin having been charged by Congress to demand us to the Court of France and having treated with us for engaging in your service, we dare think that he will be flattered to see that we have answered his Expectations & justified his choice. . . .
>
> I have the honour to be etc.
DUPORTAIL[68]

Congress prepared the following letter the next day:

Philadelphia, November 24, 1781

Sir:

Major-General du Portail will have the honor to present this. Congress, in consideration of their long and faithful services in this country, have granted permission to him and Colonels de Laumoy de Gouvion to revisit their friends in Europe for the winter.

As the merits of these gentlemen have Procured for them peculiar marks of the esteem of Congress, they wish to be distinguished by the notice of their sovereign, and for that purpose have directed that they be recommended to you, and that you be requested to present them at court in such manner as will bespeak for them the attention they justly merit.[69]

Congress also granted a furlough to Colonel Laumoy to return to France with his companions, but his exchange had not been effected, so he was obliged to remain behind. Before leaving America, General Duportail wrote the commander in chief, recommending that Colonel Laumoy be put in command of the engineering corps and of the sappers and miners as soon as released, "for the good of the service."[70] In case this could not be arranged for some reason, then the next choice would fall on Lieutenant Colonel Cambray.

Duportail specially recommended Weibert (lieutenant colonel of engineers) in this letter. This officer, who had been exchanged, had served under John Paul Jones and had proven himself a very brave man. As he lacked experience in the corps, Duportail suggested that he be sent to Fort Pitt or Albany.[71] In closing, Duportail spoke of some changes in the organization of the Corps of Sappers and Miners that experience showed would be necessary to make. However, he would attend to this matter after his return. Having made the observation, he was ready to begin his leave of absence and turn his mind toward France.

9

PEACE

Major General Duportail and Colonel Gouvion received permission in the fall of 1781 to remain in Europe six months. They returned to France after serving five years in the armies of the United States. Secretary for Foreign Affairs Robert Livingston wrote to John Jay from Passy on February 2, 1782, that "by their military skill, bravery, and good conduct, [they have] done honor to their own country and great service to ours" and that "if his majesty should think fit to bestow on these gentlemen any marks of his royal favor, it will be particular pleasing to Congress."[1]

Benjamin Franklin noted on March 4 that the "French officers who have returned to France this winter speak of our people in the handsomest and kindest manner, and there is a strong desire in many of the young noblemen to go over and fight for us. There is no restraining some of them, and several changes among the officers of their army have lately taken place in consequence."[2]

France honored Duportail with the order of Chevalier de Saint Louis in 1782. He wrote to General Washington on June 27 that he and his companions had expected to return to America within the appointed time but had been delayed, along with the Marquis de Lafayette, awaiting either news of the peace or, in case that should fail, assurances of further military aid. He added in closing, "i wish you be persuaded how much i long to join your excellency and the american army. i consider myself as an american if not by birth by a mutual adoption. the Cause of America is mine, all my pleasure is in it, and i will not leave it before we attained the success."[3]

General Duportail and Gouvion boarded the *Danae* on November 8, 1782, and left France. Duportail was bringing a letter from Lafayette to General Washington dated October 14, 1782. The *Danae* foundered in the fog in the Delaware Bay on December 16, and there was some delay before she could be refloated. She carried many packets for the army and 180,000 livres, and she brought news that the British government had agreed to preliminary articles of peace and tacitly recognized American independence. Lafayette's letter read in part,

> you must by this time know that I am kept in this country at the request of the American plenipotentiaries and with a view to be serviceable to our cause, which with me will ever be the first object. Public intelligence will be given to you by General Duportail. Those of a more secret nature I have communicated to the Secretary for Foreign Affairs, whom I have requested to send the letter to your excellency. You will be able to form your own opinion upon the situation of affairs, but though the forwardness of affairs do not permit me (consistent with the motives I have explained to you) to depart for the present from this country, yet it is my private opinion that a success is necessary before the general treaty can come to a conclusion.[4]

PROMOTIONS

During January and February 1783, General Duportail busied himself in urging the promotion of the different officers who served under his command, particularly Villefranche; L'Enfant; Cambray; and his aide-de-camp, Castaing. He corresponded with the French minister and with the Comte de Rochambeau, as well as with General Washington and the president of Congress. He intended to join General Washington at headquarters on the Hudson as soon as these important negotiations were well underway.

Colonel Gouvion had joined the army immediately at Newburg. Duportail wrote in a letter from Philadelphia to General Washington on January 29, "i am very impatient to be informed by colonel gouvion if he could get a quarter for me at camp. i will set off immediately to pay my respects to your excellency."[5] Three weeks later, on February 19, he wrote, "i was setting off for camp last Saturday . . . when I was stopped by the intelligence of the peace. . . . i have been told yesterday of your excellency proposing to make a journey to the eastward."[6]

The representatives of the United States and England signed the Preliminaries of Peace in Paris on November 30, 1782. Word reached America toward the end of January 1783. As there was every reason to believe that Congress would ratify the treaty, Duportail realized that the war was practically over and ceased to think more about joining the army at headquarters unless positively ordered to do so. The French minister, Chevalier de La Luzerne, notified Washington on April 10, 1783,

> I have to inform your Excellency, that I have just received instructions from the Minister—that in consequence of the Peace the French Troops actually here are to be sent to France without delay. If you see no cause to defer it I shall accordingly take immediate measures for their departure—I impatiently await the arrival of the Duke de Lauzun to give the necessary orders, as no definitive arrangements can be made in his absence.[7]

Duportail sent the following message on April 16, regarding the French engineers serving in the Continental Army:

> i am expecting every day orders of the court of France as they will probably recall us home and give us very little time, i wish that if your excellency thinck that if we can be of some further service to this country in this moment to communicate to me his orders and wishes. my attachment to america and in particular to your excellency will not finish with the war but only with my life and i will thinck myself very happy and much honored if i can be of some utility to a country that is in my heart next to the country to which I owe my birth.[8]

RETENTION OF FRENCH ENGINEERS

Washington replied on April 23,

> I have received your favor of the 16th instant. . . . In answer to your questions respecting the Engineers, I can only say that a Peace Establishment is now under consideration, in which it is recommended that Congress should form Military Academies & Manufactories as a part of this Establishment—should this idea be adopted, and the Plan carried into execution; it will doubtless be necessary for us to retain some of the French Engineers in America, for the first beginning of the Institution. . . . I am persuaded that none will be more agreeable than those gentlemen of your Corps who have distinguished themselves in our service with so much ability & satisfaction.[9]

Congress had already requested Duportail to express his views in writing regarding the peace establishment of the engineering branch of the army. In reporting the matter to the commander in chief, he took occasion to explain more clearly the meaning of his last communication, which Washington had assumed was an offer of continued services by the members of the Royal Corps of Engineers. Duportail's letter, dated April 29, 1783, assured Washington that "there is no appearance that those who belong to the French service will have the liberty of remaining" and that he had only meant to express his eagerness to render himself useful during the little time that remained before he and his fellow officers would be forced to return to France. He ends,

> since my last letter a committee of Congress for the establishment of peace asked me my ideas respecting my Department. i will send your excellency my memorial to make the use of it that you shall thinck proper.
>   if your excellency has no occasion for my presence in Camp, i beg leave to stay here having many little business to settle. besides it would not be worth while for so short time to send my baggage to camp and establish myself it would be very expensive and troublesome. notwithstanding I will wait for the order of your excellency and i shall execute them always with the greatest pleasure.[10]

Washington answered this letter rather coldly on May 10,

> Sir You have anticipated my wishes, in having, as you mention, communicated your sentiments on a peace establishment, so far as relates to your Department, to a Committee of Congress—as you promised to send me a copy of it, I shall be gratified by a sight of your ideas on the subject
>   As you mention it to be very inconvenient for you to come to Camp—I do not at present recollect anything of Importance enough to render your attendance here necessary.[11]

A document in the *Papers of the Continental Congress* dated May 4, 1783, shows that the French officers of the Engineer Corps were gathered in Philadelphia at this time, as Congress passed a resolution earlier in the year that required the signature of each member of the corps. The document read,

> The officers of the Corps of Engineers having met for the purpose of giving their opinion respecting the commutation of the half pay, agreeably to a resolution of Congress of the 22nd of March 1783, have

unanimously agreed to accept the Commutation agreeable to the term
of said resolution (full pay for five years instead of half pay for life.)

signed by Duportail, Gouvion, Laumoy, Cambray, Villefranche,
L'Enfant, Wuibert, Murnan and Rochefontaine.[12]

Duportail's first memorial to the commander in chief on the peace
establishment of the army has not been found among the Washington
Papers or among those of the Continental Congress. However, he wrote in
the cover letter, "i have the honor to present you the memorial mentioned
in my last letter. I composed it after the hints you have been pleased to
give me when at head quarters. i beg your excellency to let me know if i
have been happy enough to meet with your ideas, wishing not to propose
anything to Congress but through you and what you approve of."[13]

Duportail also wrote a memoir on fortifications, which he submitted
to General Washington, who forwarded it to the president of Congress on
June 7, 1783.[14] The memoir was read in Congress on June 11 and referred
to the Committee on Peace Arrangements.

Washington wrote a brief acknowledgment to General Duportail that
same day (June 7): "I have been favored with your letter of 25th May,
accompanied by your observations respecting the fortifications necessary for
the United States. I was extremely obliged by the communication, and now
enclose them under flying seal to Congress, with a letter to His Excellency
the President, which is likewise open to your inspection."[15]

Washington's letter to the President said in part,

> The sentiments expressed appear not only to be the production of a
> well informed mind, and the result of much experience aided by great
> professional knowledge, but because they seem also to be dictated by a
> disinterested zeal for the future tranquility and happiness of the United
> States.[16]
>
> Regarding the principles of defence on which Genl. Duportail has
> particularly treated in a very important point of light, cannot help rec-
> ommending a proper consideration of them in the adoption of a Peace
> Establishment, so far as they may be found practicable with our means,
> and applicable to our local circumstances. For although the subjects
> proposed are undoubtedly of very great & immediate consequence,
> & require that something should be done without delay, yet how far
> we are able at this time to enter into extensive arrangements for the
> fortification of Posts and Harbours, and the establishment of Military
> Academies etc. must be submitted to the wisdom of Congress and rest
> upon their decision.[17]

BRIGADIER GENERAL IN THE FRENCH INFANTRY

Duportail was appointed a brigadier general in the French infantry on June 13, 1783, at the age of forty. He received a bonus of 2,500 livres and commanded two regiments. Only a few official documents remain about this stage of his life; most were destroyed during the Reign of Terror.

Baron von Steuben was ordered to Québec during the summer to confer with General Frederick Haldimand, governor of Canada, about the surrender of British forts along the frontier. He asked that Major L'Enfant might accompany him. When General Duportail heard of the matter, he wrote the commander in chief, begging him to be so good "if i or the first officers of the Corps have not been so unfortunate as to lose your esteem and confidence, not to trust any person with any business that belongs to our department."[18]

Washington replied to this letter, saying that the commission was not of a nature to require an engineer and that he had not thought it important enough to send "one of your rank and abilities."[19] Villefranche ended up going with the Baron, and he later reported on the fortifications necessary on Lake Champlain.

The summer passed with no word from Congress about the French engineers, so General Duportail wrote the commander in chief on September 16,

> Dear General the officers of my department and myself have waited patiently till now with the army that Congress be pleased to take a resolution concerning them and we would wait still longer if we are not in a peculiar situation. when the army or part of it shall be dismissed the american officers can go home when they please but it is not so with us. your excellency knows that we are almost all foreigners—so to go home we must cross the atlantic. but i beg leave to observe, dear general that the winter is approaching, that in that season the opportunities for going are much more scarce, the voyage not pleasant and for many of us the distance from the sea town to our respective places of abode very great—i may add that it is of some importance for those who are attached to the service in europe to show themselves there the soonest possible. thus, dear general I take the liberty of entreating your excellency to urge the resolution of Congress respecting our department.—If the present circumstances do not permit them to take a final determination it is possible perhaps to take such measures as would set at liberty those who would wish for it without however losing irrevocably those whose service might be desired afterwards by Congress and who might

be inclined to continue them. but i entreat your excellency again most earnestly, to engage Congress to take a resolution upon this the soonest possible, for which we shall have the greatest gratitude.[20]

Washington responded immediately on September 19, "I have received your letter of the 16 instant and this day have laid it before Congress; their determination, which I hope will be speedy & agreeable to your wishes, shall be transmitted to you as soon as they come to hand."[21] Four days later he wrote again,

> I was this day in conference with a Commee of Congress upon the subject of your letter to me of the 16th inst. They discovered every disposition to relieve the Gentn. of your departmt. from the state of uncertainty in which they are prest but wished previous to their making a report to Congress to obtain your sentiments more in detail upon a proper Peace establishment for the engineering Line of the army agreeably to the idea contained in your general observations which are now before Congress—I know you will require more information than they, or I, can give you in the undecided state in which things now are before you can deliver a precise opinion but all the data I can give you to work upon is, that we ought to maintain West Point as a Post—those which the British are to surrender to us,—and such as it may be found necessary to establish West or So-west upon our interior boundary and these too upon the most economical plan.
>
> The sooner you can favor the Comee. (or me in their behalf) with your sentiments on this subject, the sooner the matter will be brought to a decision. In the mean time, if you have it in your power, you would oblige me by giving me information of the name of the Genln. in yr. departmnt. who are disposed to remain in this country upon a Peace establishment.[22]

Duportail sent the desired memorial with the following letter on September 30:

> according to the demands of the committee i have the honor to send to your excellency my ideas about the establishment of my department. i wish i may be so happy as to meet with your own. i had a peculiar intention not to say any thing more than what is necessary to take a determination upon the matter. . . .
>
> i am sorry that i cannot give to your excellency the name of the gentlemen who might be disposed to remain in this country. in the present unsettled state of the affairs their choice would be a blind one— . . . congress must pronounce first and show what they intend to do. then if

the gentlemen see that they have here an honorable, solid employment, if the united states show themselves to be a great respectable empire, or at least take proper measures for becoming so—I do not doubt that many of my department induced by inclination, and by the opportunity offered them here of doing things more important and interesting than those they could do in europe, would remain with pleasure.

I take the liberty of requesting again your excellency in the most earnest manner to use his influence with congress to have a resolution upon this the soonest possible.[23]

Duportail wrote to the president of Congress on October 6, stating that Brigadier General Laumoy, Colonel Gouvion, and himself being the "three and only officers of the royal corps of engineers who had been sent in '77 by the court on request of the american congress" now beg very earnestly to be given permission to return to France the soonest possible, especially because the "present opportunity may not present itself again for a long while." He also begs that their accounts be settled before they leave.[24]

A committee of Congress considered this letter on October 10 and reported,

> That Major General Du Portail, Brigadier General Laumoy, and Colonel Gouvion, were permitted by his Most Christian Majesty to serve in the army of the United States at an early period of the war and further suppose for this purpose furloughs were granted to them by the king of France, from time to time, and it appears that from a desire to give a repeated manifestation of his affection for attachment to the United States, the services of these Engineers were considered equally entitling them to the favour of their sovereign, as if they had been performed in the armies of France.
>
> That these Gentlemen have distinguished themselves in their profession, during their service in America, as active, intelligent, and useful officers, and considering that they entered our service with the particular approbation and consent of their Sovereign, it appears to your committee that it will be expedient to grant them some peculiar testimonies of the sense Congress entertain of their services, as well as to expedite their return to the Corps to which they are attached in France; Whereupon,
>
> Resolved, That Major General Du Portail, Brigadier General Laumoy and Colonel Gouvion, who have served with distinguished merit in the Department of Engineers, have leave to retire from the service of the United States, their affairs requiring their presence in Europe, and however desirous Congress might be of their continuing in service no arrangements in which they can be employed having been yet

compleated no arrangements having yet been made by which Congress might employ the abilities of those gentlemen, however desirous they might be of their services.

Resolved, That the Secretary at War express to the Minister Plenipotentiary of his Most Christian Majesty in America, the high sense Congress entertain of the zeal, abilities and conduct of these officers during their service in the Army of the United States, to the end that the said Minister may convey to his Court, the approbation of Congress of their distinguished merit.

Resolved, That the Superintendant of finance cause the accounts of Major General Du Portail, Brigadier General Laumoy and Colonel Gouvion, to be immediately adjusted, and advance to them respectively, such sums as the state of the public finances will, in his opinion, admit, giving them certificates on interest for the balances which may be found due to them.[25]

RESIGNATION

General Duportail resigned his commission in the Continental Army that same day and returned to France on October 10, 1783. He rejoined the French army as lieutenant colonel attached to the infantry, which was his only option to advance to higher positions of responsibility, but he had to fight hard to get rewarded. He and his companions benefited from the king's support when they left France and from the American commander in chief's and Congress's deserved praises during the American War of Independence. Fortunately, Lafayette's support was most valuable.

Before leaving America, General Laumoy requested a certificate from Washington. Washington forwarded the request to Congress on October 14, along with a detailed account of his various employments in the service of America. He also wrote about the services of General Laumoy on October 18, in part, "[T]hroughout the course of his services he has shown great knowledge of his profession and has acquitted himself with that zeal, activity and bravery which entitle him to the character of a good officer and an able Engineer."[26]

Congress ordered a few days later that their passage would be at the expense of the United States: "*Resolved*, (October 16) That the agent of Marine provide Major General du Portail, Brigadier General Laumoy, and Colonel Gouvion with a passage to France, in the ship *Washington* and that they be informed of the same."[27]

General Duportail wrote to the commander in chief very soon after Congress passed a resolution excusing them from further service. The letter began by referring to General Washington's expressions of regret to the two French officers to see them quit the service. Duportail pointed out that the same method of approach as formerly used would have to be followed if the services of any one of them were really desired. As Congress did not make any request to the French government through its minister, their only option was to return to France.

Washington replied promptly on October 18,

> Genl Laumoy and Col. Gouvion did me justice in mentioning the regret I feel at your intention of leaving this Country. The personal attraction which naturally grows out of such a length of service together, had I no other motive would occasion a regret at parting, but it is considerably heightened by your quitting the service and thereby depriving me of the hope of seeing you return to benefit the country by your abilities and experience in your profession, [interlined, thought not clearly expressed] if such an establishment as this great Empire ought to adopt for the peace of it, should be finally agreed to, but which this moment is yet undecided.
>
> It would afford me much pleasure to tell you this personally before your departure, but if I should not have this satisfaction I beg you to be assured that you carry with you every good wish I can form for you, also that I shall ever retain a grateful sense of the aids I have derived from your knowledge & advice and more especially for the repeated testimonials I have recd. of your friendship and attachment for me.[28]

Duportail's mission and that of his companions came to an end. They were still in the United States on October 18, 1783, because Laumoy received a certificate from Washington attesting to his services. General Laumoy and Colonel Gouvion probably traveled to headquarters to take their leave of Washington. They must have departed shortly after because Laumoy's letter of gratitude to Washington was addressed from Brest, where they arrived after a rapid crossing of thirty-one days.

Everybody who knew Gouvion loved him, and Washington seems to have held him in high regard. He wrote two testimonials to the French authorities, and Lafayette was particularly charged to acquaint the ministers with the high regard he enjoyed in America. The first testimonial is addressed to "His Exe. the Marq. de Bouille":

Head Quarters at Newburg 23d March 1783

Sir

Tho a stranger to your person, I am not so to your character—of the last I have the honor to rank myself among the first of your admirers.— Under the sanction of this profession, which I assure you is sincere, permit me to introduce to your Excellency's civilities Mons. Gouvion, a Colonel in the American Service of distinguished abilities and of whose intelligence, bravery and zeal I have had the most unequivocal proofs.

On whatever expedition your Excellency may embark, and in whatever enterprise engage, my warmest wishes shall attend you, and if it is possible that you may increase that military fame which is at present so high.

I have the honor etc.[29]

The second testimonial is addressed to the "Baron de Viomenil":

Hdqr. Newburg 23, March

I could not let Col. Gouvion (to whom I pray your civilities and they cannot be bestowed on a more worthy man), depart without bearing with him this testimony of my remembrance of a corps, to whom gratitude, and every other consideration—public and private has bound me—

GEORGE WASHINGTON[30]

In a final letter to his chief, Gouvion says,

Sir At the moment of leaving this country where I had the honour of serving for seven years under your command, I beg your Excellency's leave to express to you how grateful I am for all the favours which you have been pleased to bestow upon me. Although the part I acted in this happy and glorious revolution was but small, I shall always take pride in remembering that I was an American officer. the testimonies I have of the satisfaction your Excellency had of my services will in every time be dear to me. they were my only wish and I feel very happy in having obtained them.

May your Excellency experience from his country a gratitude so well deserved, but which can never be equal to the unparalleled toils, labours and cares you have sustained to save it, may you for a long while see its inhabitants enjoy . . happiness and prosperity.[31]

REPORT OF A COMMITTEE ON A
MILITARY PEACE ARRANGEMENT

Congress accepted on October 23, 1783, Duportail's September 30 memorial entitled "Report of a Committee on a Military Peace Arrangement":

> The Committee are of opinion that the principles laid down by Major General Du Portail, Chief Engineer, in the Memorial annexed to this report, so far as they respect merely the article of fortifications are in general sound and just; and that it will be expedient for Congress, as soon as they have determined upon the Corps of Engineers to instruct the head of that Corps to make a survey of the points proper to be fortified and to digest a plan, proportioned to the Military establishment of the United States, to be laid before Congress for their consideration.

A committee consisting of Hugh Williamson, William Ellery, and Samuel Osgood considered General Duportail's request of October 29, 1783, for some immediate payment for himself and other officers belonging to the Corps of Engineers whose accounts had not been settled as Congress had authorized on October 10. The pay they received for a considerable time was in depreciated money and very unequal to their actual expenses. Some of them depended on remittances from their friends in France for their support, while others less fortunate contracted considerable debts in America. Their situation was such that they did not have the means of subsisting in America nor of returning to France unless some part of the money due them was paid.

There is no response from Paymaster Pierce to Williamson's query in the *Papers of the Continental Congress*, but the committee recommended payment on January 21, 1784. The motion was adopted the following day, and Congress passed the following resolution:

> Resolved, That the superintendant of finance take order for paying to the foreign officers of the late corps of engineers, and to the foreign officers lately belonging to the legionary corps, commanded by Brigadier-General Armand, also to Major Seconde, Captain Beaulieu, late of General Pulaski's corps, and to Captain Ponthiere, late aid to the Baron Steuben, such sums on account of their pay as may be necessary to relieve them from their present embarrassments, and enable those in America to return to their native country and that he take such measures for facilitating the payment of the balances which may remain due to them as may comport with the condition of the finances of the U.S.[32]

Duportail's last letter to General Washington was sent from Paris on December 24, 1783:

Dear General i arrived here ten days ago from london; i landed at plymouth, traveled through England about three hundred miles and stayed at london five days; i intended to stay sometime longer but was prevented by different news i heard from here—your excellency will not be surprised of that tour of mine after the american war it was certainly curious to see england & to observe the effect of their misfortunes the alterations it ought to produce in their government and so for those reasons i propose to return there in two months hence there is now in that city and throughout the country another cause of fermentation. it is the affair of the east indies. as you receive probably the english papers i thinck it superfluous to give your excellency any account of it—but i will be satisfied with saying to you that after all that i heard of the situation of their affairs in that part of the world, it is a great pity that France has made peace with england so for one year more and probably they were irrecoverably lost there. it is what i imagined while in america—i cannot give you any interesting news from this place. pleasure, diversions are the first objects which strike the attention here and the person arriving should thinck that there are no other affairs in paris. to know that it is not so requires some stay so as i cannot give you anything interesting in politics i am almost tempted to give you something in the physical way but i suppose this same ship will carry you from every one or your correspondents great particulars about the *merveille* of the time. your excellency conceives that i am speaking of the air baloon the most extraordinary discovery ever made but in that very matter i am yet pretty ignorant; i had not yet time since i am here of penetrating into all the proceedings. Chv. de Chastillux to whom i delivered your letter told me that he intended to give your excellency an account of it. nobody can do it better than that gentleman.—

everybody here, dear general, asks me if you intend to come over—i give them little hope after what you told me. your excellency may be certain that he would be received in France with great pleasure but no body could have a greater satisfaction to see you than myself—you may be an object of admiration from those who are at a distance and who know only your military and political life but for those who are so happy as to be particularly acquainted with your excellency's private character you are equally an object of veneration and attachment—however if i have little hopes of seeing you in France i hope to see you in america for i am far from renouncing from that country forever. maybe i shall be able to tell you more about it a few weeks hence. i suppose this letter will find your excellency in Virginia. permit me to present my respects to Mrs. Washington and my compliments to the gentlemen our companions in the war who are so happy as to live near you. i have the honor to be etc.

Duportail[33]

Major General Duportail's letter of November 6, 1783, recommending the promotion of Captain Castaing to the rank of major by brevet, was read before Congress on December 24, 1783, and referred to a committee consisting of Jacob Read, Edward Hand, and James Monroe. They considered the matter on February 26, 1784, and reported that Captain Castaing received a promotion by brevet as an officer of a regiment in the late Massachusetts line:

> But that as his extraordinary services out of the line of duty of his regiment, as an aid de camp to Major General Duportail for four years and particularly in the defence of Charles Town in So. Carolina and the seige and reduction of York Town in Virginia and the recommendation given him by the letter of Major General Duportail deserve the acknowledgement and attention of Congress, And as the dissolution of the army prevents any inconvenience, arising on the subject of this promotion in the line of the regiment to which Capt. Castaing lately belonged, and the rank requested may prove useful to him in his own country, your Committee recommend that the request of Major General Duportail, in behalf of Capt. Castaing be granted, and that the Secretary in the War Office do make out, and enclose to Capt. Castaing the brevet of Major in the Army of the United States of America.[34]

The motion was defeated.

SERVICE IN THE FRENCH ARMY

Duportail returned to France as brigadier des armées du roi (brigadier general of the king's armies). He and Gouvion accompanied the Marquis de Lafayette to Silesia in August and September 1785 for Prussian army drills. On June 16, 1787, the king ordered Duportail to accompany the Baron de Sales to Naples and to serve under him to train the Army of the Two Sicilies for two years. He was appointed to the general staff of the French armies as Aide-Maréchal des Logis, that is, Sous-chef d'état-major des Armées (assistant quartermaster general) on June 29, 1787. He was promoted to field marshal (Maréchal de camp) on March 9, 1788, at the age of forty-four. He was noticed for his authority in suppressing a riot in the government of Rouen in Normandy without bloodshed and for his organizational abilities in merging the artillery and engineers and in the reorganization of the general staff of the army. He retired from the general staff on May 14, 1789.

He was given regional command of Flanders on March 7, 1790, and was appointed to the regional command of the departments of Eure and the lower Seine on October 15, 1790.

MINISTER OF WAR

Duportail succeeded La Tour du Pin as minister of war (November 1790–December 1791) during the French Revolution. He resigned a year later to accept a military appointment in Lorraine.

In assuming the ministry, he found the Royal Army so disorganized that it invited a complete audit. The status of the troops was a complete disaster. Out of a theoretical total of 140,965 officers, subalterns, and rank-and-file, few fought in America, and many were absent from their units. He was constrained to make a regulation on February 4, 1791, creating a corps of 100,000 auxiliaries between the ages of eighteen and forty, enlisting in the army for three years in time of war. On June 21, the assembly sent 26,000 national guardsmen to the borders.

Duportail realized on October 11, 1791, that he had only forty-four battalions of volunteers, and most of them were undermanned. He also realized that 1,932 officers had left their post in the infantry and cavalry, and he could only find 764 replacements, while the assembly decided to raise the number of troops to about 176,616 officers and soldiers.

Duportail would be criticized for a lack of muskets, even though the government decided in 1784 to cut back its orders for weapons. As national production was insufficient, his efforts to diversify the rapid acquisition of new weapons during very difficult economic times would attract unscrupulous suppliers, sometimes recommended by subordinates. There was also a lack of horses, especially for the artillery, for the same reasons. That would lead to abnormally high expenses to bring them up to code.

However, his biggest difficulty was the general lack of discipline, and he was accused of finishing his overhaul of the army by allowing soldiers to visit clubs. He believed that allowing soldiers to frequent popular clubs and organizations, where new ideas were read and discussed, would bring new ideas into the army. He hoped that this would result in better cohesion between the officers, subalterns, and enlisted men and eliminate insubordination. Duportail wanted to ensure that the army would not become an instrument of the counterrevolution.

The queen's partisans wanted to chase him out of the ministry as quickly as possible. The patriots criticized his allegiance to the king and blamed him for leaving the volunteers without arms or equipment. He would also be attacked by both the military committee of the legislature and the revolutionaries from the summer of 1791. He tendered his resignation on December 3, 1791, and it was quickly accepted. He was replaced three days later, not by the man he proposed, but by Louis Marie Jacques Amalric, Comte de Narbonne-Lara. Later, during the French Revolution, he was forewarned of threats against his life.

He was promoted to lieutenant general on January 13, 1792, and commanded the Twenty-First Division at Moulins on February 22, but he never reached his post. This assignment bore a note saying, "never reported," which indicates both the state of his health and the hatred against him. Everyone who was appointed by the king or who was in charge of a ministry was suspected of hatching plots against the nation.

The legislative assembly accused him on August 15, 1792, of having entered into negotiations with émigrés and having worked against the constitution. He left the army and concealed himself in Paris for about twenty-two months, before fleeing to the United States in 1794, where he became head of the Corps of Engineers.

10

AMERICAN CITIZEN AND FARMER

Louis Duportail and the French officers swore allegiance to the United States while serving in the Continental Army at Valley Forge in 1778. General Washington witnessed Duportail signing the document that ipso facto conferred citizenship and served the French general in good stead when he fled the Reign of Terror fifteen years later. He sought refuge in America and intended to buy land and to establish himself there. His flight from France did not permit him to bring very much. The inventory of his property after his death lists only his books, which consisted of about thirty volumes, mostly about agriculture and his need to enrich his vocabulary in these matters.

Duportail knew his adopted country better than most Americans. He rode the whole range of it on horseback from post to post during his five years in the Continental Army. He chose to establish himself around Valley Forge. Despite the miseries of that dreadful winter of 1777–1778, the natural advantages of that part of the country, its climate, and the general beauty of its wooded hills greatly impressed him. He was particularly enchanted with the streams that flowed down from the hills, the crystal-clear "great springs of water," and the majesty of the winding Schuylkill.

The region around Valley Forge was originally included in Letitia Penn Manor. The property had been divided into farms, mostly owned by members of the Society of Friends (Quakers), to which William Penn belonged, so practically all of the region was cultivated by 1778. Early in the eighteenth century, a strip of land on the right bank of the Schuylkill, known as "Swede's Ford Tract," extended a mile along the river. It extended two miles inland and had been purchased and settled by Swedes from the region of the Delaware.[1]

Definite boundaries were drawn up in 1784, and new counties made. The Swede's Ford Tract became part of Montgomery County and in the township of Upper Merion. The waters of the Schuylkill were still crystal clear and teeming with fish. The shad-fishing industry, carried on by the Swedes who settled there, thrived. All this appealed greatly to Duportail, who wished to leave behind him as far as possible the bitter memories of the last few years. He wished to possess some part of the Swede's Ford Tract and was particularly attracted to that part that followed the Swede's Ford Road. The Continental Army had marched along that highway fifteen years earlier on its way from the Whitemarsh encampment to that of the Gulph, the last resting place before taking up winter quarters at Valley Forge.

Duportail knew that road well, as he constructed a bridge of wagons floored with rails from nearby fences so the army could cross the Schuylkill at Swede's Ford. It was there that he watched the Continental Army cross on their march to winter quarters at Valley Forge. The location brought back many memories and held a particular significance for him.

PURCHASE OF A FARM

Duportail was not the only *émigré* who sought shelter from the French Revolution in the farmlands of the United States. Louis Marie and Guy de Noailles both bought farms in Montgomery County. Many other French names occur in the records, including that of James Philip Delacour, who in 1792 bought a large segment of Swede's Ford Tract. It was to him that Duportail expressed his desire to settle in that locality. Delacour sold his entire plantation of 189¼ acres "to Louis Lebegue Duportail" for the sum of "2,368 pounds and 15 shillings lawful money of Pennsylvania" on June 8, 1795.[2]

The recorded deed (in the Montgomery County Courthouse, Norristown, Pennsylvania) gives a lengthy description of the land and an accurate description of its boundaries. It states that the land runs for a considerable distance along the Swede's Ford Road, but there is no mention of its touching the river. Duportail bought a "piece of land, situate on the south east side of the road leading to Norristown ford on Schuylkill included between and bounded by said road the said river and the plantation of the said Louis Lebegue Duportail, containing by computation three acres more or less" from John and Margaret Eastburn for the sum of fifty-five pounds lawful money of Pennsylvania on September 25, 1795.[3] The river frontage thus acquired measured a little more than a quarter-mile in length, and the farm is henceforth listed as composed of 194 acres. It is important to note that while the first deed had no land directly on the river, Duportail was careful to secure the right "to half part of the shad fisheries opposite Swede's Ford Tract," as well as "free egress, ingress, and regress . . . for carrying out seins and putting fish on shore."[4]

The former major general (Maréchal de Camp) and French minister of war was now settling down to the life of an American farmer. He was certainly not married, as was customary for officers of the Royal Corps of Engineers. They were generally less fortunate or wealthy, often subject to frequent and unforeseen changes, and were not deemed suitable for young women in search of a husband. The average marriage age of these officers was forty-eight, and about a third died bachelors.

Throughout his career in the Continental Army, Duportail had servants, as was customary of officers, so he may have brought a servant and a French cook with him. There are no documents that mention servants in his retirement, but that may be because they were so common that there was no need for special mention to be made of them.

When Charles-Albert Moré, Comte de Pontgibaud, came to America to receive the arrears in his pay that he saw advertised in Europe, he found several of his old friends living in or near Philadelphia, and Duportail was one of them. Pontgibaud noted in his *Memoires* that he found Duportail living in another time, dressed in outmoded clothes, mulling over his incomprehension of events, particularly the false accusations against him in France. His mind seemed wholly absorbed in things of the past, and his costume was that of a gentleman of the old regime.

General Mathieu Dumas, Duportail's former subordinate, learned on June 18, 1797, why Duportail decided to emigrate and began proceedings to have Duportail's name struck from the list of émigrés so he could return to France. Duportail had placed all his confidence in Dumas during the Reign of Terror, and Dumas did his utmost to bring the matter to the legislature, which deemed the motives insufficient. Duportail requested again on February 24, 1798, that his name be struck from the émigré list, but the Directory of April 26, 1799, kept him on. He had to wait until the coup d'état of the 18 Brumaire to be allowed to return to France.

After Napoléon Bonaparte had become first consul, the 1792 law that banished for life émigrés on the list and condemned them to death upon return was abrogated. Napoléon probably was aware of Duportail's career as a young officer and must have also wanted the return of a man of noted loyalty and fastidiousness to the service of his country.

Duportail disposed of parts of his farm to two different purchasers in 1801 and left America for France the following year. One might suppose that he had begun to dispose of his property, intending to return to France permanently, but that was not the case.

He sold his dwelling, barn, and all improvements, along with eight acres and eight perches of land to Alexander Crawford for $730.60 on June 24, 1801. The next day, June 25, he sold eighteen acres and seventy-six perches to Samuel Holstein, a neighbor whose land joined his, for the sum of "273 pounds 15 shillings, lawful gold or silver money of America."[5] The sale included

> buildings, improvements, ways, woods, watercourses together with the benefit of the great spring of water . . . and other privileges particularly mentioned in the indenture from the said James Philip Delacour to Louis Lebegue Duportail . . . reserving . . . the right of roadway through the property [connecting his remaining property with] the Swede's Ford Road, together with the fruit and ornamental trees planted and growing on the verge of each side thereof, with liberty of planting, cultivating and pruning as many more as he or they [his heirs and assigns] may from time to time deem necessary.[6]

This last clause proves that Duportail intended to continue farming, even though he had already been notified that his disabilities as *émigré* had been removed and freedom secured for his return to France. The aforementioned deed goes on to say that special reservation is made of his right to the shad fisheries opposite Swede's Ford Tract.

These 1801 deeds anticipate continued farming activities (the farm contained about 166 acres). Later documents also reveal that Duportail had already selected a site for a dwelling that pleased him better than the original buildings bought with the farm, and he had already begun construction. In the meantime, Napoléon issued an order that all *émigré* officers return home. It is not known when or how the message was conveyed to him, but he must have received it early that year and complied with the order very quickly; the tax lists were sent out toward the end of March each year, and there was none recorded for "General Duportail, Farmer," for 1802. He left one Isaac Huddleston, a young Quaker doctor who settled in Norristown in 1793, as his agent to look after the plantation in his absence. The two men must have become friends some time earlier.[7]

DEATH

Duportail boarded the small American vessel *Sophia* in New York on July 22, 1801, along with twenty-two other people, men and women of all ages recently freed from the prison at Cayenne. He was taken by a fit of vomiting at 4:00 p.m. on 22 Thermidor (August 10) and was found dead at 2:00 a.m. the following morning, probably due to a gastric hemorrhage resulting from dysentery contracted during his imprisonment. Isaac Hand, the captain of the vessel, certified the death of the former minister of war at 7:00 a.m. on August 11 and proceeded to take an inventory of Duportail's belongings. Before four French travelers selected as witnesses, he made a report in the cabin of the deceased:

> Today August 12, 1801 at 11 AM, we the subsigned passengers on board the New York ship *Sophia*, Capt. Isaac Hand, going from New York to Havre, having been called by the said Captain to be present at the summary verification of the effects left by Mr Louis Joseph Le Begue Du Portail, a passenger aboard the said ship, deceased aboard the ship during the night of the 10th to the 11th of the month of August have taken on the duty on behalf of Mr Du Portail's family and heirs this report by which we certify that at the moment the said Mr Du Portail was found dead in his bed yesterday about 7 o'clock in the morning, the said Capt. Hand took the keys of the bag and trunks of the deceased which trunks and bags remained untouched and today at the above stated time the said Capt. opened the bag in our presence in which was found: clothing, two portfolios containing letters, a certificate of the debt of the United States toward the deceased, two certificates of English public funds, two New York banknotes, one for $20, the other for $5, 96 gold louis, some dollars and small change, a gold watch, a pair of garters with silver buckles, a parasol, three trunks two of which are in the hold.[8]

Duportail was fifty-eight years old. He undoubtedly never recovered from the illness that weakened him so much at the beginning of his ministry.

The ship captain was detained in England, along with his ship, and could not register the death himself, so he requested the four witnesses, including a notary, an invalid war officer, a merchant, and a Guadalupian without a profession, to do so. They appeared before the mayor of Le Havre on September 8, 1801.

For some unknown reason, Duportail was given an added surname of Joseph. This seemingly insignificant error most directly registered at this date would oblige his sole heir, his sister who was now remarried to an engineer, to request a correction before a civil tribunal on February 27, 1815, in order to claim the American inheritance.

THE ESTATE

After news of Duportail's death reached America, the court appointed Isaac Huddleston as administrator of the estate on February 3, 1803. His account of revenues and expenditures dated January 1804 mentions under "Disbursements" the sum of "117 pounds 17 shillings and 6 pence" given to several persons in the lifetime of Louis L. Duportail, agreeable to his instructions when he left America, in finishing a new House and Barn and digging a well, which were left unfinished by him—and other improvements on his farm, & harvesting and threshing his grain etc.[9]

Huddleston charged £37.10 for managing the estate, which, with commissions, fees, and so on, brought disbursements up to £227.17.9. This sum was paid by the sale of the accumulated hay, oats, and rye and by collecting numerous lesser and greater debts scattered among surrounding farmers. There appear to have been no outstanding obligations against the estate.

The list of books taken from the inventory of Duportail's estate included

> Smith's *Wealth of Nations*
> *Our Own Gardiner*
> *Roads and Dictionary*
> *Rural Economy*
> *Hints to Gentlemen of Property*
> Leslie's *Husbandry*
> *Inquiries on Plaster of Paris*
> *The Famous Kalendar*
> *Practical Farmer*
> *Vindication of Randolph*
> *Speech of Ames in ye House of Rs.*
> *Sketch on Rotation of Crops*
> *Progress and State of the Canal Navigation in Penna.*
> *Description of certain lands in Massachusetts*

Disquisition concerning Ancient India
On Fattening of Cattle
Douglas (a tragedy)

His French books included

Dictionnaire du jardinage
Theorie du jardinage
Boyle's Dictionary in French and English
Les éléments de la langue anglaise
Nouvelle grammaire allemande
Dictionnaire de Bromare—fifteen volumes
Guide du Voyageur en Suisse
Constitution of the French Republic
Testament politique
Map of Connecticut
A French Map
Map of Pennsylvania[10]

These books were all so worn from constant use that the appraiser found it difficult to set a value on them. The lot was finally sold for ten dollars. Duportail must have spent much of his free time poring over these books, especially whatever pertained to the cultivation of his farm. At the time of his death, his barns were full of hay, rye (threshed and unthreshed), oats, old rye straw, and more. He always kept horses, usually six, but the number and value varied during the five years the tax lists contained his name. He usually had at least four cows, but the number sometimes dropped to two, then rose to six. This shows that he was not averse to a "trade" when the right opportunity arose. His farm and dwelling were assessed at $1,746 in 1796, but the assessment rose to $1,996 in 1799, undoubtedly owing to the improvements made during that time.

The sheriff of Montgomery County sold the rest of Duportail's real estate at auction in 1805. The property and a few articles netted £63.22.47. Elisha Evans, who kept the Rising Sun Inn at the Norristown end of Schuylkill Ford, purchased the property and laid out the tract in town lots. He called the place Evansville, which was later changed to Bridgeport. The proceeds were sent to Duportail's elder brother, "A. G. Le Begue de Presle," the doctor in the Duportail family who died in 1807. It does not seem that he ever received the inheritance.

ESTATE SETTLEMENT

Duportail's attorney, Peter S. Duponceau, came to America with Beaumarchais in Beaumarchais's ship, the *Flamand*, as a young man of seventeen and arrived at Valley Forge in February 1778. He eventually became an American citizen. Beaumarchais introduced him to Baron von Steuben as interpreter, as the boy was a fluent linguist. Von Steuben and Duponceau were lodged at Cressbrook farm, two miles from Washington's headquarters; Duportail also lived there during his stay at Valley Forge. Duponceau married an American and settled in Philadelphia, where he became a successful lawyer.

Duponceau signed the report of Duportail's estate and distributed the property among his heirs. He also settled an outstanding account of Robert Porter, "administrator *de bonis non*," for "sundry sums received at various times," amounting to $3,191.91 and dated September 28, 1811.[11] After deducting fees, commissions, and other state charges, including "postage on two letters to A. G. Le Begue de Presle," Duponceau appropriated what remained of the earlier sum ($2,949.15¼) as his own lawyer's fee.

The list of heirs would only be definitively established on April 14, 1840, and included his sister, still living; a niece; and two great nieces. John C. Calhoun presented a petition to the US Senate on behalf of the heirs of Major General Duportail, Brigadier General Armand, and Major de La Colombe, requesting warrants for their bounty lands on January 7, 1841.[12]

The Committee on Public Lands met on January 19 and filed a report (no. 96), accompanied by a bill that was read and passed to a second reading. The bill directed the issuing of warrants "for the bounty land due on account of the services of Major General Duportail, Brigadier General Armand, and Major De la Colombe."[13]

The Committee on Private Land Claims requested on February 12, 1841, that the matter be referred to the Committee on Revolutionary Claims. The Committee on Revolutionary Claims read the bill (no. 55) twice on December 29, 1841, and decided to address it as a Committee of the Whole House the following day.[14] The same day, the House of Representatives, Twenty-Seventh Congress, second session, considered the bill (H.R. 55) to issue the bounty land due on account of the services of Major General Duportail, Brigadier General Armand, and Major de La Colombe. The matter apparently was still not settled by January 28, 1842, when the Senate Committee on Public Lands considered it again (S. 150 and S. 213).[15]

At the time of his unusual death, Duportail disappeared completely from human memory, in the greatest anonymity, in the greatest indifference, without earthly burial, without military honors, without a dedicated monument to his glory in service to France and the United States, and without intervention of his brothers in arms to honor and recall his memory. The media of the time forgot him completely. Only the US Army Corps of Engineers continues to remember him each year on May 11 as the man who created and commanded the prestigious corps and played such an important and decisive role for the liberty of the American people and the birth of the United States of America.

APPENDIX A:
CARGOES OF TWO OF BEAUMARCHAIS'S SHIPS SENT TO AMERICA

AMPHITRITE

Sailed from Le Havre for Dominica (Haiti) on December 14, 1776

- 52 bronze guns (four- and six-pounders), their carriages and fore-carriages, etc.
- 20,160 four-pound cannonballs
- 9,000 grenades
- 24,000 pounds of lead balls
- 2,900 spades
- 239 iron shovels
- 2,900 pickaxe mattocks
- 500 rock picks
- 484 pick heads
- 1,000 mattocks
- 300 hatchets
- 1,500 bill hooks
- 5 miner's drills
- 12 iron pincers
- 10 pistols
- 4 scoops (surgical instruments)
- 6 priming wires
- 2 iron wedges
- 4 pickaxes (sage-leaved)
- 15 crescent-shaped axes
- 5 shears
- 4 punches

- 2 rammers
- 6,132 muskets
- 255,000 gun flints
- 5,000 worms (tools for removing debris from the barrels of firearms)
- 12,648 iron balls for cartridges
- 345 grapeshot
- 1,000 pounds of tinder
- 200 levers
- 37 bales of tent covers
- 12,000 pounds of gunpowder
- 5 bales of blankets
- 925 tents
- clothing for 12,000 men
- 5,700 stands of arms

MERCURE

Sailed from Nantes on February 4, 1777

- 11,987 stands of arms
- 1,000 barrels (50 tons) of gunpowder
- 11,000 flints
- 57 bales, 4 cases, and 2 boxes of cloth
- 48 bales of woolens and linens
- 9 bales of handkerchiefs
- thread, cotton, and printed linens
- 2 cases of shoes
- 1 box of buttons and buckles
- 1 case of sherry, oil, etc.
- 1 box lawn
- 1 case of needles and silk neckcloths
- caps, stockings, blankets, and other necessary articles for clothing the troops

APPENDIX B:
CHIEFS OF THE CORPS OF
ENGINEERS, 1774–1893

Note that in this document, Duportail's name is spelled *Lewis* instead of *Louis*.

Name	Rank	Title	Date of Appointment	Where Appointed From
Richard Gridley	Colonel	Chief Engineer	June, 1775	Mass.
Rufus Putnam	"	"	Aug. 5, 1776	"
Lewis du Portail	"	"	July 22, 1777	France
Lewis du Portail	Brig. Gen.	"	Nov. 17, 1777	"
Lewis du Portail	Maj. Gen.	"	Nov. 16, 1781	"
Stephen Rochefontaine	Lt.-Col.	Comdr. Corps of Artillerists and Engineers	Feb. 26, 1795	——
Henry Burbeck	"	Comdr. 1st Regt. Corps Artillerists and Engineers	May 7, 1798	Mass.
Jonathan Williams	"	Principal Engineer	July 8, 1802	Penn.
Jonathan Williams	"	Chief Engineer	April 19, 1805	"
Jonathan Williams	Colonel	"	Feb. 23, 1808	"
Joseph G. Swift	"	"	July 31, 1812	Mass.
Walker K. Armistead	"	"	Nov. 12, 1818	Va.
Alexander Macomb	"	"	June 1, 1821	New York
Charles Gratiot	"	"	May 28, 1828	Mo. Ter.
Joseph G. Totten	"	"	Dec. 7, 1838	Conn.
J. J. Abert	"	Chief Top. Engineer	July 7, 1838	D.C.
Stephen H. Long	"	"	Sept. 9, 1861	New Hamp.
Joseph G. Totten	Brig. Gen.	Chief Engineer	Mar. 3, 1863	Conn.

Richard Delafield	"	"	April 22, 1864	New York
Richard Delafield	"	Chief of Engineers	July 13, 1866	"
Andrew A. Humphreys	"	"	Aug. 8, 1866	Penn.
Horatio G. Wright	"	"	June 30, 1879	Conn.
John Newton	"	"	Mar. 6, 1884	Va.
James C. Duane	"	"	Oct. 11, 1886	New York
Thomas L. Casey	"	"	July 6, 1888	R.I.

Source: Henry L. Abbot, "The Corps of Engineers," *Journal of the Military Service Institution of the United States* 15, no. 68 (March 1894): 413–27.

NOTES

INTRODUCTION

1. Henri Doniol, *Histoire de la participation de la France à l'établissement des États-Unis d'Amérique. Correspondance diplomatique et documents* (Paris: Imprimerie nationale, 1886–1892), 1:402–19; Elizabeth Sarah Kite, *Brigadier-General Louis Lebègue Duportail, Commandant of Engineers in the Continental Army, 1777–1783* (Baltimore: Johns Hopkins Press, 1933), 57–61.

2. Letter from London to Count de Vergennes, April 26, 1776, in Doniol, *Histoire*, 1:413–14. A letter from Arthur Lee dated June 21, 1776, stated that the British Army in America consisted of 40,000 men and a fleet of 100 ships, that they were well supplied with artillery and stores, and that they had good officers and engineers. He also emphasized the difficulty of resisting such forces without assistance from France, with officers, engineers, and large ships of war. Pierre Augustin Caron de Beaumarchais, *For the Good of Mankind: Pierre-Augustin Caron de Beaumarchais Political Correspondence Relative to the American Revolution*, comp., ed., and trans. Antoinette Shewmake (Lanham, MD: University Press of America, 1987), 136; Silas Deane, *The Deane Papers . . . 1774–[1790]*, ed. Charles Isham (New York: Printed for the Society, 1887–1890), 3:297; Record Group 76, Records Relating to French Spoliation Claims, 1791–1821.

3. Deane, *Deane Papers*, 1:119.

4. Pierre Augustin Caron de Beaumarchais, *Correspondance [de] Beaumarchais*, ed. Brian N. Morton and Donald C. Spinelli (Paris: A.-G. Nizet, 1969–), 2:241–44; Beaumarchais, *Good of Mankind*, 157; Etienne Dennery, ed., *Beaumarchais (Catalog of the 1966 Exposition)* (Paris: Bibliothèque Nationale, 1966), MS 327; H.R. Res. 220, 20th Cong., 1st Sess. (April 1828), 24–25; Francis Wharton, ed., *Revolutionary Diplomatic Correspondence of the United States* (Washington, DC: US Government Printing Office, 1889), 2:129.

5. Otis Grant Hammond, ed., *Letters and Papers of Major-General John Sullivan, Continental Army* (Concord: New Hampshire Historical Society, 1930), 1:407; US

Continental Congress et al., *Journals of the Continental Congress, 1774–1789* (Washington, DC: US Government Printing Office, 1904), vol. 8, 528, 537.

6. US Continental Congress et al., *Journals*, 8:537.

7. US Continental Congress et al., *Journals*, 8:553.

8. US Continental Congress et al., *Journals*, 8:569.

9. Duportail has been universally ignored by American historians. This seems curious when one considers that the names of de Kalb, Pulaski, von Steuben, and Kosciuszko, not to mention Lafayette and Rochambeau, are known to everyone. Perhaps Duportail was somewhat to blame for this neglect. Cold and reserved toward the other officers, he was too highly trained and his judgment too much valued by Washington for him ever to be popular. Though he avoided disparaging remarks regarding his brother officers, one senses in his memorials that he was secretly amazed at their shortcomings. He must have spoken openly of these things in his letters to the minister of war, the Comte de Saint-Germain, but these letters have not been preserved.

In writing to his successor, the Prince de Montbarey, on August 10, 1778, Duportail says,

> I have reason to fear that neither you, Monseigneur, nor your predecessor, M. de St. Germain, have seen the letters or memorials and plans of battles I have had the honor of addressing to both of you, conformably to the orders given me by M. de St. Germain to relate to him all that took place under my observation and add thereto my remarks. Probably the vessels which carried my despatches have been captured, or if not, as I always required the word of honor of those to whom I entrusted them to throw them into the sea in the event of an untoward encounter, perhaps as soon as they perceived a vessel, whether hostile or friendly, they may have begun by getting rid of my packet.

Copy in the hand of M. de La Radière, *Archives des Affaires Étrangères, États-Unis* 4, no. 37, folio 2r; Benjamin Franklin Stevens, *B. F. Stevens's Facsimiles of Manuscripts in European Archives Relating to America, 1773–1783: With Descriptions, Editorial Notes, Collations, References and Translations* (Wilmington, DE: Mellifont Press, 1970), vol. 22, no. 1936.

CHAPTER 1

1. *Duportail* is the form of the name Louis chose to sign his letters and documents. He was registered as "Le Bègue du Portail" when he entered engineering school at Mézières, but a registrar transformed it into "Le Bègue duPortail," and school documents noted him simply as "Duportail." Also, his title of chevalier does not appear on any of his civil or notarized documents. The title appears in his nomination papers for the school but was not used after the death of his father.

2. On Rue du Bouloy, now Rue de Sèvres.

3. *Archives des Affaires Étrangères, États-Unis* 4, no. 73, folio 211; Benjamin Franklin Stevens, B. F. *Stevens's Facsimiles of Manuscripts in European Archives Relating to America, 1773–1783: With Descriptions, Editorial Notes, Collations, References and Translations* (Wilmington, DE: Mellifont Press, 1970), vol. 22, no. 1936.

4. US Department of State, *The Diplomatic Correspondence of the American Revolution: Being the Letters of Benjamin Franklin, Silas Deane, John Adams, John Jay, Arthur Lee, William Lee, Ralph Izard, Francis Dana, William Carmichael, Henry Laurens, John Laurens, M. Dumas, and Others, Concerning the Foreign Relations of the United States during the Whole Revolution: Together with the Letters in Reply from the Secret Committee of Congress, and the Secretary of Foreign Affairs: Also the Entire Correspondence of the French Ministers, Gérard and Luzerne, with Congress: Published under the Direction of the President of the United States, from the Original Manuscripts in the Department of State, Conformably to a Resolution of Congress, of March 27th, 1818*, edited by Jared Sparks (Boston: N. Hale and Gray & Bowen, 1829), 1:265–66.

5. Agreement between the American Commissioners and Duportail, Laumoy, and Gouvion, copy: National Archives; draft: American Philosophical Society; transcript: National Archives. See Benjamin Franklin, *The Papers of Benjamin Franklin*, ed. Leonard W. Labaree and Whitfield J. Bell Jr. (New Haven, CT: Yale University Press, 1959), http://franklinpapers.org, 23:315.

6. *Archives des Affaires Étrangères, États-Unis* 2, no. 66, folio 9r; Stevens, *Facsimiles*, 7:652. The engineers had hoped to sail on one of Beaumarchais's ships, but four of the ships sailed before February 15, and none was ready after that date until the end of April. The *Seine*, the third of Beaumarchais's ships to sail and the last to attempt to land its cargo on the shores of North America, was the only one lost, captured by the British and part of its cargo confiscated. Most of it had landed at Martinique.

7. Lovell to Washington, July 24, 1777, in US Continental Congress et al., *Journals of the Continental Congress, 1774–1789* (Washington, DC: US Government Printing Office, 1904), 8:539, 558–59, 571, 760; George Washington, *The Papers of George Washington*, ed. Philander D. Chase, Revolutionary War Series (Charlottesville: University Press of Virginia, 1985), 10:389.

8. George Washington to Major General Horatio Gates, Coryells Ferry, July 29, 1777.

9. Washington, *Papers*, 11:225, 11:251.

10. Washington, *Papers*, 10:650. George Washington wrote to John Hancock on August 17, 1777, to inform him that Colonel Duportail had made several requests for horses and servants to accomplish their tasks and that he had to loan some to them, as they expected to find these things available at the public expense. The *Journals of Congress*, in an entry for July 5, 1777, ordered

that another warrant be drawn by the president on the auditor general, in favour of Richard Ellis, for 700 dollars, being in full of a bill drawn by his Excellency Governor Casswell, of North Carolina in part of the expenses of horses, carriages and other necessaries furnished Colonel Derford and five other French gentlemen of his party on their journey from thence to Philadelphia, to be charged to the said Governor.

11. US Continental Congress, *Papers of the Continental Congress, 1774–1789* (Washington, DC: National Archives, National Archives and Records Service, General Services Administration, 1985), vol. 8, no. 4, folio 9r. English translation signed by Duportail.

12. British National Archives, *Colonial Office Papers*, 1777, 5:2; Paul K. Walker, *Engineers of Independence: A Documentary History of the Army Engineers in the American Revolution, 1775–1783* (Washington, DC: Historical Division, Office of Administrative Services, Office of the Chief of Engineers, 1981), 175–77; Arthur P. Watts, "A Newly Discovered Letter of Brigadier-General Duportail," *Pennsylvania History: A Journal of Mid-Atlantic Studies* 1, no. 2 (April 1934): 101–6.

13. Henry Laurens to George Washington, November 19, 1777, in US Continental Congress et al., *Journals*, 9:900–901, 932; Washington, *Papers*, 12:319.

CHAPTER 2

1. William Spohn Baker, ed., *Itinerary of General Washington: From June 15, 1775, to December 23, 1783* (Lambertville, NJ: Hunterdon House, 1970), 106.

2. George Washington, letter to the president of Congress, November 16, 1778, in George Washington, *The Papers of George Washington*, ed. Philander D. Chase, Revolutionary War Series (Charlottesville: University Press of Virginia, 1985), 18:168.

3. Paul K. Walker, *Engineers of Independence: A Documentary History of the Army Engineers in the American Revolution, 1775–1783* (Washington, DC: Historical Division, Office of Administrative Services, Office of the Chief of Engineers, 1981), 178–79; Washington, *Papers*, 12:387–88. Contemporary translation by John Laurens. The original in French is signed Le Chr. du Portail.

4. Baker, *Itinerary*, 106.

5. Nathanael Greene, *The Papers of General Nathanael Greene*, ed. Richard K. Showman, Margaret Cobb, Robert E. McCarthy, Joyce Boulind, Noel P. Conlon, and Nathaniel N. Shipton (Chapel Hill: University of North Carolina Press, for the Rhode Island Historical Society, 1976), 2:229; Washington, *Papers*, 12:500.

6. Walker, *Engineers of Independence*, 179–82; Washington, *Papers*, 12:457–59. In the original French, the name is signed by the writer, Duportail. Contemporary translation by John Laurens. The omissions indicated relate to conditions that might have arisen but did not materialize.

7. Marquis de Lafayette, "Letters from the Marquis de Lafayette to Hon. Henry Laurens, 1777–1780," *South Carolina Historical and Genealogical Magazine* 7, no. 2 (April 1906): 65.

8. Washington, *Papers*, 12:506.

9. Walker, *Engineers of Independence*, 182–83; Washington, *Papers*, 12:515–16.

10. Baker, *Itinerary*, 108.

11. General orders, in Washington, *Papers*, 12:620–21.

12. May 16, 1778, in Benjamin Franklin, *The Papers of Benjamin Franklin*, ed. Leonard W. Labaree and Whitfield J. Bell Jr. (New Haven, CT: Yale University Press, 1959), http://franklinpapers.org, 26:478.

13. Frank H. Taylor, *Valley Forge: A Chronicle of American Heroism* (Philadelphia: James W. Nagle, 1905); Washington, *Papers*, 13:243.

14. Sir William Howe, *The Narrative of Lt. Gen. Sir William Howe in a Committee of the House of Commons on 29th April 1779, Relative to His Conduct during His Late Command of the King's Troops in North America, to Which Are Added Some Observations upon a Pamphlet Entitled* Letters to a Nobleman (London: H. Baldwin, 1780), 30.

15. Elizabeth S. Kite, "General Washington and the French Engineers Duportail and Companions," *Records of the American Catholic Historical Society of Philadelphia* 43, no. 2 (June 1932): 109.

16. Walker, *Engineers of Independence*, 34–36; Washington, *Papers*, 13:262–66.

17. US Continental Congress et al., *Journals of the Continental Congress, 1774–1789* (Washington, DC: US Government Printing Office, 1904), 13:305.

18. US Continental Congress, *Papers of the Continental Congress, 1774–1789* (Washington, DC: National Archives, National Archives and Records Service, General Services Administration, 1985), vol. 3, no. 147, folio 147; US Continental Congress et al., *Journals*, 10:305–6, 14:570–71; Washington, *Papers*, 10:454.

19. Brigadier General Duportail to George Washington, January 18, 1778, in Washington, *Papers*, 13:262–64.

20. George Washington to a Continental Congress Camp Committee, Valley Forge, March 1, 1778, in Washington, *Papers*, 14:5.

21. Paul H. Smith, Gerard W. Gawalt, Rosemary Fry Plakas, and Eugene R. Sheridan, eds., *Letters of Delegates to Congress, 1774–1789*, vol. 9, *February 1–May 31, 1778* (Washington, DC: Library of Congress, 1982), 13:106; US Continental Congress et al., *Journals*, 13:57–58.

22. US Continental Congress et al., *Journals*, 10:114–45.

23. Edmund Cody Burnett, ed., *Letters of Members of the Continental Congress* (P. Smith, 1963); Washington, *Papers*, 14:419–20.

24. Washington, *Papers*, 14:493–94.

25. Jared Sparks, *The Writings of George Washington: Being His Correspondence, Addresses, Messages, and Other Papers, Official and Private, Selected and Published from the Original Manuscripts with a Life of the Author, Notes, and Illustrations* (Boston: American Stationers' Company, John B. Russell, 1834), 5:325; George Washington, *The Writings of George Washington from the Original Manuscript Sources, 1745–1799: Prepared under the Direction of the United States George Washington Bicentennial Commission and Published by Authority of Congress*, ed. John C. Fitzpatrick (Washington, DC: US Government Printing Office, 1931), 11:288.

26. Washington, *Papers*, 14:567.

27. Brigadier General Duportail to George Washington, Valley Forge, c. April 20, 1778, in Washington, *Papers*, 14:562.

28. Brigadier General Duportail to George Washington, Valley Forge, c. April 29, 1778, in Washington, *Papers*, 14:562.

29. Walker, *Engineers of Independence*, 191–95; Washington, *Papers*, 14:559–66.

30. Washington, *Papers*, 14:593–94.

31. Greene, *Papers*, 2:381–85; Washington, *Papers*, 15:83–87. The rationale was omitted.

32. US Department of State, *The Diplomatic Correspondence of the American Revolution: Being the Letters of Benjamin Franklin, Silas Deane, John Adams, John Jay, Arthur Lee, William Lee, Ralph Izard, Francis Dana, William Carmichael, Henry Laurens, John Laurens . . . and Others, Concerning the Foreign Relations of the United States during the Whole Revolution: Together with the Letters in Reply from the Secret Committee of Congress, and the Secretary of Foreign Affairs: Also the Entire Correspondence of the French Ministers, Gérard and Luzerne, with Congress: Published under the Direction of the President of the United States, from the Original Manuscripts in the Department of State, Conformably to a Resolution of Congress, of March 27th, 1818*, edited by Jared Sparks (Boston: N. Hale and Gray & Bowen, 1829), 2:262; Francis Wharton, ed., *Revolutionary Diplomatic Correspondence of the United States* (Washington, DC: US Government Printing Office, 1889), 2:468–69.

33. Washington, *Papers*, 15:414–17; Greene, *Papers*, 2:434–37.

34. Walker, *Engineers of Independence*, 195–99; Washington, *Papers*, 15:439–40.

35. Elizabeth S. Kite, *Brigadier-General Louis Lebègue Duportail, Commandant of Engineers in the Continental Army, 1777–1783* (Baltimore: Johns Hopkins Press, 1933), 46.

36. Kite, *Brigadier-General Duportail*, 77.

37. Washington, *Papers*, 15:514–15, 15:517.

CHAPTER 3

1. US Continental Congress et al., *Journals of the Continental Congress, 1774–1789* (Washington, DC: US Government Printing Office, 1904), 2:59.

2. George Washington, *The Papers of George Washington*, ed. Philander D. Chase, Revolutionary War Series (Charlottesville: University Press of Virginia, 1985), 13:225. The letter is dated October 7 in George Washington's papers, but it was undoubtedly October 8. In the original, one date is written over the other. Washington probably had it copied without first comparing it with the letter to Radière, which was sent first.

3. Elizabeth S. Kite, *Brigadier-General Louis Lebègue Duportail, Commandant of Engineers in the Continental Army, 1777–1783* (Baltimore: Johns Hopkins Press, 1933), 83.

4. Kite, *Brigadier-General Duportail*, 83–84.

5. Major General Israel Putnam to George Washington, Headquarters, Highlands, New York, January 13, 1778, in Washington, *Papers*, 13:229.

6. Edward C. Boynton, *The History of West Point* (New York: D. Van Nostrand, 1864), 61.

7. Washington, *Papers*, 14:219.

8. George Washington to Major General Alexander McDougall, in Washington, *Papers*, 14:236.

9. George Washington to Major General Alexander McDougall, in Washington, *Papers*, 14:412.

10. On November 17, 1777, Congress raised "Monsr. de la Radiere to the rank of Colonel . . . in the army of the United States . . . to be employed as heretofore in the capacity of engineer" (US Continental Congress et al., *Journals*, 9:932).

11. Washington, *Papers*, 14:497.

12. Washington, *Papers*, 14:587–88.

13. Washington, *Papers*, 15:590–93.

14. Edmund Cody Burnett, ed., *Letters of Members of the Continental Congress* (P. Smith, 1963), 3:462; US Continental Congress et al., *Journals*, 10:476. August 18, 1778.

15. Washington, *Papers*, 16:452–54.

16. Washington, *Papers*, 16:386, 16:468. Translation in Alexander Hamilton's writing.

17. Washington, *Papers*, 16:536, 16:594–98. Endorsed "M. Duportail on the North in the Highlands. 13th September 1778." The contemporary translation in the handwriting of John Laurens is preserved in the Washington Papers at the Library of Congress under the date of August 13. The month is taken from the docket on the translation. The French text is dated "13 aout [August]." This is definitely a mistake, as Washington's order was not issued until August 27, and John Laurens was in Rhode Island on August 13, until early September. Duportail's report was delivered to Washington before September 9.

18. George Washington to Brigadier General Duportail, Fort Clinton, West Point, September 19, 1778. Washington, *Papers*, 17:46.

19. Washington, *Papers*, 17:46.

20. Washington, *Papers*, 18:168. The foregoing letter offers strong proof of Washington's appreciation of the services of the French engineers and his desire that they might be retained in the service of the United States. The president of Congress and a majority of its members were friendly to France and to the alliance and would have wished that every courtesy be shown these French officers. There was a powerful minority, however, that dreaded French influence and that sought always to delay measures and to frustrate every motion that would tend to emphasize the importance of the alliance [Paul K. Walker, *Engineers of Independence: A Documentary History of the Army Engineers in the American Revolution, 1775–1783* (Washington, DC: Historical Division, Office of Administrative Services, Office of the Chief of Engineers, 1981), 216–19].

Three letters of Duportail to the Comte d'Estaing have the dates of October 24, 1778; October 29, 1778; and October 30, 1778. These are in the Archives de la Marine; photocopies in the Library of Congress.

21. Washington, *Papers*, 17:181–84.

22. Washington, *Papers*, 17:476–77, 17:504.

23. Kite, *Brigadier-General Duportail*, 136.

24. Jared Sparks, *The Writings of George Washington: Being His Correspondence, Addresses, Messages, and Other Papers, Official and Private, Selected and Published from the Original Manuscripts with a Life of the Author, Notes, and Illustrations* (Boston: American Stationers' Company, John B. Russell, 1834), 6:97–98.

25. Washington, *Papers*, 17:653.

26. Burnett, *Letters*, 1779. James Lovell wrote to Horatio Gates on March 1, 1779, "As to Du Portail's Plan for the Continent at large the whole Treasury of Spain is essential to it."

CHAPTER 4

1. US Continental Congress et al., *Journals of the Continental Congress, 1774–1789* (Washington, DC: US Government Printing Office, 1904). January 15, 1779. The one enclosing a January 27 letter to him from General Duportail "on the subject of fortifying Boston" is in neither the *Papers of the Continental Congress* nor Fitzpatrick's edition of his writings, but a file copy of it is in the Washington Papers at the Library of Congress.

2. Francis Wharton, ed., *Revolutionary Diplomatic Correspondence of the United States* (Washington, DC: US Government Printing Office, 1889), 3:5.

3. George Washington, *The Papers of George Washington*, ed. Philander D. Chase, Revolutionary War Series (Charlottesville: University Press of Virginia, 1985), 19:83–85.

4. Washington, *Papers*, 19:145–46, 19:155.

5. Board of War to President Reed, War Office, February 22, 1779, Pennsylvania Archives, 1st ser., 7:201.

6. Elizabeth S. Kite, *Brigadier-General Louis Lebègue Duportail, Commandant of Engineers in the Continental Army, 1777–1783* (Baltimore: Johns Hopkins Press, 1933), 137–38.

7. Washington, *Papers*, 19:655–56, 19:753.

8. Washington, *Papers*, 19:645–46.

9. George Washington, *The Writings of George Washington from the Original Manuscript Sources, 1745–1799: Prepared under the Direction of the United States George Washington Bicentennial Commission and Published by Authority of Congress*, ed. John C. Fitzpatrick (Washington, DC: US Government Printing Office, 1931), 14:399.

10. Washington, *Papers*, 19:754.

11. Washington, *Writings*, 15:255.

12. Washington, *Writings*, 15:446.

13. Nathanael Greene, *The Papers of General Nathanael Greene*, ed. Richard K. Showman, Margaret Cobb, Robert E. McCarthy, Joyce Boulind, Noel P. Conlon, and Nathaniel N. Shipton (Chapel Hill: University of North Carolina Press, for the Rhode Island Historical Society, 1976), 4:262–63.

14. Kite, *Brigadier-General Duportail*, 140–43; Paul K. Walker, *Engineers of Independence: A Documentary History of the Army Engineers in the American Revolution, 1775–1783* (Washington, DC: Historical Division, Office of Administrative Services, Office of the Chief of Engineers, 1981), 226–28.

15. Washington, *Writings*, 16:93.

16. Washington, *Writings*, 16:93, 16:111, 16:139.

17. Manuscript Department, US Military Academy Library, translated by Lt. Col. Donald Dunne; Walker, *Engineers of Independence*, 229–32. Evidently, there was a map that accompanied this report, but it has not been located.

This draft, written in French and destined for Minister of War Conrad Alexandre Gérard is a major witness to Duportail's talents as a fortification engineer. In addition to depicting his expertise in this area and his technical skills, he knows how to perfectly analyze tactical possibilities of the terrain and possesses knowledge of the forces involved in the maneuvers that each party could engage.

18. Washington, *Writings*, 16:356.

19. The full report is in the Washington Papers under the date of September 25, 1779.

20. Samuel Hazard, ed., *The Register of Pennsylvania* 4, no. 8 (August 22, 1829): 118.

21. After careful analysis, James Brown Scott, *De Grasse à Yorktown* (Paris: Institut Français de Washington, 1931), concludes that Arnold's treason was as essential to the success of the revolution as his actions prior to Saratoga.

22. The Battle of Saratoga was won before France made an alliance with America. It could not have been attempted, however, without the ammunition and other military stores secretly sent from France during the winter and spring of 1777. The French foreign minister, the Comte de Vergennes, never admitted this aid, but the archives show beyond any shadow of a doubt that it was his plan from the beginning to "lay," as he expressed it, "stepping stones" in the hope it would enable France to bridge the difficulties that prevented an earlier acknowledgment of American independence. It was also part of his plan to test the sincerity and vigor of the American people by sending them the means of resistance in a way that could be repudiated, should events turn out differently from his hopes.

Beaumarchais handled the secret aid. Two shiploads arrived at Portsmouth, New Hampshire, during the spring of 1777, and four more reached the continent during the summer, by way of the West Indies. The British captured one ship with her cargo in the fall. The last one brought the famous Baron von Steuben, with his French aide-de-camp, Peter Stephen Duponceau, then a lad of seventeen, who later became an American citizen and studied law. He became famous in his own right, as well as wealthy. Duportail's heirs chose him to settle the general's estate in 1810. Duponceau died in 1844.

For a thorough treatment of the extent of French aid, see Norman Desmarais, *America's First Ally: France in the Revolutionary War* (Philadelphia: Casemate, 2019).

23. Washington, *Writings*, 16:319–20.

24. Howard Lee Landers, *The Virginia Campaign and the Blockade and Siege of Yorktown, 1781: Including a Brief Narrative of the French Participation in the Revolution Prior to the Southern Campaign*, Senate document 273 (Washington, DC: US Government Printing Office, 1931), 51.

25. The substance of the conversation on this occasion was taken down by Colonel Alexander Hamilton, who acted as interpreter during the interview. It is given under date of September 16, 1779, in Wharton, *Revolutionary Diplomatic Correspondence*, 3:318–22.

26. US Continental Congress et al., *Journals*, Library of Congress ed. Entered only in the secret journals.

27. John C. Fitzpatrick, *George Washington Himself: A Common-Sense Biography Written from His Manuscripts* (Indianapolis: Bobbs-Merrill, 1933), shows that after the loss of New York in 1776, Washington's constant desire was to regain possession of this central stronghold of the Atlantic coast.

28. Jared Sparks, *The Writings of George Washington: Being His Correspondence, Addresses, Messages, and Other Papers, Official and Private, Selected and Published from the Original Manuscripts with a Life of the Author, Notes, and Illustrations* (Boston: American Stationers' Company, John B. Russell, 1834), 6:378–79.

29. Washington, *Writings*, 16:483–84.

30. Washington, *Writings*, 16:4–6.

31. Brigadier General Louis Le Bèque Du Portail and Lieutenant Colonel Alexander Hamilton to George Washington, Great Egg Harbor Landing, New Jersey, October 26, 1779, in Alexander Hamilton, *The Papers of Alexander Hamilton*, ed. Harold C. Syrett and Jacob E. Cooke (New York: Columbia University Press, 1961), 1:212.

32. Washington, *Writings*, 16:28. Published in full in Alexander Hamilton, *The Works of Alexander Hamilton*, ed. Henry Cabot Lodge (New York: G. P. Putnam's Sons, 1904), 9:181.

33. This evidently refers to a note sent in the letter. Washington says that Mr. Henry Laurens, late president of Congress, had had the goodness to send him the note, which he enclosed. Mr. Laurens was from South Carolina; therefore, rumors from Georgia might easily reach him. There is no indication what was in the note.

34. Washington, *Writings*, 16:93–94.

35. Probably the chief cause of the disaster at Savannah was the treachery of a deserter from the American ranks who went over to the enemy the night of the eighth. He informed the enemy of the assault and that the real attack would be to the right; the onslaught to the left would be merely a feint. See Justin Winsor, ed., *Narrative and Critical History of America* (Boston: Houghton Mifflin, 1884), 6:470.

36. Washington, *Writings*, 16:110–11.
37. Washington, *Writings*, 16:247–48.
38. Washington, *Writings*, 17:56.
39. *Archives du Ministère des Affaires Étrangères: Correspondance politique, États-Unis* 12, supplement, folio 108; Kite, *Brigadier-General Duportail*, 160; Elizabeth S. Kite, "General Washington and the French Engineers Duportail and Companions," *Records of the American Catholic Historical Society of Philadelphia* 43, no. 1 (March 1932): 25.
40. *Archives du Ministère des Affaires Étrangères*, folio 109.
41. Kite, *Brigadier-General Duportail*, 161.
42. Greene, *Papers*, 5:178; Washington, *Writings*, 17:271.
43. *Archives du Ministère des Affaires Étrangères*, folio 109; Kite, *Brigadier-General Duportail*, 164; Kite, "General Washington," 29. Full text also in Serge Le Pottier, *Duportail, Ou, Le Génie De Washington* (Paris: Economica, 2011), 161–63.

CHAPTER 5

1. George Washington, *The Writings of George Washington from the Original Manuscript Sources, 1745–1799: Prepared under the Direction of the United States George Washington Bicentennial Commission and Published by Authority of Congress*, ed. John C. Fitzpatrick (Washington, DC: US Government Printing Office, 1931), 17:362–65.
2. Washington, *Writings*, 17:339–40. Washington included Colonel Radière in his request, but he reminds Congress at the end of the letter that Radière had died of an illness at West Point on October 30, 1779.
3. Samuel Huntington to George Washington, Library of Congress, in Paul H. Smith, Gerard W. Gawalt, Rosemary Fry Plakas, and Eugene R. Sheridan, eds., *Letters of Delegates to Congress, 1774–1789*, vol. 14, *October 1, 1779–March 31, 1780* (Washington, DC: Library of Congress, 1987); US Continental Congress, *Papers of the Continental Congress, 1774–1789* (Washington, DC: National Archives, National Archives and Records Service, General Services Administration, 1985), vol. 4, no. 147, folio 63; US Continental Congress et al., *Journals of the Continental Congress, 1774–1789* (Washington, DC: US Government Printing Office, 1904), 16:33, 16:39–40, 16:43–44, 16:46, 16:48–52, 16:55–56.
4. Washington, *Writings*, 17:421.
5. Published in full in Alexander Hamilton, *The Works of Alexander Hamilton: Comprising His Correspondence and His Political and Official Writings, Exclusive of the Federalist, Civil and Military* (New York: C. S. Francis, 1851), 1:108.
6. US Continental Congress, *Papers*, 1:36, folio 65; US Continental Congress et al., *Journals*, 16:234.
7. Washington, *Writings*, 18:163.
8. Washington, *Writings*, 18:164.

9. Jared Sparks, *The Writings of George Washington: Being His Correspondence, Addresses, Messages, and Other Papers, Official and Private, Selected and Published from the Original Manuscripts with a Life of the Author, Notes, and Illustrations* (Boston: American Stationers' Company, John B. Russell, 1834), 6:494; Washington, *Writings*, 18:178–79.

10. US Continental Congress et al., *Journals*, 16:316; Washington, *Writings*, 18:178.

11. Elizabeth S. Kite, *Brigadier-General Louis Lebègue Duportail, Commandant of Engineers in the Continental Army, 1777–1783* (Baltimore: Johns Hopkins Press, 1933), 171.

12. George Washington, *The Writings of George Washington*, pt. 2, *Correspondence and Miscellaneous Papers* (Charleston, SC: Nabu Press, 2012), 7:26.

13. See Jared Sparks, ed., *Correspondence of the American Revolution: Being Letters of Eminent Men to George Washington, from the Time of His Taking Command of the Army to the End of His Presidency* (Boston: Little, Brown, 1853), 450–53.

14. Samuel Huntington to George Washington, in *Archives du Ministère des Affaires Étrangères: Correspondance politique, États-Unis* 13, supplement, folio 107; Elizabeth S. Kite, "General Washington and the French Engineers Duportail and Companions," *Records of the American Catholic Historical Society of Philadelphia* 44, no. 1 (March 1932): 40–41; Smith et al., *Letters of Delegates*, vol. 15, *April 1, 1780–August 31, 1780*; US Continental Congress, *Papers*, item 164, folios 350–53; US Continental Congress et al., *Journals*, 17:609–10; Paul K. Walker, *Engineers of Independence: A Documentary History of the Army Engineers in the American Revolution, 1775–1783* (Washington, DC: Historical Division, Office of Administrative Services, Office of the Chief of Engineers, 1981), 277–79. The last two paragraphs are not given in the translation conserved in the *Papers of the Continental Congress*. They are made from the French copy sent to Luzerne.

15. Kite, "General Washington," 41.

16. Kite, "General Washington," 41; *Archives du Ministère des Affaires Étrangères: Correspondance politique, États-Unis* 12, folio 247.

17. *Archives du Ministère des Affaires Étrangères* 13, folio 117.

18. US Continental Congress et al., *Journals*, 17:609.

19. Washington, *Writings*, 19:249.

20. Washington, *Writings*, 19:234. The letter written by Robert Hanson Harrison was read in Congress on July 26 and referred to the Board of War. It was endorsed, "Nothing to be done by the Board." The three enclosures mentioned are filed with this letter from Washington in the *Papers of the Continental Congress*.

21. Washington, *Writings*, 20:69, 20:243, 20:269.

22. US Continental Congress et al., *Journals*, 17:609–10; Washington, *Writings*, 19:234, 19:249–50, 20:69, 20:243, 20:268–69, 20:315, 20:323.

23. Sparks, *Writings*, 7:290.

24. Sparks, *Writings*, 7:323.

25. Washington, *Writings*, 20:323.

26. Balfour to William Moultrie, February 8, 1781, in William Moultrie, *Memoirs of the American Revolution, So Far as It Related to the States of North and South Carolina, and Georgia,* Eyewitness Accounts of the American Revolution (New York: David Longworth, 1802); Nathanael Greene, *The Papers of General Nathanael Greene,* ed. Richard K. Showman, Margaret Cobb, Robert E. McCarthy, Joyce Boulind, Noel P. Conlon, and Nathaniel N. Shipton (Chapel Hill: University of North Carolina Press, for the Rhode Island Historical Society, 1976), 6:471n. The report that Duportail brought was correct.

27. Greene, *Papers,* 7:189.

CHAPTER 6

1. US Continental Congress et al., *Journals of the Continental Congress, 1774–1789* (Washington, DC: US Government Printing Office, 1904), 4:61.

2. US Continental Congress et al., *Journals,* 8:539.

3. Paul K. Walker, *Engineers of Independence: A Documentary History of the Army Engineers in the American Revolution, 1775–1783* (Washington, DC: Historical Division, Office of Administrative Services, Office of the Chief of Engineers, 1981), 34–36; George Washington, *The Papers of George Washington,* ed. Philander D. Chase, Revolutionary War Series (Charlottesville: University Press of Virginia, 1985), 13:262–66.

4. "Louis Duportail to the President of Congress, November 13, 1777," and "Louis Duportail to the President of Congress, Camp White plaines, 27th' August 1778," in US Continental Congress, *Papers of the Continental Congress, 1774–1789* (Washington, DC: National Archives, National Archives and Records Service, General Services Administration, 1985), roll 51; Walker, *Engineers of Independence;* Washington, *Papers,* 13:262–63.

5. Washington, *Papers,* 16:439.

6. Paul H. Smith, Gerard W. Gawalt, Rosemary Fry Plakas, and Eugene R. Sheridan, eds., *Letters of Delegates to Congress, 1774–1789,* vol. 9, *February 1–May 31, 1778* (Washington, DC: Library of Congress, 1982), 106n8; US Continental Congress et al., *Journals of the Continental Congress, 1774–1789* (Washington, DC: US Government Printing Office, 1904), 13:57–58.

7. US Continental Congress et al., *Journals,* 21:1120.

8. US Continental Congress et al., *Journals,* 13:305–6; Washington, *Papers,* 19:266–67, 19:278, 19:695.

9. Paul H. Smith, Gerard W. Gawalt, and Ronald M. Gephart, eds., *Letters of Delegates to Congress, 1774–1789,* vol. 12, *February 1–May 31, 1779* (Washington, DC: Library of Congress, 1985), 463; US Continental Congress et al., *Journals,* 14:570–71; Walker, *Engineers of Independence.* See also Smith et al., *Letters of Delegates,* 9:722–23.

10. Washington, *Papers*, 20:421, 535. For the nomination of these men and their eventual appointment, see "General Orders, 13 March," and n2 to that document.

11. George Washington, *The Writings of George Washington from the Original Manuscript Sources, 1745–1799: Prepared under the Direction of the United States George Washington Bicentennial Commission and Published by Authority of Congress*, ed. John C. Fitzpatrick (Washington, DC: US Government Printing Office, 1931), 15:491.

12. Washington, *Writings*, 15:491–92.

13. "Louis Duportail to Joseph Reed, President of the Supreme Executive Council of Pennsylvania, West point, 10th September, 1779." See Du Portail to President Reed, West Point September 10, 1779, Pennsylvania Archives, 1st ser., 7:690–91; Walker, *Engineers of Independence*, chap. 2, n11, n12.

14. Founders Online, "To George Washington from Captain William McMurray et al., 26 May 1780," https://founders.archives.gov/documents/Washington/03-26-02-0130.

15. Founders Online, "From George Washington to Samuel Huntington, 27 January 1780," https://founders.archives.gov/documents/Washington/03-24-02-0227; Washington, *Writings*, 17:444.

16. US Continental Congress, *Papers*, vol. 4, no. 147, folio 97; US Continental Congress et al., *Journals*, 17:133, Monday, February 7, 1780; Washington, *Writings*, 17:443–45.

17. *Archives du Ministère des Affaires Étrangères: Correspondance politique, États-Unis*, 10:39; Paul H. Smith, Gerard W. Gawalt, Rosemary Fry Plakas, and Eugene R. Sheridan, eds., *Letters of Delegates to Congress, 1774–1789*, vol. 14, *October 1, 1779–March 31, 1780* (Washington, DC: Library of Congress, 1987), 484; US Continental Congress, *Papers*, item 95, 1:76–83; Washington, *Papers*, 11:493–94.

18. Washington, *Writings*, 22:124–25, 22:127, 22:143.

19. US Continental Congress, *Papers*, item 38, folios 355–66; US Continental Congress, *Papers*, item 78, 8:31–34, 8:43–46; US Continental Congress et al., *Journals*, 25:668–69, 25:695, 25:700.

20. US Continental Congress et al., *Journals*, 24:324.

21. Founders Online, "To George Washington from Anne-César, Chevalier de La Luzerne, 21 November 1783," https://founders.archives.gov/documents/Washington/99-01-02-12090.

22. Jean Baptiste Donatien de Vimeur, Comte de Rochambeau, Papers without date, end of 1783, Manuscripts Division, Library of Congress.

23. These two letters are in US Continental Congress, *Papers*, vol. 8, no. 152, folios 337–39.

24. Elizabeth S. Kite, *Brigadier-General Louis Lebègue Duportail, Commandant of Engineers in the Continental Army, 1777–1783* (Baltimore: Johns Hopkins Press, 1933), 246–47.

25. Kite, *Brigadier-General Duportail*, 247.

26. Jules Marsan, *Beaumarchais et les Affaires d'Amérique: Lettres Inédites* (Paris: É. Champion, 1919), 4.

27. Kite, *Brigadier-General Duportail*, 248.

28. Major General Duportail handed this document to the Comte de Rocham-beau a few days before leaving for France to deliver to Luzerne. Rochambeau, Papers without date.

29. Rochambeau, Papers without date.

30. Kite, *Brigadier-General Duportail*, 249–50.

31. Kite, *Brigadier-General Duportail*, 251.

32. Kite, *Brigadier-General Duportail*, 251.

33. Kite, *Brigadier-General Duportail*, 251.

34. Kite, *Brigadier-General Duportail*, 251.

35. Peter Charles L'Enfant, Papers, Manuscripts Division, Library of Congress.

36. John Schuyler, *Institution of the Society of the Cincinnati: Formed by the Officers of the American Army of the Revolution, 1783, with Extracts, from Proceedings of Its General Meetings and From the Transactions of the New York State Society* (New York: Douglas Taylor, 1886), 22–23.

37. J. J. Jusserand, introduction to *L'Enfant and Washington, 1791–1792*, by Elizabeth S. Kite (Baltimore: Johns Hopkins Press, 1929).

38. See Jusserand, introduction.

39. US Continental Congress et al., *Journals*, 26:64.

40. Founders Online, "To George Washington from William Heath, 21 February 1782," https://founders.archives.gov/documents/Washington/99-01-02-07853.

41. Kite, *Brigadier-General Duportail*, 241–42.

42. Washington, *Writings*, 24:42–43.

43. Washington, *Writings*, 24:308.

44. Washington, *Writings*, 25:74–75.

45. Jean B. Gouvion, April 16, 1783, Opinion on Post-War Army, George Washington Papers, Series 4: General Correspondence, Library of Congress, Washington, DC, https://www.loc.gov/resource/mgw4.091_0463_0468/?sp=1.

46. US Continental Congress, *Papers*, no. 38, folios 355–66; Walker, *Engineers of Independence*, 349–53.

CHAPTER 7

1. Elizabeth S. Kite, *Brigadier-General Louis Lebègue Duportail, Commandant of Engineers in the Continental Army, 1777–1783* (Baltimore: Johns Hopkins Press, 1933), 183.

2. Kite, *Brigadier-General Duportail*, 183.

3. *Archives du Ministère des Affaires Étrangères: Correspondance politique, États-Unis* 13, folios 119s; Kite, *Brigadier-General Duportail*, 184; Elizabeth S. Kite, "General Washington and the French Engineers Duportail and Companions," *Records of the American Catholic Historical Society of Philadelphia* 43, no. 2 (June 1932): 121. This memoir is dated at the bottom, "New Windsor, April 30, 1781." The memoir

becomes all the more striking when we consider that General Washington and Congress were on the point of arriving at the same conclusions.

4. US Continental Congress et al., *Journals of the Continental Congress, 1774–1789* (Washington, DC: US Government Printing Office, 1904), vol. 20, 774.

5. Kite, *Brigadier-General Duportail*, 228–29.

6. Kite, *Brigadier-General Duportail*, 229–30.

7. Kite, *Brigadier-General Duportail*, 230. Very difficult handwriting to decipher.

8. George Washington, *The Writings of George Washington from the Original Manuscript Sources, 1745–1799: Prepared under the Direction of the United States George Washington Bicentennial Commission and Published by Authority of Congress*, ed. John C. Fitzpatrick (Washington, DC: US Government Printing Office, 1931), 22:73–74.

9. Kite, *Brigadier-General Duportail*, 231.

10. US Continental Congress, *Papers of the Continental Congress, 1774–1789* (Washington, DC: National Archives, National Archives and Records Service, General Services Administration, 1985), vol. 2, no. 148, folio 289. The report adds, "On question to agree to order their exchange 5 ayes, 3 noes, lost." The question is on folio 292: "Resolved, That the Commissary General of prisoners immediately cause Colonels and of the Corps of Engineers to be exchanged." See US Continental Congress et al., *Journals*, 21:1008, Monday, September 24, 1781.

11. US Continental Congress et al., *Journals*, 21:1086.

12. Kite, *Brigadier-General Duportail*, 232.

13. US Continental Congress et al., *Journals*, 21:1111.

14. US Continental Congress, *Papers*, vol. 2, no. 148, folio 465.

15. US Continental Congress et al., *Journals*, 21:1140–41.

16. US Continental Congress et al., *Journals*, 21:1086.

17. US Continental Congress, *Papers*, vol. 16, no. 78, folio 507.

18. Extract from a letter of Sir Guy Carleton to Comte de Rochambeau, sent by the latter to Washington.

19. Kite, *Brigadier-General Duportail*, 235.

20. Kite, *Brigadier-General Duportail*, 236.

21. Washington, *Writings*, 25:75.

22. US Continental Congress et al., *Journals*, 23:697.

23. US Continental Congress et al., *Journals*, 23:462.

24. Kite, *Brigadier-General Duportail*, 238.

25. US Executive Treasury Department, "Statement of Claims of Foreign Officers on the United States Remaining Unsatisfied at the Close of 1794," Miscellaneous Records, 1794–1817, Manuscripts Division, Library of Congress. Kosciusko came to America in 1798 to secure his claim of $12,280.54. No other engineers are mentioned in the list. Three of Lafayette's special friends who came over with him on the *Victoire*, de Gimat, Captain Capitaine, and the Chevalier de La Colombe, served all through the war but never called for the sums advertised as due them. The Chevalier de La Colombe was taken prisoner with Lafayette by the Austrians

and remained with him in the prison of Olmütz. He was alive after the debts were advertised in Europe. Why the money was not called for remains a mystery.

CHAPTER 8

1. George Washington, *The Writings of George Washington*, ed. W. C. Ford (New York: G. P. Putnam's Sons, 1889), 9:103.
2. Benjamin Franklin, *The Papers of Benjamin Franklin*, ed. Leonard W. Labaree and Whitfield J. Bell Jr. (New Haven, CT: Yale University Press, 1959), http://franklinpapers.org, 34:280.
3. George Washington to John Laurens, April 9, 1781, in George Washington, *The Writings of George Washington*, pt. 2, *Correspondence and Miscellaneous Papers* (Charleston, SC: Nabu Press, 2012), 8:7.
4. Colonel John Laurens's mission to France was to clarify America's needs for King Louis XVI, who was already aware of them. The king planned to increase his aid by demanding 30 million livres from the French clergy when they met at their quinquennial assembly in Paris in June 1780. The funds would allow the colonies to prosecute the war more vigorously. As the king had requested and received seven million livres the previous year, his new demand was met with great astonishment.

The king's commissioner who brought the demand before the assembly emphasized the king's efforts to improve the administration of his kingdom and to make the people happier since his accession to the throne. He reminded them of the king's wise procedures (which they admired) and how the king's economic undertakings made it possible to meet the interest on the loans for military expenses. He also noted that the king created a formidable fleet, the greatest France had ever possessed—all without raising taxes. However, prosecuting the war required more funds.

After the commissioner had finished, the promoteur of the assembly rose and spoke in sympathy with his audience about how decreased revenues and the immense debt already incurred caused hardships and advised moderation of the king's liberalities. He then expressed his interest in seeing France fight for the common cause and his confidence that the king would find means to continue the aid.

The mention of the "common cause" alluded to King Louis's July 28, 1778, innovation in maritime law, concerning the navigation of neutral vessels in time of war. This laid the foundation for the famous League of Neutrals in 1780, proclaimed by Catherine II of Russia and acceded to by all the nations of Europe except England. The assembly voted unanimously in favor of meeting the king's demand.

Colonel Laurens still had plenty to do. First, he had to impress upon the king's ministers the dire straits in which America found herself at that moment and, at the same time, to strengthen their conviction that America would become a great nation able to defend herself and repay her generous benefactor, once free from British domination. Colonel Laurens acquired the confidence of some of the ministers who bolstered his vigorous initiative. Together, they collected supplies valued at two million livres and put them aboard ships. These supplies came from the "free gift" of the king.

Colonel Laurens also received 2.5 million livres in specie to be taken onboard the *Résolu,* on which he would also sail. He was also permitted to ship 1.5 million livres in specie on an American vessel loaded with supplies at Amsterdam. Benjamin Franklin had been able to induce France to guarantee both the principal and interest of the "Holland loan" that was designated to pay for those supplies.

John Adams is sometimes credited for the Holland loan because he went to Holland to secure such a loan. The Dutch were unwilling to risk their money in such an uncertain cause as that of the United States at that time. However, when Colonel Laurens arrived in Paris, his influence and the confidence that his ability and business integrity inspired persuaded France to borrow the money herself and guarantee the interest. Holland had no objection to loaning the money under these circumstances.

Laurens was in a hurry to rejoin Washington's army with the money and supplies and could not to tend to the details of completing the business, so John Adams arranged for the loan. See US Continental Congress, *Papers of the Continental Congress, 1774–1789* (Washington, DC: National Archives, National Archives and Records Service, General Services Administration, 1985), no. 165, folios 116 et seq. and 146 et seq., May 15, 1781. (John Adams later negotiated a subsequent loan of a much smaller amount.)

5. Nathanael Greene to Washington, January 13, 1781; Nathanael Greene to Giles, January 25, 1781; Thomas Bee to William Jackson, February 5, 1781, and February 9, 1781, in Nathanael Greene, *The Papers of General Nathanael Greene,* ed. Richard K. Showman, Margaret Cobb, Robert E. McCarthy, Joyce Boulind, Noel P. Conlon, and Nathaniel N. Shipton (Chapel Hill: University of North Carolina Press, for the Rhode Island Historical Society, 1976); Paul H. Smith, Gerard W. Gawalt, and Ronald M. Gephart, eds., *Letters of Delegates to Congress, 1774–1789,* vol. 16, *September 1, 1780–February 28, 1781* (Washington, DC: Library of Congress, 1989), 692; US Continental Congress et al., *Journals of the Continental Congress, 1774–1789* (Washington, DC: US Government Printing Office, 1904), 18:676.

6. George Washington, *The Writings of George Washington from the Original Manuscript Sources, 1745–1799: Prepared under the Direction of the United States George Washington Bicentennial Commission and Published by Authority of Congress,* ed. John C. Fitzpatrick (Washington, DC: US Government Printing Office, 1931), 21:217–18. Washington wrote to the Comte de Rochambeau, now at Newport, Rhode Island, a few days earlier to introduce Lieutenant Colonel Gouvion and another French officer, Colonel Gimat. They both had permission to go to Rhode Island to pay their respects to the Comte and to see their countrymen. Washington noted they were "officers who have served with distinction in our army, and who, by

their personal qualities as well as their military merit, have acquired my particular esteem."

7. Washington, *Writings*, 21:265–66.

8. Washington, *Writings*, 21:325. Admiral Destouches assumed command of the French fleet after Admiral Ternay's death, so Washington made a sudden visit to Newport to arrange dispatching the fleet to Virginia. Lafayette had already been sent there to offset the depredations of Benedict Arnold, who had defected to the British. Arnold intended to establish a post at Portsmouth at the mouth of the Elizabeth River and use it as a command post to do as much damage as possible to the region west of the Chesapeake. The French fleet would support immensely Lafayette's efforts to deter Arnold. See James Brown Scott, *De Grasse à Yorktown* (Paris: Institut Français de Washington, 1931), 63. See also Howard Lee Landers, *The Virginia Campaign and the Blockade and Siege of Yorktown, 1781: Including a Brief Narrative of the French Participation in the Revolution Prior to the Southern Campaign*, Senate document 273 (Washington, DC: US Government Printing Office, 1931), 38, last paragraph.

9. Elizabeth S. Kite, *Brigadier-General Louis Lebègue Duportail, Commandant of Engineers in the Continental Army, 1777–1783* (Baltimore: Johns Hopkins Press, 1933), 192.

10. Paul K. Walker, *Engineers of Independence: A Documentary History of the Army Engineers in the American Revolution, 1775–1783* (Washington, DC: Historical Division, Office of Administrative Services, Office of the Chief of Engineers, 1981), 294–96.

11. Walker, *Engineers of Independence*, 296.

12. Washington, *Writings*, 21:433.

13. Washington, *Writings*, 21:427.

14. Jared Sparks, *The Writings of George Washington: Being His Correspondence, Addresses, Messages, and Other Papers, Official and Private, Selected and Published from the Original Manuscripts with a Life of the Author, Notes, and Illustrations* (Boston: American Stationers' Company, John B. Russell, 1834), 8:57.

15. Walker, *Engineers of Independence*, 296–98.

16. June 23, 1780, in James Thacher, *Military Journal of the American Revolution, from the Commencement to the Disbanding of the American Army: Comprising a Detailed Account of the Principal Events and Battles of the Revolution, with Their Exact Dates, and a Biographical Sketch of the Most Prominent Generals* (Hartford, CT: Hurlbut, Williams, 1862; New York: *New York Times* and Arno Press, 1974).

17. Papers of George Washington, general orders, July 6, 1781, in Washington, *Writings*, 22:232.

18. Sparks, *Writings*, 8:97–98, shows the addressee of the letter as the president of Congress.

19. Henri Doniol, *Histoire de la participation de la France à l'établissement des États-Unis d'Amérique. Correspondance diplomatique et documents* (Paris: Imprimerie nationale, 1886–1892), 5:513.

20. Kite, *Brigadier-General Duportail*, 197.

21. Doniol, *Histoire*, 5:514–16; Scott, *De Grasse*, 149–53.

22. George Washington to Jean-Baptiste Donatien de Vimeur, Comte de Rochambeau, July 25, 1781, in Washington, *Writings*, 22:416.

23. Senate Documents, 71st Cong., 3rd Sess. (December 1, 1930–March 4, 1931) (Washington: Government Printing Office, 1931), 2:159.

24. Senate Documents, 2:159.

25. Landers, *Virginia Campaign*, 159ss.

26. Washington, *Writings*, 22:425.

27. Washington, *Writings*, 22:425. This note was written by Washington on the back of Duportail's letter. The draft was copied and sent by one of his aides.

28. Walker, *Engineers of Independence*, 298–99.

29. Walker, *Engineers of Independence*, 298.

30. Kite, *Brigadier-General Duportail*, 202.

31. Joseph Plumb Martin, *The Adventures of a Revolutionary Soldier* (n.p.: Madison and Adams Press, 2019), 161.

32. Martin, *Adventures*, 161.

33. Washington, *Writings*, 22:501. When Admiral Graves returned to New York after abandoning the search for Colonel Laurens, he learned that a French fleet of twenty-eight vessels was fitting out at Martinique for North America. Rear Admiral Hood reached Sandy Hook on the twenty-eighth with a large fleet from the British West Indies. That same day, Clinton, Graves, and Hood held a council on Long Island, when they received intelligence that Barras had left Newport with his whole squadron on the twenty-fifth. They decided immediately to combine their forces to pursue both Barras and Grasse. However, Graves had to wait until the thirty-first to get his ships over the bar at Sandy Hook. Grasse arrived in the Chesapeake that same day. See Landers, *Virginia Campaign*, 159ss.

34. Founders Online, "[Diary Entry: 14 August 1781]," https://founders.archives.gov/documents/Washington/01-03-02-0007-0004-0010.

35. George Washington to François-Joseph-Paul, Comte de Grasse-Tilly, August 17, 1781, in Washington, *Writings* (Fitzpatrick), 23:8.

36. William Spohn Baker, ed., *Itinerary of General Washington, from August 24, 1777 to June 20, 1778* (East Sussex, UK: Gardners Books, 2007).

37. Washington, *Writings*, 23:1, 23:79–80.

38. Letter of Grasse in George Washington, *Correspondence of General Washington and Comte de Grasse, 1781, August 17–November 4: With Supplementary Documents from the Washington Papers in the Manuscripts Division of the Library of Congress*, ed. the Institut Français de Washington (Washington, DC: US Government Printing Office, 1931), document 211, 8–11. Scott, *De Grasse*, 243ss, discusses at length the significance of Grasse's intended action.

39. The letter is published in full in US Senate, *Correspondence*, document 211, 12–14.

40. Emil Reich, *Foundations of Modern Europe: Twelve Lectures Delivered in the University of London* (London: G. Bell and Sons, 1904). See Landers, *Virginia Cam-*

paign, chap. 15, for a full and authoritative description of this battle, with maps and more. A letter from Benjamin Franklin to his grandson tells of the effect produced by the news when it reached Europe. He writes,

Versailles, Oct. 23, '81.

My Dear Child

. . . Inclos'd I send you the last Paper from London by which you will see there has been an Action between the French and English Fleets off Chesapeake. It appears even by their own Account that the English have been drubb'd and oblig'd to leave the French in possession of the Bay, and at Liberty to carry on their Operations against Cornwallis. By other Accounts M. Rochambeau was near joining the Marquis de la Fayette so that if Cornwallis has not made the best of his way into Carolina, he will probably be taken with his whole force. [Benjamin Franklin, *The Papers of Benjamin Franklin*, ed. Leonard W. Labaree and Whitfield J. Bell Jr. (New Haven, CT: Yale University Press, 1959), http://franklinpapers.org, 35:639].

41. Washington, *Writings*, 22:101–2.

42. Sparks, *Writings*, 8:155–56.

43. George Washington to Marie-Joseph-Paul-Yves-Roch-Gilbert du Motier, Marquis de Lafayette, September 10, 1781, in Washington, *Writings*, 23:10.

44. Founders Online, "To George Washington from Marie-Joseph-Paul-Yves-Roch-Gilbert du Motier, Marquis de Lafayette, 8 September 1781," https://founders.archives.gov/documents/Washington/99-01-02-06933.

45. Founders Online, "To Washington from Lafayette, 8 September 1781."

46. Founders Online, "To Washington from Lafayette, 8 September 1781."

47. Letter of October 29, 1781, in Kite, *Brigadier-General Duportail*, 219; US Continental Congress, *Papers*, vol 10, no. 152, folio 373.

48. George Washington, *Correspondence of General Washington and Comte de Grasse, 1781, August 17–November 4: With Supplementary Documents from the Washington Papers in the Manuscripts Division of the Library of Congress*, ed. The Institut Français de Washington (Washington, DC: US Government Printing Office, 1931), 35.

49. Elizabeth S. Kite, "General Washington and the French Engineers Duportail and Companions," *Records of the American Catholic Historical Society of Philadelphia* 44, no. 2 (June 1933): 149.

50. Washington, *Writings*, 23:188.

51. Landers, *Virginia Campaign*, 191.

52. Landers, *Virginia Campaign*, chap. 17; Washington, *Writings*, 22:140–41.

53. Great Britain found herself isolated in world politics only once during the last three centuries: when the American colonies were fighting for their independence. French diplomacy influenced Spain and Holland to side with France and America. This eventually led to the formation of the League of Armed Neutrality,

which also included Sweden, Prussia, and Russia and, in turn, led to the victory of the colonies. See John J. Meng, *The Comte De Vergennes: European Phases of His American Diplomacy (1774–1780)* (Washington, DC: Catholic University of America, 1932).

54. Washington, *Writings*, 22:246.
55. Washington, *Writings*, 23:268–69.
56. Given in full in US Senate, *Correspondence*, 146–47.
57. M. le Chevalier,

permettez moy l'honneur de vous presenter un plan des attacques d'York. Je me proposais au commencement de la siège de vous en faire suivre les progrès par mes lettres, mais je me suis trouvé accablé de besogne, et d'ailleurs le colonel armand m'a annoncé que nous aurions le plaisir de vous voir. le jour que l'ennemy a offert des termes je suis tombé malade d'une dissentere qui m'a oté l'usage de la plume pour une dizaine de jours. je commencais a m'en remettre.

toutes reflections faites je prends la résolution d'aller en france par la premiere frégate. dans cette circumstance, Monsieur le Chevalier, j'ai recours à vos bontés et je crois que vous pouvez me rendre service. il sera de la plus grande importance pour moy d'emporter le grade de major-general. cela seul peut assurer en France celui de brigadier; or, le general washington, sans peut-etre pouvoir en faire la demande positive au Congres, luy écrira de façon a luy faire probablement [ ] l'idée de me le donner. peut être sans vous compromettre, vous pourriez faire le reste. il me semble qu'après un coup si magnifique, il serait extraordinaire que le commandant des ingénieurs n'acquit pas un grade; en europe cela sera monstrueux—mais ici on est attaché a l'ordre du tableau d'une façon très ridicule. mon départ pour la France a une autre circonstance qui devrait rendre la chose encore plus aisée, enfin ma qualité d'étranger et de français (dans ce moment, avec des gens tant soit peu sensibles et reconnaissants ce devrait être un bien beau titre) tout cela devrait rendre la chose bien aisée. je demande pour gouvion la commission de colonel, celle de major pour Rochefontaine, au reste je comte partir pour philadelphi apres demain mais j'irai lentement et je voudrais bien que mon affaire fut faite au moins bien en train. je prends la liberté de vous demander des secours, comptant toujours sur les bontés dont vous m'avez déja donné tant de preuves. Je vous previens, M. le Chevalier qu'il y a un certain [membre au] bureau de guerre qui je crois ne m'aime pas beaucoup sans qui je sache pourquoy—mais j'ai des raisons de le croire ainsi. apres tout un mot de votre part suffira probablement pour leur persuader de faire les choses et *de bonne grace* sans attendre des sollicitations de ma part, qui m'oteraient le mérite pour eux et que je n'ay pas d'ailleurs le temps de faire—ne pouvant rester plus de cinq ou six jours à philadelphie. le temps me presse un peu et je finis en vous priant de recevoir les assurances etc.

DUPORTAIL

(*Archives du Ministère des Affaires Étrangères: Correspondance politique, États-Unis* 13, supplement, folio 191)
58. US Continental Congress, *Papers*, vol. 10, no. 152, folio 373.
59. Washington, *Writings*, 23:307–8.
60. US Continental Congress, *Papers*, vol. 10, no. 152, folios 365–66; Washington, *Writings*, 23:307–9.

61. John Hanson to Louis Le Begue Duportail. See Paul H. Smith, Gerard W. Gawalt, and Ronald M. Gephart, eds., *Letters of Delegates to Congress: 1774–1789*, vol. 18, *September 1, 1781–July 31, 1782* (Washington, DC: Library of Congress, 1991), 202.

62. US Continental Congress, *Papers*, item 16 folios 123–24; US Continental Congress et al., *Journals*, 21:1121.

63. US Continental Congress, *Papers*, item 152, 10:309–73; US Continental Congress et al., *Journals*, 21:1099; Washington, *Writings*, 23:294–99, 23:307–8. Also a letter of November 19 from Major General Duportail in no. 164, folio 354.

64. Washington does not seem to have complied with Duportail's request on this occasion. When the Royal Engineers left America in 1783 after the close of the war, Washington sent a message to the Marquis de Ségur in their favor.

65. Founders Online, "To George Washington from Antoine-Jean-Louis Le Bègue de Presle Duportail, 24 November 1781," https://founders.archives.gov/documents/Washington/99-01-02-07442.

66. This report is in US Continental Congress, *Papers*, vol. 2, no. 148, folio 475; US Continental Congress et al., *Journals*, 21:1129. For the resolves announcing the promotions of three French officers in the Corps of Engineers (Louis le Bègue Duportail, Jean-Baptiste de Gouvion, and the Chevalier de Rochefontaine) and commending Washington for the steps he had taken for the "liberation of the southern states from the power of the enemy," see US Continental Congress et al., *Journals*, 21:1121, 21:1131.

67. This resolution is in US Continental Congress, *Papers*, vol. 2, no. 148, folio 478.

68. US Continental Congress, *Papers*, no. 164, folios 362–63.

69. Francis Wharton, ed., *Revolutionary Diplomatic Correspondence of the United States* (Washington, DC: US Government Printing Office, 1889), 4:868.

70. Elizabeth S. Kite, "General Washington and the French Engineers Duportail and Companions," *Records of the American Catholic Historical Society of Philadelphia* 44, no. 3 (September 1933): 273.

71. Doniol, *Histoire*, 2:401–2, speaks of an engineer named Weibert, undoubtedly the same as here. He says, "the 4 april [1777] M. de Noailles transmitted a petition to Versailles of three officers who had been the first to leave: Laiaut de Boisbertrand, Millin de la Brosse, the engineer Weibert, and that of two seargents, prisoners in England."

CHAPTER 9

1. Francis Wharton, ed., *Revolutionary Diplomatic Correspondence of the United States* (Washington, DC: US Government Printing Office, 1889), 5:144.

2. US Continental Congress et al., *Journals of the Continental Congress, 1774–1789* (Washington, DC: US Government Printing Office, 1904), 216; Wharton, *Revolutionary Diplomatic Correspondence*, 5:214.

3. Elizabeth S. Kite, *Brigadier-General Louis Lebègue Duportail, Commandant of Engineers in the Continental Army, 1777–1783* (Baltimore: Johns Hopkins Press, 1933), 254.

4. Nathanael Greene, *The Papers of General Nathanael Greene*, ed. Richard K. Showman, Margaret Cobb, Robert E. McCarthy, Joyce Boulind, Noel P. Conlon, and Nathaniel N. Shipton (Chapel Hill: University of North Carolina Press, for the Rhode Island Historical Society, 1976), 12:335; Wharton, *Revolutionary Diplomatic Correspondence*, 5:814.

5. Kite, *Brigadier-General Duportail*, 255.

6. Founders Online, "To George Washington from Antoine-Jean-Louis Le Bègue de Presle Duportail, 19 February 1783," https://founders.archives.gov/documents/Washington/99-01-02-10672.

7. Kite, *Brigadier-General Duportail*, 256.

8. Founders Online, "To George Washington from Antoine-Jean-Louis Le Bègue de Presle Duportail, 16 April 1783," https://founders.archives.gov/documents/Washington/99-01-02-11074.

9. George Washington, *The Writings of George Washington from the Original Manuscript Sources, 1745–1799: Prepared under the Direction of the United States George Washington Bicentennial Commission and Published by Authority of Congress*, ed. John C. Fitzpatrick (Washington, DC: US Government Printing Office, 1931), 26:355.

10. Kite, *Brigadier-General Duportail*, 258.

11. Washington, *Writings*, 26:415–16.

12. US Continental Congress, *Papers of the Continental Congress, 1774–1789* (Washington, DC: National Archives, National Archives and Records Service, General Services Administration, 1985), vol. 31, no. 149, folio 393.

13. Paul K. Walker, *Engineers of Independence: A Documentary History of the Army Engineers in the American Revolution, 1775–1783* (Washington, DC: Historical Division, Office of Administrative Services, Office of the Chief of Engineers, 1981), 328.

14. Memoir on Fortifications

Should the United States of America have, within its borders, fortified ports which would require a regular siege either by land or by sea to capture? If they should have them, how many and what principles should be followed in establishing all the other fortifications of this country according to its present state, the nature of its forces and those of America? Eighteen months ago, an officer, my compatriot, proposed, in a memoir, that the United States should not have fortified places, that they should only use field fortifications as necessary. It then appeared to me that many people in the administration had adopted this idea.

Regardless of the situation in which this officer found himself, it was easy to discover his motives in proposing such a system. We have to admit that there is something which could create an illusion in supporting his reasoning. He alleged that if the United States had fortifications and the enemy seized them, they could occupy them with few forces and it would become more difficult to expel them than from places that are totally exposed.

We certainly cannot disagree with that, but, for the same reason, we cannot deny that it would also be more difficult for the enemy to first route the Americans from these fortifications to occupy them. The question seems to basically come down to this: is it better to keep one's house well locked? It is not better to leave the doors open to be able to more easily chase thieves who might take possession of it.

If this were the case, fortifications would not be necessary anywhere, no more in Europe than in America. The particular circumstances in which America finds itself require more fortification according to the same rationale of the memoir's author.

He says that the fortifications would require garrisons drawn from the regular army or from the militia which are already inadequate for the many sites where we should be prepared to face an enemy who can move rapidly from one end of the continent to the other by means of their vessels. But it is precisely for this reason that it would be good to fortify the most important locations on the coast so that we might resist an enemy with few men and give the troops time to muster to come to their aid before they are destroyed.

But let's look at the reasoning of those who don't want the United States to have fortifications to see if they hold any validity. Behold. It's as if the United States built more fortifications, forts which the present state of their population, the number of their troops, their arsenals of all types could not furnish or supply, in a word, which they cannot defend.

Certainly, the enemy could suddenly attack some of the fortifications which are insufficiently supplied, seize them and occupy them. But if the United States only have places and forts which they can easily supply and defend, they would certainly have the advantage. I'll even say that they cannot do without them.

In fact, America's grandeur is primarily based on trade, but trade requires vessels to go to foreign countries. It needs to receive foreign vessels in its ports. It needs to begin to establish a navy to protect its coasts and the merchant marine. It therefore needs shipyards, stores, all kinds of warehouses, everything, most of which needs to be collected in the same place for mutual aid.

But if these sites are exposed, the enemy could come destroy these works. That will make all the work and expenses useless. N.B. let's remove all the difficulties. If the fortified ports of the United States could be impregnable, the warnings would be useless. Nobody would doubt that having them was a great advantage.

But, we might ask, can we have impregnable places? Can we make them? Undoubtedly, if absolutely necessary, there is no impregnable place. If we want to suppose that the attacking force were in condition and resolved to sacrifice the number of men, the quantity of munitions, money, etc. necessary to do so. But the means of all forces are limited. They can sacrifice 3, 4, 6, 10,000 men, if you want, and the time and everything necessary in proportion. But they would not sacrifice 15, 20, 25,000 men if this loss would not be rewarded by the taking of the city.

Therefore, if a place is fortified in such a way as to require a greater loss of men and other things than the attacking force is willing to make, it is clear that the place is impregnable for them. It is in this sense that the United States can have them and even have only them. This is how.

In Europe, we estimate that it requires an army of eight or nine times stronger than the garrison to besiege an ordinary place, that is fortified according to the common principles of the art and which does have any particular advantage of location,

Thus, a garrison built for 4000 men at a mediocre site can only be besieged by an army of more than 30,000 men. But what European power could send an army of 30,000 men to a single location in America? Certainly not the British.

But that is not all. I was speaking about a location such as our fortified cities of Europe, most of which were not originally destined to be fortifications, which are not in favorable locations or whose sites haven't been optimized. Their initial fortifications were constructed in the infancy of the art and then improved according to circumstances, sometimes according to certain principles sometimes others.

But here, where there is nothing constructed or on a hill 10 or 11 miles long, we can select the most advantageous sites. I am convinced that we could have some places which, with very few supplies, would truly not fear any European power.

According to all this, I therefore propose the United States fortify well three ports: one in the North, another in the South, and a third between the two. The reasons for this distribution are self-evident (note C). The sites would be entirely enclosed and in a state to sustain a regular siege by land. On the other hand, I don't know which places would be most suitable for their construction. Maybe Boston and Charlestown would be suitable. For the place in the middle, we could think of Philadelphia.

But Philadelphia would require much work and expense. It is very close to the North River which offers a very strong settlement or one which could easily be made so. I do not speak here of New York because I do not know it well enough. On the other hand, I believe, given its location, it will always belong to whoever is master of the sea.

But if the works we are constructing now at West Point were constructed solidly and with suitable modifications, instead of field works, the North River above this location all the way to Albany could provide a safe harbor for this state's entire navy.

But we must assure that it is only a refuge. A warship or a few frigates at the mouth of the river would suffice to prevent your ships from exiting and thus render them totally useless. That is the flaw of all the ports on the rivers which are large enough for ships to remain there without being master of the shores.

Boston and Charlestown, supposing they are otherwise suitable, would not have this defect. I would desire therefore that the third fortified port not have it also. It should go straight to the sea. I hope that the coasts of Pennsylvania, Maryland and Virginia offer some convenient locations. That's what needs to be studied.

Now we have another thing to consider. Suppose that we have three well-fortified ports where most of our merchant vessels, privateers, frigates, allied fleets have nothing to fear from the enemy in time of war, that they are always well supplied and have, in themselves or nearby, sufficient people to defend them, would we do nothing at all for the safety of the others?

Would we leave such cities exposed so that little enemy fleets could reach them without difficulty, take or burn the vessels there and even ravage the cities? Certainly not! But here are the principles which should guide us in this matter.

We have said that the inconvenience of constructing many fortifications in a sparsely populated land, compared to its extent, is that the enemy could find a way to seize some of these fortified locations, allowing them to remain in the region much more easily.

But if we could fortify these sites in such a way that our fortifications would give us the means to block an enemy from capturing them and not allow them to occupy them safely, it is clear that we would have attained the goal.

It is only a matter of knowing whether the matter is possible. It is certainly not everywhere, at every site, but it is at many. Let's assure that we want to put ourselves in safety here from naval forces, fleets. Any fortification which would prevent warships from entering a port, to land nearby, would achieve our purpose without then being turned against us.

For example, I'll cite Philadelphia. The forts which were nearby would have prevented the British from going up river to the city and when they took possession of it by land, the forts would serve them nothing to remain there. Also, they destroyed these forts. Therefore, that is the touchstone by which we would test the deployment of the fortifications for the sites under consideration.

We will ask ourselves, supposing that the enemy somehow captured these places, whether it would be convenient for them to destroy our fortifications. When we think they must do so or, in a word, that they would be useless, we will conclude that our fortifications are well-placed.

These are the principles according to which we would fortify all the other ports or important places on the American coast (except our three large ports). In this manner, supposing the worst case scenario which is that the Americans, for some reason, were not prompt and did not have the means to use the constructed works to repulse the enemy, we would at least have the pleasure of seeing that our works would be totally useless to them.

However, there is still a problem with what I propose in this memoir. Perhaps the plan of three well-fortified ports that might be the cradle of this continent's Navy, which encompass all the arsenals etc. might go against the rights of the different states. Each of these states being sovereign, doesn't it belong to them alone to provide for its defense as it sees fit, to build forts or not? In sum, to construct such fortifications as it pleases? Wouldn't the construction of three fortified places arouse the jealousy of the other states against the three which possess them?

I don't know if these inconveniences are true or false. I don't know enough about the Constitution of the United States to make any judgment on that. All that I can say is that I believe that the strength of the United States depends on its interior union, that in regard to war, the 13 states should consider themselves as one. It would then be easy to show this truth, but I will content myself only with making it in regard to fortification.

The general Congress should not meddle, in any way, in the construction of fortifications of the continent; that each state in particular, having only limited means, be charged with working to its defense as it sees fit and you will soon see a multitude of little fortifications constructed, defective in many ways.

As it will not join forces with the neighboring states, many of these fortifications will become useless or even detrimental to the state where they are located or to neighboring states.

Instead, without considering the borders separating the states, considering the United States as a single power, a general plan of defense of the continent is formulated according to the knowledge of the country, then any constructed fortification would be infinitely better placed or many fewer would be constructed. They could all have the necessary conditions for grandeur, strength, etc. and thus contribute more effectively to the defense of the continent in general. That is the goal which we propose.

Note A—The present time does not give us proof of what I just proposed. We fear that the enemy would head to Boston by land as well as by sea; and as this city is not in the state of defense, the Continental Army is obliged to detach itself from New York and divide itself so that at least part of it might go to New England, in time of need, to join with the local militias to save the capital.

Several considerable drawbacks arise from this division. First it is clear that if Boston were sufficiently fortified to hold out for a fortnight, the Continental Army would have the time to arrive. Consequently, it would no longer have reason to be hindered in its operations.

It could change its position and make movements only after the real movements of the enemy without hindering itself by its feints, by the rumors which spread and even by the appearances which support them. What I just said about Boston should also be understood about all other important locations.

Note B—As long as the United States do not have any navy, it is necessary that the fleets of their allies protect them against those of their enemies. But can the friendly fleets come in this region if they cannot find safe harbor, ports where they will have nothing to fear either from the land or from the sea, where, after a long navigation, after combats, they might resupply, refresh themselves and find all sorts of stores to do that.

Note C—If the United States currently had a port in the South capable of receiving the French fleets, isn't it evident that they would acquire large facilities for expeditions against the British Isles?

Note D—The three fortified locations that I proposed in this memoir would be the natural residences of the Continental troops engaged in time of peace. They would find an occasion to perfect the service and maintain military spirit.

These three sites which would contain the largest part of the navy, the troops, the stores, etc. and which would always be under the immediate direction of Congress would prevent any ambitious plans of the different states, would fortify the general government and restrain the bonds of political union.

"Memoir presented to Congress by Monsieur du Portail," translated by Norman Desmarais. Benjamin Perley Poore, Faucher de Saint-Maurice, and Jean Gervais Protais Blanchet, *Collection de manuscrits contenant lettres, mémoires, et autres documents historiques relatifs à la Nouvelle-France: Recueillis aux archives de la province de Québec, ou copiés a l'étranger* (Québec: Impr. A. Cote et Cie, 1883–1885), 4:438–45.

15. Kite, *Brigadier-General Duportail*, 260.

16. US Continental Congress et al., *Journals*, 25:74n; Washington, *Writings*, 26:480n.

17. Washington, *Writings*, 26:479–80.

18. Kite, *Brigadier-General Duportail*, 261.

19. Kite, *Brigadier-General Duportail*, 261.

20. US National Archives and Records Service, *Papers of the Continental Congress, 1774–1789* (Washington, DC: National Archives and Records Service, General Services Administration, 1971), RG188, item 169, 9:370.

21. Elizabeth S. Kite, "General Washington and the French Engineers Duportail and Companions," *Records of the American Catholic Historical Society of Philadelphia* 44, no. 4 (December 1933): 332.

22. Founders Online, "George Washington to Antoine-Jean-Louis Le Bègue de Presle Duportail, 23 September 1783," https://founders.archives.gov/documents/ Washington/99-01-02-11845; Washington, *Writings*, 27:161–62.

23. Founders Online, "To George Washington from Antoine-Jean-Louis Le Bègue de Presle Duportail, 30 September 1783," https://founders.archives.gov/ documents/Washington/99-01-02-11871.

24. US Continental Congress, *Papers*, vol. 8, no. 78, folio 61.

25. US Continental Congress, *Papers*, vol. 2, no. 19, folio 167. Duportail's letter of October 6 is in US Continental Congress, *Papers*, vol. 8, no. 78, folio 31. See also US Continental Congress et al., *Journals*, 25:669.

26. Kite, *Brigadier-General Duportail*, 272.

27. US Continental Congress, *Papers*, vol. 2, no. 36, folio 237; US Continental Congress et al., *Journals*, 25:695.

28. Washington, *Writings*, 27:201–2.This draft was signed by Washington, but it has a marginal note that is impossible to know whether it was copied on the letter sent. If an organization, such as the one adopted by Congress for time of peace, it should refer to this memorial, but that is not decided at this time.

29. Founders Online, "From George Washington to François-Claude-Amour, marquis de Bouillé. 23 March 1783," https://founders.archives.gov/documents/ Washington/99-01-02-10897.

30. Founders Online, "From George Washington to Antoine-Charles du Houx, baron de Vioménil. 23 March 1783," https://founders.archives.gov/documents/ Washington/99-01-02-10905.

31. Kite, *Brigadier-General Duportail*, 275.

32. US Continental Congress, *Papers*, item 78, vol. 1, no. 19, folios 95–97; US Continental Congress et al., *Journals*, 25:771; 26:42–44. Duportail's letter is in US Continental Congress, *Papers*, vol. 8, no. 78, folio 43. Armand's letter is in US Continental Congress, *Papers*, no. 164, folio 489.

33. Kite, *Brigadier-General Duportail*, 275–77.

34. US Continental Congress, *Papers*, vol. 2, no. 19, folio 171; US Continental Congress, *Papers*, vol. 8, no. 78, folio 505; US Continental Congress et al., *Journals*, 26:42–43; Washington, *Writings*, 27:280.

CHAPTER 10

1. Archives of the Montgomery County Historical Society.

2. Deed recorded at the Montgomery County Courthouse, Norristown, Pennsylvania, quoted in Elizabeth S. Kite and Peter S. Duponceau, "General Duportail at Valley Forge," *Pennsylvania Magazine of History and Biography* 56, no. 4 (1932): 350.

3. Deed recorded at the Montgomery County Courthouse, Norristown, Pennsylvania, quoted in Kite and Duponceau, "General Duportail," 350.

4. Deed recorded at the Montgomery County Courthouse, Norristown, Pennsylvania, quoted in Kite and Duponceau, "General Duportail," 350.

5. Kite and Duponceau, "General Duportail," 352.

6. Kite and Duponceau, "General Duportail," 352–53.

7. M. Auge, *Biographies of Montgomery County Men* (Norristown, PA: n.p., 1879).

8. Serge Le Pottier, *Duportail, Ou, Le Génie De Washington* (Paris: Economica, 2011), 275.

9. Kite and Duponceau, "General Duportail," 353.

10. The papers connected with the settlement of the estate of General Duportail are kept on file in the office of the Register of Wills, Montgomery County Courthouse, Norristown, Pennsylvania.

11. Kite and Duponceau, "General Duportail," 354.

12. *Journal of the Senate of the United States of America, 1789–1873* (January 7, 1841): 87.

13. US Congress, *Documents Relating to the Foreign Relations of the United States*, vol. 23 (Washington, DC: US Government Printing Office, 1905); US Government Printing Office, *United States Congressional Serial Set*, vol. 377 [95] (Washington, DC: US Government Printing Office, 1841).

14. *Journal of the House of Representatives of the United States, 1840–1841* (February 12, 1841): 269; *Journal of the House of Representatives of the United States, 1841–1842* (December 29, 1841): 104; *Journal of the Senate of the United States of America, 1789–1873* (December 22, 1841): 47.

15. *Journal of the House of Representatives of the United States, 1841–1842* (August 24, 1842):, 1395; *Journal of the Senate of the United States of America, 1789–1873* (January 19, 1841): 114; *Journal of the Senate of the United States of America, 1789–1873* (January 28, 1842); *Journal of the Senate of the United States of America, 1789–1873* (July 28, 1842): 129; *Journal of the Senate of the United States of America, 1789–1873* (August 23, 1842): 596.

GLOSSARY

abatis. Sharpened branches pointing out from a fortification at an angle toward the enemy to slow or disrupt an assault.

accoutrement. Piece of military equipment carried by soldiers in addition to their standard uniform and weapons.

bar shot. A double shot consisting of two half-cannonballs joined by an iron bar, used in sea-warfare to damage masts and rigging.

bastion. A fortification with a projecting part of a wall to protect the main walls of the fortification.

bateau. A light flat-bottomed riverboat with sharply tapering stern and bow.

battalion. The basic organizational unit of a military force, generally five hundred to eight hundred men. Most regiments consisted of a single battalion that was composed of ten companies.

battery. 1. Two or more similar artillery pieces that function as a single tactical unit. 2. A prepared position for artillery. 3. An army artillery unit corresponding to a company in an infantry regiment.

bayonet. A long blade that can be attached to the end of a musket and used for stabbing.

blunderbuss. A short musket with a large bore and wide muzzle capable of holding a number of musket or pistol balls, used to fire shot with a scattering effect at close range. It is very effective for clearing a narrow passage, door of a house or staircase, or in boarding a ship.

bomb. An iron shell, or hollow ball, filled with gunpowder. It has a large touch hole for a slow-burning fuse that is held in place by pieces of wood and fastened with a cement made of quicklime, ashes, brick dust, and steel filings worked together with glutinous water. A bomb is shot from a mortar mounted on a carriage. It is fired in a high arc over fortifications

245

and often detonates in the air, raining metal fragments with high velocity on the fort's occupants.

bombproof. A structure built strong enough to protect the inhabitants from exploding bombs and shells.

brig. A small, two-mast sailing vessel with square-rigged sails on both masts.

brigade. A military unit consisting of about eight hundred men.

broadside. 1. The firing of all guns on one side of a vessel as simultaneously as possible. 2. A large piece of paper printed on one side for advertisements or public notices.

canister or cannister shot. A kind of case shot consisting of a number of small iron balls packed in sawdust in a cylindrical tin or canvas case, in four tiers between iron plates.

carronade. A short, stubby piece of artillery, usually of large caliber, having a chamber for the powder like a mortar, chiefly used on shipboard.

chain shot. A kind of shot formed of two balls or half-balls, connected by a chain, chiefly used in naval warfare to destroy masts, rigging, and sails.

chandeliers. Large and strong wooden frames used instead of a parapet. Fascines are piled on top of each other against it to cover workmen digging trenches. Sometimes they are only strong planks with two pieces of wood perpendicular to hold the fascines.

chevaux-de-frise. Obstacles consisting of horizontal poles with projecting spikes to block a passageway, used on land and modified to block rivers to enemy ships.

cohorn or coehorn. A short, small-barreled mortar for throwing grenades.

company. The smallest military unit of the army consisting of about 45 to 110 men commanded by a captain, a lieutenant, an ensign, and sometimes by a second lieutenant. A company usually has two sergeants, three or four corporals, and two drums.

Crown forces. The allied forces supporting King George III. They consisted primarily of the British army, Hessian mercenaries, Loyalists, and Native Americans.

cutter. 1. A single-mast sailing vessel similar to a sloop but having its mast positioned further aft. 2. A ship's boat, usually equipped with both sails and oars. In the eighteenth century, the terms *sloop* and *cutter* seem to have been used almost interchangeably.

demilune. Fortification similar to a bastion but shaped as a crescent or half-moon rather than as an arrow.

dragoon. A soldier who rode on horseback like cavalry. Dragoons generally fought dismounted in the seventeenth and eighteenth centuries.

earthworks. A fortification made of earth.

embrasure. A slanted opening in the wall or parapet of a fortification designed for the defender to fire through it on attackers.

envelopment. An assault directed against an enemy's flank. An attack against two flanks is a double envelopment.

espontoon. *See* spontoon.

fascine. A long bundle of sticks tied together, used in building earthworks and strengthening ramparts.

flèche. A work of two faces, usually raised in the field, to cover the quarter guards of the camp or advanced posts.

fraise. Sharpened stakes built into the exterior wall of a fortification to deter attackers.

gabion. A cylindrical basket made of wicker and filled with earth for use in building fortifications.

general engagement. An encounter, conflict, or battle in which the majority of a force is involved.

grapeshot. A number of small iron balls tied together to resemble a cluster of grapes. When fired simultaneously from a cannon, the balls separate into multiple projectiles. The shot usually consisted of nine balls placed between two iron plates.

grenadier. 1. A soldier armed with grenades. 2. A specially selected foot soldier in an elite unit selected on the basis of exceptional height and ability.

gun. A cannon. Guns were referred to by the size of the shot they fired. A three-pounder fired a three-pound ball; a six-pounder fired a six-pound ball.

Hessian. A German mercenary soldier who fought with the British army. Most of the German soldiers came from the kingdom of Hesse-Cassel, hence the name. Other German states that sent soldiers included Brunswick, Hesse-Hanau, Waldeck, Ansbach-Bayreuth, and Anhalt-Zerbst.

howitzer. A cannon with a short barrel and a bore diameter greater than thirty millimeters and a maximum elevation of 60°, used for firing shells at a high angle of elevation to reach a target behind cover or in a trench.

hussars or huzzars. Horse soldiers resembling Hungarian horsemen. They usually wore furred bonnets adorned with a cock's feather; a doublet with a pair of breeches, to which their stockings are fastened; and boots. They were armed with a saber, carbines, and pistols.

jaeger. A hunter and gamekeeper who fought with the Hessians for the British army. They wore green uniforms, carried rifles, and were expert marksmen.

langrage. A particular kind of shot, formed of bolts, nails, bars, or other pieces of iron tied together and forming a sort of cylinder that corresponds with the bore of the cannon.

letter of marque. 1. A license granted by a monarch authorizing a subject to take reprisals on the subjects of a hostile state for alleged injuries. 2. Later, legal authority to fit out an armed vessel and use it in the capture of enemy merchant shipping and to commit acts that would otherwise have constituted piracy. *See also* privateer.

light infantry. Foot soldiers who carried lightweight weapons and minimal field equipment.

loophole. Aperture or slot in defenses, through which the barrels of small arms or cannon can be directed at an outside enemy.

Loyalist. An American who supported the British during the American Revolution; also called Tory.

magazine. A structure to store weapons, ammunition, explosives, and other military equipment or supplies.

man-of-war. A warship.

matross. A private in an artillery unit who needed no specialized skills. Matrosses usually hauled cannon and positioned them. They assisted in the loading, firing, and sponging of the guns.

militia. Civilians who are part-time soldiers who take military training and can serve full time for short periods during emergencies.

minuteman. Member of a special militia unit called a Minute Company. A minuteman pledged to be ready to fight at a minute's notice.

mortar. A cannon with a relatively short and wide barrel, used for firing shells in a high arc over a short distance, particularly behind enemy defenses. They were not mounted on wheeled carriages.

musket. A firearm with a long barrel, large caliber, and smooth bore. It was used between the sixteenth and eighteenth centuries, before rifling was invented.

open order. A troop formation in which the distance between the individuals is greater than in close order (which is shoulder to shoulder). Also called extended order.

parapet. Earthen or stone defensive platform on the wall of a fort.

parley. A talk or negotiation, under a truce, between opposing military forces.

parole. A promise given by a prisoner of war, either not to escape or not to take up arms again as a condition of release. Individuals on parole can remain at home and conduct their normal occupations. Breaking parole makes one subject to immediate arrest and often execution. From the French *parole*, which means "one's word of honor."

privateer. An armed vessel owned and crewed by private individuals and holding a government commission known as a letter of marque, authorizing the capture of merchant shipping belonging to an enemy nation. *See* letter of marque.

rampart. An earthen fortification made of an embankment and often topped by a low protective wall.

ravelin. A small outwork fortification shaped like an arrowhead or a *V* that points outward in front of a larger defense work to protect the sally port or entrance.

redan. Lines or faces forming salient and reentering angles flanking one another and generally used on the side of a river that runs through a garrisoned town.

redoubt. A temporary fortification built to defend a prominent position, such as a hilltop.

regiment. A permanent military unit usually consisting of two or three companies. British regiments generally consisted of ten companies, one of which was grenadiers. Some German regiments consisted of two thousand men.

regular. Belonging to or constituting a full-time professional military or police force as opposed to, for example, the reserves or militia.

ropewalk. A long, narrow building where rope is made.

round shot. Spherical ball of cast iron or steel for firing from smoothbore cannon; a cannonball. The shots were referred to by the weight of the ball: a nine-pound shot weighed nine pounds; a twelve-pound shot weighed twelve pounds. Round shot was used principally to batter fortifications. The balls could be heated ("hot shot") and fired at the hulls of ships or buildings to set them on fire. The largest balls (thirty-two- and sixty-four-pounders) were sometimes called "big shot."

sapper. A soldier who specializes in making entrenchments and tunnels for siege operations.

saucisson. 1. A kind of fascine, longer than the common ones. They serve to raise batteries and to repair breaches. They are also used in making epaulements and stopping passages and in making traverses over a wet ditch and so on. 2. A long pipe or bag, made of cloth or leather, about an inch and a half in diameter, filled with powder going from the chamber of a mine to the entrance of the gallery. It serves to give fire to the mine.

shell. An explosive projectile fired from a large-bore gun, such as a howitzer or mortar. *See also* bomb, howitzer, and mortar.

ship of the line. A large warship with sufficient armament to enter combat with similar vessels in the line of battle. A ship of the line carried sixty to one hundred guns.

shot. A bullet or projectile fired from a weapon. *See also* bar shot, canister shot, chain shot, grapeshot, round shot, sliding bar shot, and star shot.

sliding bar shot. A projectile similar to a bar shot. A sliding bar shot has two interlocked bars that extend almost double the length of a bar shot, thereby increasing the potential damage to a ship's rigging and sails.

spike [a gun]. To destroy a cannon by hammering a long spike into the touch hole or vent, thereby rendering it useless.

spontoon. A type of half-pike or halberd carried by infantry officers in the eighteenth century (from about 1740).

stand of arms. A complete set of arms (musket, bayonet, cartridge box, and belt) for one soldier.

star shot. A kind of chain shot.

Tory. A Loyalist, also called Refugee and Cow-Boy. The Whigs usually used the term in a derogatory manner.

trunnions. Two pieces of metal sticking out of the sides of an artillery piece. They serve to hold the artillery piece on the carriage and allow it to be raised or lowered. The trunnions are generally as long as the diameter of the cannonball and have the same diameter.

Whig. Somebody who supported independence from Great Britain during the American Revolution. The name comes from the British liberal political party that favored reforms and opposed many of the policies of the king and Parliament related to the American War for Independence.

WORKS CITED

Abbot, Henry L. "The Corps of Engineers," *Journal of the Military Service Institution of the United States* 15, no. 68 (March 1894): 413–27.

Archives des Affaires Étrangères, États-Unis.

Archives du Ministère des Affaires Étrangères: Correspondance politique, États-Unis.

Auge, M. *Biographies of Montgomery County Men.* Norristown, PA: n.p., 1879.

Baker, William Spohn, ed. *Itinerary of General Washington: From June 15, 1775, to December 23, 1783.* Lambertville, NJ: Hunterdon House, 1970.

———, ed. *Itinerary of General Washington, from August 24, 1777 to June 20, 1778.* East Sussex, UK: Gardners Books, 2007.

Beaumarchais, Pierre Augustin Caron de. *Correspondance [de] Beaumarchais.* Edited by Brian N. Morton and Donald C. Spinelli. Paris: A.-G. Nizet, 1969– .

———. *For the Good of Mankind: Pierre-Augustin Caron de Beaumarchais Political Correspondence Relative to the American Revolution.* Compiled, edited, and translated by Antoinette Shewmake. Lanham, MD: University Press of America, 1987.

Boynton, Edward C. *The History of West Point.* New York: D. Van Nostrand, 1864.

British Archives. Record Group 76. Records Relating to French Spoliation Claims, 1791–1821.

British National Archives. *Colonial Office Papers,* vol. 5.

Burnett, Edmund Cody, ed. *Letters of Members of the Continental Congress.* Gloucester, UK: P. Smith, 1963.

Deane, Silas. *The Deane Papers . . . 1774–[1790].* Edited by Charles Isham. New York: Printed for the Society, 1887–1890.

Dennery, Etienne, ed. *Beaumarchais (Catalog of the 1966 Exposition).* Paris: Bibliothèque Nationale, 1966.

Desmarais, Norman. *America's First Ally: France in the Revolutionary War.* Philadelphia: Casemate, 2019.

Doniol, Henri. *Histoire de la participation de la France à l'établissement des États-Unis d'Amérique. Correspondance diplomatique et documents.* Paris: Imprimerie nationale, 1886–1892.

Fitzpatrick, John C. *George Washington Himself: A Common-Sense Biography Written from His Manuscripts*. Indianapolis: Bobbs-Merrill, 1933.

Founders Online. "[Diary Entry: 14 August 1781]." https://founders.archives.gov/documents/Washington/01-03-02-0007-0004-0010.

———. "From George Washington to Antoine-Charles du Houx, baron de Vioménil, 23 March 1783." https://founders.archives.gov/documents/Washington/99-01-02-10905.

———. "From George Washington to Antoine-Jean-Louis Le Bègue de Presle Duportail, 23 September 1783." https://founders.archives.gov/documents/Washington/99-01-02-11845

———. "From George Washington to François-Claude-Amour, marquis de Bouillé. 23 March 1783." https://founders.archives.gov/documents/Washington/99-01-02-10897.

———. "From George Washington to Samuel Huntington, 27 January 1780." https://founders.archives.gov/documents/Washington/03-24-02-0227.

———. "To George Washington from Anne-César, Chevalier de La Luzerne, 21 November 1783." https://founders.archives.gov/documents/Washington/99-01-02-12090.

———. "To George Washington from Antoine-Jean-Louis Le Bègue de Presle Duportail, 24 November 1781." https://founders.archives.gov/documents/Washington/99-01-02-07442.

———. "To George Washington from Antoine-Jean-Louis Le Bègue de Presle Duportail, 19 February 1783." https://founders.archives.gov/documents/Washington/99-01-02-10672.

———. "To George Washington from Antoine-Jean-Louis Le Bègue de Presle Duportail, 16 April 1783." https://founders.archives.gov/documents/Washington/99-01-02-11074.

———. "To George Washington from Antoine-Jean-Louis Le Bègue de Presle Duportail, 30 September 1783." https://founders.archives.gov/documents/Washington/99-01-02-11871.

———. "To George Washington from Captain William McMurray et al., 26 May 1780." https://founders.archives.gov/documents/Washington/03-26-02-0130.

———. "To George Washington from Marie-Joseph-Paul-Yves-Roch-Gilbert du Motier, Marquis de Lafayette, 8 September 1781." https://founders.archives.gov/documents/Washington/99-01-02-06933.

———. "To George Washington from William Heath, 21 February 1782." https://founders.archives.gov/documents/Washington/99-01-02-07853.

Franklin, Benjamin. *The Papers of Benjamin Franklin*. Edited by Leonard W. Labaree and Whitfield J. Bell Jr. New Haven, CT: Yale University Press, 1959. http://franklinpapers.org.

Greene, Nathanael. *The Papers of General Nathanael Greene*. Edited by Richard K. Showman, Margaret Cobb, Robert E. McCarthy, Joyce Boulind, Noel P. Conlon, and Nathaniel N. Shipton. Chapel Hill: University of North Carolina Press, for the Rhode Island Historical Society, 1976.

Hamilton, Alexander. *The Papers of Alexander Hamilton*. Edited by Harold C. Syrett and Jacob E. Cooke. New York: Columbia University Press, 1961.

———. *The Works of Alexander Hamilton*. Edited by Henry Cabot Lodge. New York: G. P. Putnam's Sons, 1904.

———. *The Works of Alexander Hamilton: Comprising His Correspondence and His Political and Official Writings, Exclusive of the Federalist, Civil and Military*. New York: C. S. Francis, 1851.

Hammond, Otis Grant, ed. *Letters and Papers of Major-General John Sullivan, Continental Army*. Concord: New Hampshire Historical Society, 1930.

Hazard, Samuel, ed. *The Register of Pennsylvania* 4, no. 8 (August 22, 1829).

H.R. Res. 220, 20th Cong., 1st Sess. (April 1828).

Howe, Sir William. *The Narrative of Lt. Gen. Sir William Howe in a Committee of the House of Commons on 29th April 1779, Relative to His Conduct during His Late Command of the King's Troops in North America, to Which Are Added Some Observations upon a Pamphlet Entitled* Letters to a Nobleman. London: H. Baldwin, 1780.

Journal of the House of Representatives of the United States, 1840–1841.

Journal of the Senate of the United States of America, 1789–1873.

Jusserand, J. J. Introduction to *L'Enfant and Washington, 1791–1792*, by Elizabeth S. Kite. Baltimore: Johns Hopkins Press, 1929.

Kite, Elizabeth S. *Brigadier-General Louis Lebègue Duportail, Commandant of Engineers in the Continental Army, 1777–1783*. Baltimore: Johns Hopkins Press, 1933.

———. "General Washington and the French Engineers Duportail and Companions." *Records of the American Catholic Historical Society of Philadelphia* 43, no. 1 (March 1932): 1–33.

———. "General Washington and the French Engineers Duportail and Companions." *Records of the American Catholic Historical Society of Philadelphia* 43, no. 2 (June 1932): 97–141.

———. "General Washington and the French Engineers Duportail and Companions." *Records of the American Catholic Historical Society of Philadelphia* 43, no. 3 (September 1932): 193–219.

———. "General Washington and the French Engineers Duportail and Companions." *Records of the American Catholic Historical Society of Philadelphia* 43, no. 4 (December 1932): 289–319.

———. "General Washington and the French Engineers Duportail and Companions." *Records of the American Catholic Historical Society of Philadelphia* 44, no. 1 (March 1933): 1–46.

———. "General Washington and the French Engineers Duportail and Companions." *Records of the American Catholic Historical Society of Philadelphia* 44, no. 2 (June 1933): 118–50.

———. "General Washington and the French Engineers Duportail and Companions." *Records of the American Catholic Historical Society of Philadelphia* 44, no. 3 (September 1933): 262–88.

———. "General Washington and the French Engineers Duportail and Companions." *Records of the American Catholic Historical Society of Philadelphia* 44, no. 4 (December 1933): 311–55.

Kite, Elizabeth S., and Peter S. Duponceau. "General Duportail at Valley Forge." *Pennsylvania Magazine of History and Biography* 56, no. 4 (1932): 341–54.

Lafayette, Marquis de. "Letters from the Marquis de Lafayette to Hon. Henry Laurens, 1777–1780." *South Carolina Historical and Genealogical Magazine* 7, no. 2 (April 1906): 53–68.

Landers, Howard Lee. *The Virginia Campaign and the Blockade and Siege of Yorktown, 1781: Including a Brief Narrative of the French Participation in the Revolution Prior to the Southern Campaign*, Senate document 273. Washington, DC: US Government Printing Office, 1931.

L'Enfant, Peter Charles. Papers, Manuscripts Division, Library of Congress.

Le Pottier, Serge. *Duportail, Ou, Le Génie De Washington*. Paris: Economica, 2011.

Marsan, Jules. *Beaumarchais et les Affaires d'Amérique: Lettres Inédites*. Paris: É. Champion, 1919.

Martin, Joseph Plumb. *The Adventures of a Revolutionary Soldier*. N.p.: Madison and Adams Press, 2019.

Meng, John J. *The Comte De Vergennes: European Phases of His American Diplomacy (1774–1780)*. Washington, DC: Catholic University of America, 1932.

Moultrie, William. *Memoirs of the American Revolution, So Far as It Related to the States of North and South Carolina, and Georgia*. Eyewitness Accounts of the American Revolution. New York: David Longworth, 1802.

Pennsylvania Archives, lst ser.

Poore, Benjamin Perley, Faucher de Saint-Maurice, and Jean Gervais Protais Blanchet. *Collection de manuscrits contenant lettres, mémoires, et autres documents historiques relatifs à la Nouvelle-France: Recueillis aux archives de la province de Québec, ou copiés a l'étranger*. Quebec: Impr. A. Cote et Cie, 1883–1885.

Reich, Emil. *Foundations of Modern Europe: Twelve Lectures Delivered in the University of London*. London: G. Bell and Sons, 1904.

Rochambeau, Jean Baptiste Donatien de Vimeur, Comte de. Papers. Without date, end of 1783. Manuscripts Division, Library of Congress.

Schuyler, John. *Institution of the Society of the Cincinnati: Formed by the Officers of the American Army of the Revolution, 1783, with Extracts, from Proceedings of Its General Meetings and From the Transactions of the New York State Society*. New York: Douglas Taylor, 1886.

Scott, James Brown. *De Grasse à Yorktown*. Paris: Institut Français de Washington, 1931.

Senate Documents, 71st Cong., 3rd Sess. December 1, 1930–March 4, 1931. Washington: Government Printing Office, 1931.

Smith, Paul H., Gerard W. Gawalt, and Ronald M. Gephart, eds. *Letters of Delegates to Congress, 1774–1789*. Vol. 12, *February 1–May 31, 1779*. Washington, DC: Library of Congress, 1985.

————, eds. *Letters of Delegates to Congress, 1774–1789*. Vol. 16, *September 1, 1780–February 28, 1781*. Washington, DC: Library of Congress, 1989.

————, eds. *Letters of Delegates to Congress: 1774–1789*. Vol. 18, *September 1, 1781–July 31, 1782*. Washington, DC: Library of Congress, 1991.

Smith, Paul H., Gerard W. Gawalt, Rosemary Fry Plakas, and Eugene R. Sheridan, eds. *Letters of Delegates to Congress, 1774–1789*. Vol. 9, *February 1–May 31, 1778*. Washington, DC: Library of Congress, 1982.

————, eds. *Letters of Delegates to Congress, 1774–1789*. Vol. 14, *October 1, 1779–March 31, 1780*. Washington, DC: Library of Congress, 1987.

Sparks, Jared, ed. *Correspondence of the American Revolution: Being Letters of Eminent Men to George Washington, from the Time of His Taking Command of the Army to the End of His Presidency*. Boston: Little, Brown, 1853.

————. *The Writings of George Washington: Being His Correspondence, Addresses, Messages, and Other Papers, Official and Private, Selected and Published from the Original Manuscripts with a Life of the Author, Notes, and Illustrations*. Boston: American Stationers' Company, John B. Russell, 1834.

Stevens, Benjamin Franklin. *B. F. Stevens's Facsimiles of Manuscripts in European Archives Relating to America, 1773–1783: With Descriptions, Editorial Notes, Collations, References and Translations*. Wilmington, DE: Mellifont Press, 1970.

Taylor, Frank H. *Valley Forge: A Chronicle of American Heroism*. Philadelphia: James W. Nagle, 1905.

Thacher, James. *Military Journal of the American Revolution, from the Commencement to the Disbanding of the American Army: Comprising a Detailed Account of the Principal Events and Battles of the Revolution, with Their Exact Dates, and a Biographical Sketch of the Most Prominent Generals*. Hartford, CT: Hurlbut, Williams, 1862; New York: *New York Times* and Arno Press, 1974.

US Congress. *Documents Relating to the Foreign Relations of the United States*, vol. 23. Washington, DC: US Government Printing Office, 1905.

US Continental Congress. *Papers of the Continental Congress, 1774–1789*. Washington, DC: National Archives, National Archives and Records Service, General Services Administration, 1985.

US Continental Congress, et al. *Journals of the Continental Congress, 1774–1789*. Washington, DC: US Government Printing Office, 1904.

US Department of State. *The Diplomatic Correspondence of the American Revolution: Being the Letters of Benjamin Franklin, Silas Deane, John Adams, John Jay, Arthur Lee, William Lee, Ralph Izard, Francis Dana, William Carmichael, Henry Laurens, John Laurens, M. Dumas, and Others, Concerning the Foreign Relations of the United States during the Whole Revolution: Together with the Letters in Reply from the Secret Committee of Congress, and the Secretary of Foreign Affairs: Also the Entire Correspondence of the French Ministers, Gérard and Luzerne, with Congress: Published under the Direction of the President of the United States, from the Original Manuscripts in the Department of State, Conformably to a Resolution of Congress, of March 27th, 1818*. Edited by Jared Sparks. Boston: N. Hale and Gray & Bowen, 1829.

US Executive Treasury Department. Miscellaneous Records, 1794–1817. Manuscripts Division, Library of Congress.

US Government Printing Office. *United States Congressional Serial Set*, vol. 377 [95]. Washington, DC: US Government Printing Office, 1841.

US National Archives and Records Service. *Papers of the Continental Congress, 1774–1789.* Washington, DC: National Archives and Records Service, General Services Administration, 1971.

Walker, Paul K. *Engineers of Independence: A Documentary History of the Army Engineers in the American Revolution, 1775–1783.* Washington, DC: Historical Division, Office of Administrative Services, Office of the Chief of Engineers, 1981.

Washington, George. *Correspondence of General Washington and Comte de Grasse, 1781, August 17–November 4: With Supplementary Documents from the Washington Papers in the Manuscripts Division of the Library of Congress.* Edited by the Institut Français de Washington. Washington, DC: US Government Printing Office, 1931.

———. Papers. Series 4: General Correspondence. Library of Congress, Washington, DC. https://www.loc.gov/resource/mgw4.091_0463_0468/?sp=1.

———. *The Papers of George Washington.* Edited by Philander D. Chase. Revolutionary War Series. Charlottesville: University Press of Virginia, 1985.

———. *The Writings of George Washington.* Edited by W. C. Ford. New York: G. P. Putnam's Sons, 1889.

———. *The Writings of George Washington.* Part 2, *Correspondence and Miscellaneous Papers.* Charleston, SC: Nabu Press, 2012.

———. *The Writings of George Washington from the Original Manuscript Sources, 1745–1799: Prepared under the Direction of the United States George Washington Bicentennial Commission and Published by Authority of Congress.* Edited by John C. Fitzpatrick. Washington, DC: US Government Printing Office, 1931.

Wharton, Francis, ed. *Revolutionary Diplomatic Correspondence of the United States.* Washington, DC: US Government Printing Office, 1889. 6 vols.

Winsor, Justin, ed. *Narrative and Critical History of America.* Boston: Houghton Mifflin, 1884.

BIBLIOGRAPHIC ESSAY

Names of French nobles present particular difficulties for American researchers. First, they tend to have multiple surnames and titles, making it difficult to select an access point. Consider, for example, the famous Marie Jean Paul Joseph du Motier, Marquis de Lafayette, or Jean-Baptiste Donatien de Vimeur, Comte de Rochambeau, and our protagonist, Louis Le Bègue (Lebèque or Lebègue) de Presle Duportail. Second, while the American and French Revolutions fought to overthrow the nobility, France was more radical, ignoring all titles. So, in our example, one would search by name [du Motier, de Vimeur or Le Bègue (Lebèque or Lebègue)], sometimes with the article, sometimes without, in France but by title in America [Lafayette, Rochambeau, or Duportail]. Notice also that American practice includes the article as part of the name [Lafayette instead of la Fayette and Duportail instead of du Portail). In some cases, the individuals adopted American practices.

France has relatively few documents about Duportail, to her embarrassment. The Directory sequestered many of Duportail's writings during the French Revolution. The existing documents are widely dispersed. They may be found in the diplomatic archives of the Ministry of Foreign Affairs (archives diplomatiques du Ministère des Affaires Étrangères), the archives of the Bibliothèque Nationale de France, the French national archives, the municipal archives of Le Havre, the registre de catholicité du Diocese d'Orléans, and the archives départementales du Loiret.

Some of the cited memorials, letters, cards, drawings, and maps cannot be found. Some were seized by the British. Others were tossed in the ocean to prevent their capture by the British. Many of the surviving documents are located in the Library of Congress, the National Archives and Records Administration, the Association of Military Engineers, the headquarters of the Army Corps of Engineers in Washington, the National Historic Park of Pennsylvania in Philadelphia and Valley Forge, Cornell University, Yale University, the US Military Academy at West Point, and the New York Historical Society.

Some biographical dictionaries include a biography of Duportail, such as the following:

> Bodinier, Gilbert. *Dictionnaire Des Officiers Généraux De L'armée Royale, 1763–1792*. Paris: Archives & Culture, 2009.

> Herringshaw, Thomas William. *Herringshaw's National Library of American Biography: Contains Thirty-Five Thousand Biographies of the Acknowledged Leaders of Life and Thought of the United States; Illustrated with Three Thousand Vignette Portraits*. Chicago: American Publishers' Association, 1909.

> Lasseray, André. *Les Français Sous Les Treize Étoiles, 1775–1783*. Macon, France: Imprimerie Protat frères; se trouve à Paris chez D. Janvier, 1935.

Also see subject encyclopedias, like Harold E. Selesky, ed., *Encyclopedia of the American Revolution: Library of Military History*, 2nd ed. (Detroit: Charles Scribner's Sons, 2006), initially compiled by Mark Mayo Boatner. These sources usually draw on the only monographic biography of Duportail.

Elizabeth S. Kite, of the Institut Français de Washington (DC) authored *Brigadier-General Louis Lebègue Duportail, Commandant of Engineers in the Continental Army, 1777–1783* (Baltimore: Johns Hopkins Press, 1933). It is the seminal work quoted by biographical dictionaries and encyclopedia articles, but it has long since been out of print. The first four chapters of the book were also published about the same time in the *Records of the American Catholic Historical Society* 43, nos. 1–4, as "General Washington and the French Engineers Duportail and Companions." Elizabeth S. Kite's and Peter S. Duponceau's "General Duportail at Valley Forge" was initially published in the *Pennsylvania Magazine of History and Biography* 56, no. 4 (1932): 341–54. It became chapter 12, "Duportail, American Citizen and Farmer," of Kite's book.

Serge Le Pottier, a French engineer assigned to the US Army Corps of Engineers and the US Military Academy at West Point as liaison officer, was astounded to learn that the corps was founded by a Frenchman. He discovered the important role of the French engineers and Duportail's crucial contributions to American independence. Le Pottier translated most of Kite's work into French, with a view to make this man known in France [Serge Le Pottier, *Duportail, Ou, Le Génie De Washington* (Paris: Economica, 2011)].

Most of these books do not identify the sources of the documents they reproduce. When they do, the citations are often incomplete, citing the work but not the volume and page number. Paul K. Walker, *Engineers of Independence: A Documentary History of the Army Engineers in the American Revolution, 1775–1783* (Washington, DC: Historical Division, Office of Administrative Services, Office of the Chief of Engineers, 1981), reprints a collection of documents by engineers and general officers during the American Revolution. They are arranged chronologically to chronicle the origins and development of the Army Corps of Engineers. Each document ends with a brief citation of source, such as "Washington Papers, roll 26 (microfilm)," or "Kite, Duportail, pp. 201–2." This book is not a biography of any of the engineers, but it does contain several of Duportail's memorials and letters.

Scholars researching Duportail undoubtedly encounter the name of Jean-Baptiste Louvet de Couvray (or Couvrai; 1760–1797). Born in Paris, the son of a stationer, he became a bookseller's clerk before becoming a novelist promoting revolutionary ideas. He was also a playwright, journalist, politician, and diplomat and first attracted attention with the first part of his novel *Les Amours du chevalier de Faublas* (Paris, 1787), part of his *Histoire du chevalier de Faublas* (*The Adventures of the Chevalier de Faublas*). It was translated into English in 1793 as *Love and Patriotism! or The Extraordinary Adventures of Mons. Duportail, Late Major-General in the Army of the United States: Interspersed with Many Surprising Incidents in the Life of the Late Count Pulaski.* The account went through several editions and variant titles, such as

1. *Vie Du Chevalier De Faublas*
2. *The Interesting History of the Baron de Lovzinski, Written by Himself: With a Relation of the Most Remarkable Occurrences in the Life of the Celebrated Count Pulaski, Well Known as the Champion of American Liberty, and Who Bravely Fell in Its Defence before Savannah, 1779: Interspersed with Anecdotes of the Late Unfortunate King of Poland*
3. *Love and Patriotism! or, The Extraordinary Adventures of M. Duportail, Late Major-General in the Armies of the United States: Interspersed with Many Surprising Incidents in the Life of the Late Count Pulauski*

De Couvray's *Love and Patriotism*, his best-known novel, is disguised as Duportail's account to his friend, the Baron de Faublas, about his friendship with Kazimierz (Casimir) Pułaski (also spelled Pulauski and Pulawski). It is a stilted romance, purporting to relate Duportail's adventures in Poland, where his title, according to the author, was Baron de Lovzinski. The author also says Duportail went to Poland after the American Revolution. A subplot details the adventures of Duportail's daughter and "Pulawski," who is described as having died at the siege of Savannah in 1779 and who appears to have been the father of Lodoiska, Duportail's wife. In reality, there are no records indicating that Duportail ever married or fathered any children. There was certainly none named as his heirs or beneficiaries. Moreover, besides the grotesque absurdity of its contents, the book's style is so different from that of Duportail's other writings that it could not have been written by him.

Since the publication of Kite's biography, several critical editions of the papers of some of the important players have been published, greatly facilitating research. Some are still in the course of publication. These sources include:

Deane, Silas. *The Deane Papers . . . 1774–[1790].* Edited by Charles Isham. New York: Printed for the Society, 1887–1890.

Franklin, Benjamin. *The Papers of Benjamin Franklin.* Edited by Leonard W. Labaree and Whitfield J. Bell Jr. New Haven, CT: Yale University Press, 1959. http://franklinpapers.org/.

Greene, Nathanael. *The Papers of Nathanael Greene.* Edited by Richard K. Showman, Margaret Cobb, Robert E. McCarthy, Joyce Boulind, Noel P. Conlon, and Nathaniel N. Shipton. Chapel Hill: University of North Carolina Press for the Rhode Island Historical Society, 1976.

Laurens, Henry. *The Papers of Henry Laurens.* 1st ed. Edited by Philip M. Hamer. Columbia: Published for the South Carolina Historical Society by the University of South Carolina Press, 1968.

Washington, George. *The Papers of George Washington.* Edited by Philander D. Chase. Revolutionary War Series. Charlottesville: University Press of Virginia, 1985.

As *The Papers of George Washington* is only up to 1778, *The Writings of George Washington from the Original Manuscript Sources, 1745–1799: Prepared under the Direction of the United States George Washington Bicentennial Commission and Published by Authority of Congress,* edited by John C. Fitzpatrick (Washington, DC: US Government Printing Office, 1931), and *The Diaries of George Washington, 1748–1799*, edited by John C. Fitzpatrick (Boston: Houghton Mifflin, 1925), still remain the standard sources.

The Internet also provides access to important resources, such as the *Journals of the Continental Congress* and *The Papers of Benjamin Franklin*, greatly facilitating research.

INDEX

abatis, 80

academy, 130–32, 137. *See also* Mézières

Albany, 24, 77, 183

Alexander, William. *See* Stirling, William Alexander (Earl of Stirling)

André, John, 9, 83

Arbuthnot, Marriot, 155

Armstrong, John, 14, 20, 22, 47; Valley Forge, 17

Arnold, 69, 83, 156; treason, 126

Articles of War, 113

artillery, 4, 7, 13, 24, 103, 109, 130–33, 145, 199; battalions, 45; command, 4; Dobb's Ferry, 82; organization, 117; West Point, 79, 81. *See also* cannon

Baldwin, Jeduthan, 92

Balfour, Nesbit, 108

Baltimore, 166, 169

Banister, John, 36

Barras, Jacques-Melchior Saint-Laurent, Comte de, 117, 126, 158, 161–63, 168

batteries, 62, 65, 66, 68, 78, 82, 88, 131, 160, 171; New York, 163; Stony Point, 75; West Point, 64, 79, 81

Beaumarchais, 4, 5, 12, 122, 208

Board of War, 57, 58, 72, 97, 99–101, 107, 112–14, 116, 117, 136, 144, 145, 181

Boston, 27, 59, 60, 68–72, 94, 162, 166

Brahm, Ferdinand J. S. de, 118, 121

brevet, 118–22, 124, 148, 180, 181, 198

Burgoyne, John, 53, 104, 118; exchange, 143

Byron, John, 83

Cadwalader, John, 22

Cambray-Digny Louis Antoine Jean Baptiste Chevalier de, 12, 118, 120, 141–42, 183, 186; appeal, 148; exchange, 108, 117, 140–41, 143–44, 147–48, 176; French service, 149; pay, 149, 189; petition, 146; prisoner, 174; promotion, 124, 175; return to France, 149

Camden, SC, 58, 108, 118

cannon, 75–76, 78, 89; West Point, 61, 79–80; Yorktown, 171. *See also* artillery

Cape Henlopen, DE, 85

Cape Henry, VA, 166, 170

Cape May, NJ, 88

Castaing, Peter de, 12, 100, 119; promotion, 121, 181–82, 186, 198

Charleston (Charlestown/Charles Town), SC, 68, 72, 83–84, 91, 94–95, 98–99, 100–102, 104–6, 108, 118, 121–23, 139–40, 145–46, 149, 154–56, 174, 182, 198

Charlestown, MA, 68

Chastellux, François-Jean de Beauvoir, chevalier de, 161, 170, 197

Chesapeake Bay, 74, 141, 156, 161–62, 165, 167–69

Chester, PA, 20–21, 23, 51

Choisy, Claude Gabriel marquis de, 126

Clinton, Henry, 53, 56, 78, 92, 99, 106–7, 161

Clinton, George, 58, 104

commandant, 13, 32, 73–74, 113–14, 118, 127, 151, 157, 161, 174

communication, 21, 45, 47, 58, 74–77, 87–88, 92, 172, 182, 188–89; West Point, 82

communication trench, 172

Conciliatory Bills, 36, 48

Connecticut, 56, 60, 117, 126, 158, 207

Conway, Thomas, 36

Conway cabal, 118

Cornwallis, Charles, 75, 161–62, 167–69; Yorktown, 171

Corny, Ethis de, 174

Corps of Engineers, 2–8, 11, 13, 31–33, 57, 73, 109–10, 112–14, 116–17, 120–21, 125, 133, 137, 149, 157, 179, 180, 182, 188, 196, 200, 203, 209; disbanded, 137; structure, 129

Coudray, Philippe Charles Jean Baptiste Tronson du, 4, 13–15, 31, 121–22

Council of War, 49, 54, 74

Cox hill, NY, 163

Custis, John Park, 180

Deane, Silas, 5, 13, 33, 44, 46, 48, 70, 109

defense, 24, 26, 33, 36, 53–54, 60, 62–63, 65, 68–69, 73–74, 80–81, 115, 126, 131, 163, 173; Boston, 68; Charlestown, 98, 103, 198; Delaware, 60, 67, 69; Gulph, 25; Hudson, 57, 60, 76; New York, 87, 163; principles, 189; Valley Forge, 24; West Point, 65, 66, 74, 81

defenses, 14, 26–9, 50, 53, 69, 74, 84, 94, 170, 171; Charleston, 101; Delaware, 72; Fort Herkimer, 127, 158; Highlands, 81–82; Hudson, 54; Valley Forge, 28, 35; West Point, 53, 61–63, 80, 81; Yorktown, 170, 171

Delaware Bay, 185

Delaware River, 14, 20–21, 44–45, 47, 49–51, 59–60, 66–67, 69, 72–74, 85, 88, 185, 201

desertion, 44–45

Dorchester Heights, MA, 68

Dumas, Mathieu, 203

Duponceau, Peter Stephen, 122, 208

Ellery, William, 196

Erskine, Robert, 33

exchange, 7, 104, 106–8, 122, 140–48, 152, 176, 183

fascines, 29, 86, 110, 158–60, 166, 171

field works, 131

Fishkill, NY, 58

Fleury, François-Louis Teissèdre de, 12, 122

Folger, John, 47–48

Forman, George Foreman, 162

Fort Arnold, 62, 65

Fort Charles, 163

Fort Clinton, 55–56, 66, 78–79

Fort Herkimer, 117, 127, 158

Fort Independence, 63–64

Fort Montgomery, 53
Fort Putnam, 61–63, 65, 78–79
Fort Schuyler, 158
Fort Ticonderoga, 14, 53
Fort Tryon, 163
Fort Washington, 161, 164
Fort Webb, 62
fortification, 4, 13, 23, 29, 39, 40, 57, 69, 70, 72, 124, 131, 134; memoir, 189; principles, 8, 189; system, 67
French alliance, 5

gabions, 158, 160, 171
garrison, 4, 75, 80; Rhode Island, 86; structure, 129; West Point, 78
Gates, Horatio, 14, 17, 36, 47, 57, 58, 59, 69, 74, 85, 86, 87, 89, 94, 108, 118; Newport, 87; North Carolina, 104
general actions, 39
Genton Jean-Louis-Ambroise. *See* Villefranche Jean-Louis-Ambroise de Genton Chevalier de
Gérard, Conrad-Alexandre, 51
Germaine, George Germain, 155
Germantown, PA, 17, 53
Gloucester, VA, 126
Gouvion, Jean-Baptiste de, 8, 9, 16, 31, 82, 91, 94, 101, 110, 120, 129, 166, 177, 179, 186, 189, 194; agreement, 11; alias, 12; gratitude, 71; leave of absence, 176, 182, 185, 192; Newport, 153; Order of the Cincinnati, 125; pay, 150, 193; promotion, 175, 176, 178, 180; rank, 15; retention, 97; return to France, 117, 193, 195; school of engineering, 112; Silesia, 198; Stony and Verplanck Points, 81, 87; Virginia, 157; Yorktown, 170, 174
Grasse, François-Joseph-Paul Comte de Grasse-Tilly, 141, 146, 152, 154, 156, 158, 161, 162, 165, 170, 174

Graves, Samuel, 162, 163, 168
Greene, Nathanael, 17, 20, 22, 26, 47, 50, 58, 93, 95, 107, 108, 118, 152
Gridley, Richard, 13, 109
Gulph, PA, 24–26, 202

Haldimand, Frederick, 190
Hamilton, Alexander, 72, 73, 87, 88, 90, 98, 148, 149; Delaware capes, 85
Hand, Edward, 126, 198, 205
Hand, Isaac, 205
Hanson, John, 20, 180
Harlem River, NY, 161, 164
Harrison, Robert Hanson, 20
Havard, John Jr., 29
Heath, William, 68, 69, 88, 127, 165
Hood, Samuel Hood, 1st Viscount, 168
Hopewell, PA, 50
Howe, Robert, 83; West Point, 101
Howe, William, 21, 23, 24, 27, 36, 38, 41–43, 48, 83, 101, 126
Huddleston, Isaac, 204, 206
Hudson Highlands, 51, 53, 54, 56, 57, 60, 64, 81, 84, 87, 91, 120, 125, 126, 151, 157, 160, 161, 186
Hynson, Joseph, 48

independence, 8, 12, 36, 46, 48, 63, 139, 140, 152, 186
Irvine, William, 21, 22

Jay, John, 185
Jefferson, Thomas, 113
Jones, John Paul, 183

Kalb, Johann Baron de, 20, 22, 47, 104; Valley Forge, 17
Kingsbridge, NY, 46, 161, 163
Knox, Henry, 17, 20, 22, 47, 50, 76, 170, 179

Kosciusko, Andrew Thaddeus, 57, 58, 62, 65, 66, 74, 83, 94, 118–120, 126, 157

L'Enfant, Pierre, 13, 118, 122, 190; exchange, 108, 118, 121, 142, 148; Order of the Society of the Cincinnati, 125; pay, 189; prisoner, 174; promotion, 120, 122–24, 148, 186
Lafayette, Marie-Jean-Paul Joseph-Yves-Roch-Gilbert du Motier Marquis de, 5, 13, 17, 20, 22, 47, 50, 108, 126, 157, 165, 168–170, 185, 186, 193, 194; leave of absence, 185; Silesia, 198; Virginia, 156; Yorktown, 167, 169
Lake Champlain, 53, 190
Laumoy, Jean Baptiste Joseph Comte de, 8, 9, 10, 16, 59, 102, 142, 175, 189, 194; agreement, 11; alias, 12; Boston, 69; Charleston, 72, 91, 99, 104; Delaware, 74; exchange, 108, 117, 140, 141, 144, 146, 147, 176; gratitude, 71; leave of absence, 182, 183, 192; Order of the Cincinnati, 125; pay, 193; petition, 146, 174; retention, 97; return to France, 117, 193, 194
Laurel hill, NY, 163
Laurens, John, 14, 20, 37, 50, 90, 107, 122, 151, 152, 158, 162, 166
Laurens, Henry, 35, 59
Lauzun, Armand Louis de Gontaut–Biron, Duc de, 160, 187
Lee, Charles, 13, 17, 69
Lee, Richard Henry, 85, 88, 100
Lewes, DE, 85, 88
Lincoln, Benjamin, 72, 84, 94, 99, 100, 107, 145, 149, 160, 170; Charlestown, 102–4; Savannah, 90
Little Egg Harbor, NJ, 83, 88
Livingston, Robert, 185

Long Island, NY, 87, 88, 164, 165
Luzerne, Anne-César Chevalier de la, 84, 92, 102, 104, 117, 120, 139, 141, 177, 181, 187

magazines, 37, 45, 47, 49, 74, 75; West Point, 61
Malcom, William Malcolm, 60
Marbois, François Barbé-Marbois, marquis de Barbé-Marbois, 91, 93, 94, 104
Martin, Joseph Plumb, 116, 165
Massachusetts, 84, 121, 198, 206
Maxwell, William, 20, 22
McDougall, Alexander, 56–59, 127; Hudson, 76
McMurray, 115
Mendham, 95, 96
Mézières, military academy, 2, 3, 13, 31, 129
Mifflin, Thomas, 14, 47; Valley Forge, 17
military academy, 130. *See also* academy
militia, 15, 23, 42, 86; Charlestown, 103; Pennsylvania, 84
Mohawk River, 128
Monmouth, NJ, 50, 69, 162
Monroe, James, 198
Morris, Robert, 96, 166
Morristown, NJ, 90, 92–96, 99
Mount Vernon, VA, 170
Muhlenberg, John Peter Gabriel, 20, 22
Murnan, Jean-Bernard Gauthier de, 12, 34, 68, 113, 125, 126, 189

Nevin, Daniel, 116, 117, 120
New Jersey, 48, 50, 90, 94, 96, 165
New Windsor, NY, 54, 65, 92, 154, 156–58, 160
New York (City), 27, 37, 46, 48, 49, 51, 53, 55, 59, 74, 76, 77, 83–87,

92, 104, 107, 120, 126, 139, 146, 149, 152, 154–58, 160–66, 174, 205; evacuation 104
Newark, NJ, 97
Newburg, NY, 125, 128, 133, 147, 186
Newport, RI, 59, 69, 83, 86, 87, 91, 93, 117, 126, 152–54, 158, 161, 162, 165
Noailles, Guy de, 202
Norristown, PA, 202, 204, 207
North Carolina, 12, 58, 104, 107, 174

Order of the Society of the Cincinnati, 125
Osgood, Samuel, 196

Parsons, Samuel Holden, 56–58
Patterson, Samuel, 22
Paulus Hook, NJ, 97
pay, 11, 32, 34, 67, 113, 119, 121, 122, 129, 131, 137, 144–46, 165, 188, 189, 196, 203; engineers, 15, 109–11, 113; sappers and miners, 30
peace, 33, 36, 130, 135, 185–89, 194, 197
peace establishment, 187–89
Peekskill, NY, 59, 126, 160
Petersburg, VA, 108
Philadelphia, PA, 4, 11–14, 17, 21, 22, 24–27, 36, 41, 42, 48–51, 53, 59, 60, 66, 67, 69, 70, 72, 73, 83–85, 88, 91, 99, 100, 104, 106–8, 124, 140, 141, 152, 153, 157, 165, 166, 177, 180, 182, 186, 188, 203, 208
Phillips, William, 105
Phillipsburg, NY, 160
Pin, La Tour du, 199
Pinckney, Charles Cotesworth, 144
Pluckemin, NJ, 95
Pontgibaud, Charles-Albert Moré Comte de, 203
Poor, Enoch, 20, 22, 50
Portsmouth, VA, 12, 154, 155, 164

Potter, James, 22
Prevost, Augustine, 123, 143
Princeton, NJ, 50
prisoners of war, 118, 140; Charleston, 103
promotion, 8, 33, 106, 113, 119, 121, 122, 124, 127, 129, 130, 175, 177, 179–82, 186, 198
Pulaski, Kazimierz (Casimir), 21
Putnam, Israel, 39, 54–56, 62, 63, 65, 78
Putnam, Rufus, 13, 255

Radière, Louis-Guillaume-Servais des Hayes de la, 8, 10, 16, 54, 57, 58; agreement, 11; alias, 12; death, 91; Delaware, 73; Fort Montgomery, 53; gratitude, 71; Hudson, 55; pay, 150; promotion, 110; rank, 15; retention, 97; West Point, 55
Rawdon, Francis, 155
Read, Jacob, 198
recruiting, 21, 114, 116
redoubt, 32, 68, 78–90, 172; Savannah, 90; West Point, 61
Reed, Joseph, 22, 72, 73, 114
Reign of Terror, 190, 201, 203
Rhode Island, 59, 86, 87, 153; evacuation, 87
Rochambeau, Jean Baptiste Donatien de Vimeur Comte de, 83, 93, 117, 120, 122, 123, 146–48, 152, 154, 156–58, 160–63, 165, 166, 170, 186
Rochefontaine, Étienne Nicolas Marie Béchet de Rochefontaine (later known as Stephen Rochefontaine), 12, 118, 124, 180, 189; French service, 120; promotion, 178; rank, 123; Yorktown, 174
Rockhill, NY, 78, 79
Rocky Hill, NJ, 50
Roderigue Hortalez et Cie., 4
Roxbury, MA, 68

Royal Corps of Engineers, 2–5, 8, 110, 188, 203; agreement, 11

Sandy Hook, NJ, 85, 88, 154, 162, 168
sappers and miners, 13, 29, 32, 82, 101, 110, 113–15, 117, 132, 156, 160, 165, 183
Saratoga, NY, 36, 37, 53, 57, 83, 107, 118, 143; Convention, 143
saucissons, 158–60
Savannah, GA, 73, 83, 88–91, 122, 123
Schreiber, Jacob, 145; petition, 146; prisoner, 174
Schuyler, Philip, 90
Schuylkill River, 14, 21, 23, 24, 201, 202, 207
Scott, Charles, 20, 22; Valley Forge, 17
Ségur, Philippe Henri, Marquis de, 149
siege, 29, 89, 110, 121–23, 127, 131, 149, 158; Charlestown, 104, 122; New York, 165; Yorktown, 113, 123, 144, 155, 174, 177, 178–79
Skinner, Abraham, 107, 143
Smallwood, William, 20, 22
Sourland Hills, NJ, 50
South Carolina, 59, 72, 84, 94, 98, 118, 141, 149, 152, 182
Spuyten Duyvil, NY, 163
Staten Island, NY, 143
Steuben, Friedrich Wilhelm von, 47, 108, 122, 190, 196, 208; Valley Forge, 17
Stirling, William Alexander (Earl of Stirling), 20, 22, 26, 47; Valley Forge, 17
Stony Point, NY, 74–76, 81, 82, 87, 91
subsistence, 21, 34, 42, 45, 47, 92; engineers, 113; Savannah, 90

Sullivan, John, 20, 22, 26, 50, 59, 60, 85, 94, 126
Swede's Ford, PA, 24, 201–4

Ternay, Charles Louis d'Arsac Chevalier de, 154; death, 158
Thatcher, James, 160
Thompson, William, 107
Treaty of Alliance, 5, 35, 46, 48

Valley Forge, PA, 24, 26, 28, 29, 35, 36, 49, 50, 55, 57, 59, 68, 96, 125, 201, 202, 208
Varnum, James Mitchell, 20, 22
Vauban, Sébastien Le Prestre de, 2, 81, 136
Vergennes, Charles Gravier, Comte de, 4, 117, 149, 152
Verplanck Point, NY, 74, 81, 87
Villefranche, Jean-Louis-Ambroise de Genton Chevalier de, 13, 31, 74, 82, 118, 119, 121, 123, 126; chief of the Corps of Engineers, 117; Delaware, 73; Fort Herkimer, 158; French service, 120; Lake Champlain, 190; Newport, 153; Order of the Cincinnati, 125; pay, 150, 189; promotion, 120, 124, 127, 128, 148, 186; West Point, 94, 126, 128, 147
Virginia, 36, 108, 113, 154–56, 161, 164–66, 170, 182, 197, 198

Wadsworth, Peleg, 113
Waterbury, David, 107
Wayne, Anthony, 17, 20, 22, 74, 82
Weedon, George, 20, 22
Weibert. *See* Wuibert
West Indies, 4, 12, 83, 154, 156, 158, 165, 167
West Point, NY, 53, 55–58, 61, 63–66, 74, 78, 80–83, 85, 89–91, 94, 101, 118, 119, 126, 128, 147, 165, 191

Wethersfield, CT, 117, 158, 161
White Plains, NY, 51, 60
Whitemarsh, PA, 17, 23, 24, 39, 202
Williams, Otho Holland, 113
Williamsburg, VA, 170
Williamson, Hugh, 196
Wilmington, DE, 20, 21, 174
Woodford, 20, 22
Woodford, William, 17

Wuibert, 13, 118, 189

York River, 126, 169
Yorktown, VA, 24, 26, 31, 37, 46,
   49, 59, 69, 76, 86, 88, 91, 95,
   108, 113, 121, 123, 124, 126–28,
   143, 144, 151, 155, 161, 165–67,
   170–75, 177–80, 182, 198, 205;
   campaign, 143